Lesbian & Gay Youth

Care & Counseling

Caitlin Ryan   Donna Futterman

COLUMBIA UNIVERSITY PRESS   NEW YORK

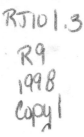
Columbia University Press
Publishers Since 1893
New York   Chichester, West Sussex
Copyright © 1998 Caitlin Ryan and Donna Futterman

Library of Congress Cataloging-in-Publication Data
Ryan, Caitlin.
    Lesbian and gay youth: care and counseling / Caitlin Ryan, Donna
Futterman.
        p. cm.
    Includes bibliographical references and index.
    ISBN 0-231-11190-8. —ISBN 0-231-11191-6 (pbk.)
    1. Gay teenagers—Medical care. 2. Gay teenagers—Health and
hygiene. I. Futterman, Donna. II. Title.
    RJ101.3.R9   1998
    362.1'086'64—dc21   97-52339
                                                              CIP

∞™

Casebound editions of Columbia University Press books are printed on permanent and durable acid-free
paper.

Printed in the United States of America

c 10 9 8 7 6 5 4 3 2 1
p 10 9 8 7 6 5 4

Contents

Foreword

Adolescents face many barriers in accessing appropriate primary care. Among the most underserved are lesbian, gay, and bisexual youth who are often neglected by traditional systems of care.

In its mission of increasing access to care for vulnerable populations, the Health Resources and Services Administration (HRSA), an agency of the U.S. Department of Health and Human Services, convened a national working conference to address the full range of primary health care and prevention needs for these underserved adolescents. Sponsored by HRSA's Bureau of Primary Health Care, Division of Programs for Special Populations, the conference was held December 4-5, 1994. Conference steering committee members and participants included nationally recognized experts in adolescent health, social services, and primary care. This provider's guide evolved from that meeting.

In attempting to develop a report to educate providers on the needs of lesbian and gay adolescents, it soon became apparent that a much more inclusive and carefully referenced document would have to be written. This extensively researched and comprehensive guide provides a much needed resource for responding to the primary care needs of these most vulnerable youth.

This guide is intended to serve as a basic resource for primary care providers, enabling them to confidently and effectively provide appropriate quality care to lesbian, gay and bisexual youth and their families. In addition to physicians, nurses, social workers, psychologists, and other primary care providers, this guide provides essential information for individuals serving adolescents in a variety of settings.

I would like to acknowledge the work of Dr. Donna Futterman, who served as my co-chair for the 1994 working conference, Caitlin Ryan, and members of the conference steering committee who ensured the meeting's success. Caitlin and Donna have created a guide that will made a critical difference in the lives of lesbian, gay, and bisexual youth. They deserve a very special thank you for this major contribution to the state-of-the art of adolescent health care.

Joan Holloway
Director, Division of Programs for Special Populations
Bureau of Primary Health Care
Health Resources and Services Administration

Preface

Every book has a story and this one is no different. In the spring of 1994 when Joan Holloway, Director of the Division of Programs for Special Populations, at HRSA asked for help with an initiative for lesbian and gay youth, very little information was available on primary care for lesbian and gay adolescents. Concerned about the dearth of knowledge, Joan decided to convene a conference to identify care needs of lesbian and gay youth, with the intent of developing guidelines for primary care providers in a variety of settings.

For the next six months, we worked closely with a steering committee of experts on lesbian and gay youth to plan a conference that would address these goals (Appendix A). Steering committee members developed a series of protocols for care delivery which were further refined by participants at HRSA's Conference on the Primary Care Needs of Lesbian and Gay Adolescents and are included in this book (Appendix F). The conference was a resounding success and we began to work on guidelines to enhance the quality of care available to lesbian, gay, and bisexual adolescents. It did not take long before we realized that a much more basic step was needed. Without a standard reference guide to provide background information, substantive references, and detailed information on the stressors, health needs, experiences, and developmental challenges facing lesbian and gay youth, providers lacked the context for appropriate assessment and treatment. So we decided to write this book.

Drawing on years of practice and the work of many researchers and providers, we developed a basic framework for understanding the needs and experiences of lesbian and gay adolescents. Although the book was initially intended for health and mental health providers, it is written in an accessible, easy-to-read format suitable for educators, parents, advocates, and anyone who wants or needs to know about these issues.

As with any major life experience, writing a book requires the support and encouragement of many people. This would never have become a reality without the inspiration and vision of Joan Holloway and the enthusiastic support of Deborah Parham and Maria Lago of HRSA. We would like to thank the conference steering committee who shared their time and expertise in shaping the conference and who provided helpful comments on our initial report—Joanne Haas, Neal Hoffman, Joyce Hunter, Frances Kunreuther, Darrel LeMar, David Ocepek, Gary Remafedi, Janet Shalwitz, and particularly Andy Boxer, who nurtured the book through every developmental stage. Thanks also to Kate Perkins, who helped coordinate the conference. Special thanks to Don Greydanus, Linda Belfus, and the American Academy of Pediatrics for making sure that adolescent medicine acknowledges and addresses the needs of lesbian and gay youth. And thanks to the editors and staff at Columbia University Press—in particular, Susan Pensak, John Michel, and Alexander Thorp—for their support and assistance in getting this into the hands of readers who can make a difference.

The authors wish to express their appreciation for the grant from the Health Resources and Services Administration which supported the conference and enabled them to write a report from which this book evolved.

Finally, we would like to thank our families, friends, and colleagues for their on-going support. I would especially like to thank Ellen Ratner, Ann Garfinkle, Judy Bradford, Lori Wiener, Hank Carde, Gary Raymond, Dottie Bailey, Vic Basile, Eliz-abeth Stirling, Winfield Scott, Audrey Denson, and Judy Weinraub. And for sharing this journey as well as for her considerable expertise, compassion, and commitment, I want to acknowledge Donna Futterman, whose practice wisdom informed this book and makes a daily difference in the lives of adolescents, particularly lesbian, gay, and bisexual youth.

—Caitlin Ryan

Working on this project has been both a challenge and an honor. It has been a special privilege to work with Caitlin Ryan, an insightful clinician, gifted writer, and long-term leader on gay and lesbian health issues. Thanks also go to my colleagues at Montefiore Medical Center: Karen Hein, Susan Coupey, S. Kenneth Schonberg, and Elaine Brennan, with a very special acknowledgment to Neal Hoffman. I also want to express my deep appreciation to the staff of the Adolescent AIDS Program for their commitment and excellence. My heartfelt thanks to my family, my parents, Alvin and Muriel Futterman, and most especially my life partner, Virginia Casper, and our son Evan, the loves of my life, who have always been there for me.

—Donna Futterman

We offer this book with our hope that it will empower, guide, and help providers, decision makers, teachers, and advocates make a difference in the quality of care provided to all adolescents, but particularly those who are most underserved—lesbian, gay, and bisexual youth.

Introduction

We are the community of tomorrow. How we are treated now, our experiences now, who we are able to become will affect the world of tomorrow. Even though we're young and gay, we're people just like you.

Chris, age 17

Until the 1990s, lesbian, gay, and bisexual youth remained largely invisible, even within the lesbian and gay community. Their exclusion from research studies, health and mental health literature, professional training and the media was perpetuated by myths and misconceptions about adolescent identity development that perceived lesbian or gay identity as an adult phenomenon: what was, at best, "just a passing phase" and, at worst, a pervasive disorder. Adolescents were considered too young to be able to form a sexual identity or be sure that they were not really heterosexual.

As lesbian and gay providers struggled to develop youth service organizations and document experiences and identify needs, lesbian, gay, and bisexual youth increasingly moved from the margins to the mainstream. They began to organize, to write and speak about their lives, to challenge stereotypes and to self-identify as lesbian and gay or "come out" at younger ages. In spite of perceptions among many adults that lesbian/gay identity could only be consolidated in adulthood, increasing numbers of adolescents confirm their awareness of sexual identity in childhood and adolescence. However, fear of negative and hostile reactions from parents, teachers, providers, and friends prevents many from disclosing their identity to others. And lack of awareness that adolescents may be lesbian, gay, or bisexual also prevents an accurate discussion of health risks and needs and inhibits provision of quality care.

Ironically, while media attention on lesbian and gay youth has increased and support services are more widely available even in many non-urban areas, the lack of attention to the health and mental health needs of lesbian, gay, and bisexual youth in mainstream health services and research reinforces their invisibility and heightens vulnerability as a socially stigmatized minority and medically underserved population.

Lesbian and gay youth face the same health and mental health challenges as their heterosexual peers, with the addition of social and health challenges associated with having a stigmatized identity. During the past 20 years, a substantial body of knowledge, expertise, and practice wisdom has been developed by providers working with lesbian, gay, and bisexual youth and young adults. What has been missing is a single resource that synthesizes and combines this information in one place for providers, parents, advocates, educators, and lay readers.

Lesbian and Gay Youth: Care and Counseling is such a resource, providing for the first time comprehensive guidelines for the care and counseling of lesbian, gay, bisexual, and transgendered youth, together with a compact review of the most recent information and research on lesbian and gay health and mental health, identity development, and peer and family issues. The book is designed as a minicourse in three sections that combine background information, state-of-the-art research, practical guidelines and reference information, together with a series of appendixes on clinical care, HIV counseling and testing, suggested reading materials for providers, family, and youth and community resources. Initially published as the June 1997 issue of the American Academy of Pediatrics' peer-reviewed journal, *Adolescent Medicine: State*

of the Art Reviews, Lesbian and Gay Youth: Care and Counseling is written in an
easy-to-read, user-friendly style that emphasizes clarity, practicality, and comprehen-
siveness.

Part 1 provides an overview of lesbian and gay adolescents' needs and experiences with a discussion of identity development, health concerns, and confidentiality.
Unlike much information on lesbian and gay youth, which often focuses on their
problems, *Lesbian and Gay Youth: Care and Counseling* is written from the perspective of *all* adolescents, which allows lesbian, gay, and bisexual youth to be seen in
the context of adolescents in general. When isolated as a separate group, lesbian and
gay youth are often presented and perceived as multiproblem, having many health and
mental health concerns. Seen in the context of their heterosexual peers, the developmental challenges experienced by lesbian, gay, and bisexual youth are normalized.

Like their heterosexual peers, lesbian and gay youth have the same health and
developmental needs; what is different is the addition of another primary developmental task—learning to manage a stigmatized identity. Chapters 2 and 3 show how
prejudice and fear of homosexuality (stigma) are internalized and have social, behavioral and health-related consequences. Stigma, not deficit, is what separates lesbian
and gay adolescents from their heterosexual peers, and some gay youth, such as ethnic
and racial minorities, are doubly or triply stigmatized. Although this concept is not
new, this section clearly describes the impact of stigma so readers understand its
powerful effects on the lives of young people. Chapter 2 also presents a detailed
description of identity development, including an in-depth discussion of identity development in ethnic/racial minority lesbian, gay, and bisexual youth and their struggle
to balance and integrate multiple identities and allegiances.

Building on the reader's growing understanding of the effects of stigma on self-
concept and behavior, Part 2 provides a comprehensive discussion of primary care
and prevention needs, including guidance on health and mental health assessment and
care. This section also provides important new and previously unpublished information, including:

- Clinical care protocols for primary care, HIV, and mental health care for lesbian, gay, and bisexual youth.
- Anticipatory guidance information for parents and youth on developmental issues and concerns for lesbian, gay, and bisexual adolescents.
- Policy statements related to mental health services and "reparative" therapy
  from the major mental health professional associations.
- Guidance on gender identity disorder, psychiatric hospitalization, and preventing inappropriate diagnoses and mental health care.
- Information on the health and mental health needs of neglected populations,
  including transgendered youth and lesbian and gay youth who are disabled and
  severely mentally ill.
- Guidance on making referrals and assessing the capacity of providers and agencies to serve lesbian and gay youth.
- New findings on suicide among gay, lesbian, and bisexual youth and a practical
  critique of the problems with earlier suicide data.

Part 3 provides an overview of HIV infection in adolescents, including risk behaviors,
prevention, and care, together with guidelines for HIV counseling and testing with
adolescents that address developmental needs and the decision to test and protocols
for medical and psychosocial care, counseling, and testing.

Clinical care protocols discussed throughout the text are included in the appendixes along with suggested readings and resources for providers, parents, and youth.

In addition, each chapter includes extensive references for additional follow-up on specific areas.

Guidelines reflect current knowledge of adolescent identity development and thus focus on lesbian and gay youth, although treatment approaches and concerns generally apply to other non-heterosexual youth as well. Available research on bisexuality is limited and has focused mainly on adults. As a result, little is known about bisexual identity development during adolescence, even though the term has been used to describe some adolescent behavior and experiences, and is discussed in this book. Even less is known about identity development in transgendered youth. By providing an overview of current research and practice wisdom, this book seeks to focus attention on the care and counseling needs of all non-heterosexual or sexual minority youth and to stimulate much-needed research into their development, care, and support needs.

Lesbian and Gay Youth: Care and Counseling is the first hands-on guide that provides health and mental health care to lesbian and gay youth and young adults. In addition to offering specific guidelines for care and providing guidance on how to approach such sensitive topics as sexual behavior, substance use, and suicide, the book includes a comprehensive review of the literature that will interest researchers, scholars, and general readers alike. Given its depth and breadth of information and practical focus, the book is a unique resource for training health and mental health providers and for enabling parents and advocates to assist in monitoring and ensuring quality care for a group of adolescents that has previously been neglected and ignored.

Lesbian and Gay Youth: Care and Counseling was written to fill a missing gap in the literature on adolescents and young adults and to help bring the needs of lesbian and gay youth into the medical mainstream. In the hands of providers, counselors, parents, and educators, prominent practitioners and community leaders have predicted that "this book will save lives."

Part 1

Overview: Lesbian and Gay Adolescents—Experiences and Needs

The primary care needs of lesbian and gay adolescents cannot be considered separate and apart from the needs of adolescents in general. Adolescence is a time of significant physical, emotional, and cognitive changes. These include exploration of new roles and experiences; formation of sexual identity; self-definition through peers and through interaction with others; and development of autonomy, career, and occupational goals. Because adolescence is also a time when habits and behavioral patterns are established and reinforced, including coping responses, decision-making ability, and attitudes about health and self-care, the experiences that adolescents have with health care providers are particularly important. They form the basis for future provider-client relationships, communication patterns, and help-seeking behaviors.

Like their peers, lesbian and gay adolescents face many health challenges. Their unique vulnerabilities, stressors, and health problems are addressed throughout this resource guide. Provision of care and service delivery, however, should be provided within the context of care for all adolescents.

Part 1 provides a comprehensive overview of the needs and experiences of lesbian and gay adolescents, including information about identity development, experiences with stigma and discrimination, and a general overview of health and mental health concerns. Although each part can be read and used separately, this section provides important background information to help the reader understand the context for providing primary care services to lesbian and gay youth and to those who are questioning their sexual identity. Since concerns about confidentiality are high for all adolescents, particularly lesbian and gay youth, a separate chapter is included about confidentiality and legal issues in treating adolescents.

CHAPTER 1

Adolescent Health Challenges

Adolescents, in general, have many unmet physical and emotional needs. A recent federal assessment of adolescent health concerns estimates that 1 in 5 of the nation's more than 40 million youth suffers from at least one serious health problem,[20] while as many as 1 in 4 are believed to be at high risk for school failure, delinquency, early unprotected sexual intercourse, or substance abuse. Nevertheless, access to care is limited: among all age groups, adolescents are the most uninsured and underinsured group and are the least likely to receive office-based medical care or to use primary care services.[9,16]

Poverty remains a significant factor in limiting health care options. One out of 7 adolescents in the United States, including more than half of all ethnic minority children, lives in poverty; of these, 1 in 3 lacks medical coverage. Nearly 5 million adolescents are uninsured, while millions more lack coverage for important health care needs. Uninsured youth are twice as likely as adolescents with insurance to report poor or fair health status, to suffer from chronic disabling conditions, or to be ethnic and racial minorities.[6,15] Although low-income youth are also at increased risk for teen pregnancy, STDs (including HIV), substance abuse, unintentional injuries, and homicide, they are only half as likely to receive health services as adolescents from higher-income families.[19]

Although most adolescent mortality and morbidity is preventible, health challenges facing this population continue to rise. Suicide and homicide, the second and third leading causes of death in adolescents, have increased significantly. During the past three decades, adolescent homicide rates have more than doubled, and suicide rates have tripled. The incidence of sexually transmitted diseases (in particular, HIV) and the proportion of sexually active youth have steadily increased. Seventy percent of all adolescents have had sexual intercourse by twelfth grade, and 1 out of 4 reports having four or more partners.[5] Each year, approximately 3 million adolescents contract an STD,[5] and 1 million teens become pregnant. Nevertheless, less than 22% of sexually active youth report consistent use of condoms, which significantly increases risk for sexually transmitted diseases, including HIV.[16]

Although AIDS is the sixth leading cause of death in youth, ages 15–24, the full impact of the epidemic is obscured by the lengthy incubation period—approximately 10 years from infection to onset of disease. More than 1 out of 5 cases of AIDS are reported in young adults, ages 20–29; most were likely infected in their teens. Between 1990 and 1992, the number of new AIDS cases among 13- to 24-year-olds grew by 70%. Initiation of sexual activity at increasingly younger ages, high rates of STDs and teen pregnancy, and frequency of substance use place adolescents at very high risk for HIV infection.

In addition to sexual experimentation, many adolescents explore use of alcohol and other drugs. At least 90% of high school seniors report some alcohol use; moreover, 1 out of 3 reports heavy drinking within the past two weeks.[1,11] One in 5 has used marijuana or other drugs, while 1 in 3 reports cigarette use during the past month (and 1 in 5 smokes daily). Rates of substance use and other behaviors with potentially severe health outcomes are significantly higher for out-of-school youth,[4] who comprise 10–15% of the adolescent population.[8]

Vulnerabilities and health risks are especially high among runaways and adolescents who are institutionalized or incarcerated in juvenile facilities. Each year, approximately 1.2 million adolescents run away from home. One out of 4 will become street youth, who often use drugs and may resort to prostitution for survival.[6] At high risk for suicide, many are abused and neglected and have serious health and emotional problems. Risk for HIV infection is extremely high: in a New York shelter, 1 out of 12 homeless 20-year-olds was found to be infected, and a San Francisco clinic for homeless youth found that among 14- to 20-year-olds, 1 out of 8 was infected.[7] Similarly, a high proportion of adolescents in juvenile correctional facilities have been abused and neglected; in some studies, as many as 75% of detained and incarcerated youth had been sexually abused. Many have serious emotional disorders and high rates of substance abuse, suicide, and STDs (including HIV).[2] Both groups face significant barriers to care.

Despite having poorer overall health status, ethnic and racial minority youth are less likely than white peers to receive needed health or mental health care.[3,10] Differences in access persist, regardless of health insurance availability, income, or need. Minority youth are at higher risk for serious health problems and poor outcomes, are less likely to have health insurance or a routine source of care for health maintenance or acute care needs, and are more likely to live in poverty than white youth.

Adolescents with chronic, disabling health or mental health problems face additional barriers to care. Included are the nearly 2 million American teens, ages 10–18, who suffer from disabilities that limit their activities. These range in severity from having an impact on recreation or sports to restricting major activities. Although adolescents with disabling conditions are more likely to use inpatient and outpatient services than nondisabled peers, they are also more likely to live in poverty and to be covered by public health plans (primarily Medicaid). One out of 7 has no health coverage, and many lack adequate coverage to meet their broad range of needs.[14]

Although physicians may not be aware of the sexual orientation of many or even most of their clients, lesbian and gay adolescents, like their heterosexual peers, present with these and other primary care needs and are likely included in their current caseload; very few, however, identify themselves as lesbian or gay to their provider. In some stress-related categories, such as substance abuse and suicide, they are reported to be overrepresented. And although most lesbians and gay men ultimately lead satisfying and productive lives, lesbian and gay adolescents face unique challenges to identity development, social acceptance, and survival.

Lesbian and Gay Adolescents: Vulnerabilities and Challenges

The struggle to develop and integrate a positive adult identity—a primary developmental task for all adolescents—becomes an even greater challenge for lesbian and gay youth, who learn from earliest childhood the profound stigma of a homosexual identity. Unlike many of their heterosexual peers, lesbian and gay adolescents have no built-in support system or assurances that their friends and family will not reject them if they share their deepest secret.

Shunned by the social institutions that routinely provide emotional support and positive reinforcement for children and adolescents—families, religious organizations, schools, and peer groups—lesbian and gay adolescents must negotiate many important milestones without feedback or support.[12] They must learn to identify, explore, and ultimately integrate a positive adult identity despite persistent negative stereotypes of lesbian and gay people. They must learn to accept themselves, to find intimacy and meaning through relationships, work, and connection with the broader community. They also must learn to protect themselves against ridicule, verbal and physical abuse, and exposure. And until they develop relationships with accepting adults and peers, they must do this alone. The social and emotional isolation experienced by lesbian and gay youth is a unique stressor that increases vulnerability and risk for a range of health and mental health problems.[13,17,18]

From a very early age, negative attitudes about homosexuality are communicated and reinforced through social institutions and the media. Children learn to think that being "gay" is deviant, "unnatural," and intolerable. They learn from a variety of credible sources—their families, teachers, religious leaders, friends—that being lesbian or gay means living alone, being rejected and ostracized, forgoing a meaningful career or satisfying intimate relationships, and not being accepted or integrated into the broader society. Through a variety of deprecating stereotypes, they learn that being lesbian or gay means living a half-life; by the time they enter early adolescence, when social interaction and sexual strivings coincide with formulating an adult identity, they have learned to hide same-sex feelings, attractions, and behaviors from others and often from themselves.

Prejudice, fear, and hatred of homosexuals (or *homophobia*) are also internalized. As adolescents struggle to reconcile societal myths and misconceptions about homosexuality with a growing sense of dread that they might be lesbian or gay, these internalized feelings of stigma and self-hatred increase existing vulnerabilities, affect self-esteem, and, for many gay youth, restrict life choices. The extent to which lesbian and gay adolescents find supportive relationships with peers and adults and develop positive coping skills will determine their successful adaptation to stigma and their quality of life. Access to a caring, nonjudgmental provider who will provide appropriate services and referrals will help lesbian, gay, and bisexual adolescents to negotiate difficult challenges and to develop appropriate skills for self-care and survival.

References

1. Adger H: Problems of alcohol and other drug use and abuse in adolescents. J Adolesc Health Care 12:606, 1991.
2. Brown RT: Health needs of incarcerated youth. Bull NY Acad Med 70:208, 1993.
3. Bui KV, Takeuchi DT: Ethnic minority adolescents and the use of community mental health care services. Am J Community Psychol 29:403, 1992.
4. Centers for Disease Control: Health risk behaviors among adolescents who do and do not attend school—U.S., 1992. MMWR 43:129, 1994.
5. Eng T, Butler W (eds): The Hidden Epidemic: Confronting Sexually Transmitted Diseases. Institute of Medicine. Committee on Prevention and Control of STDs. Washington, DC, National Academy Press, 1997.
6. Farrow JA, Deisher RW, Brown R: Introduction (Special issue on homeless and runaway youth). J Adolesc Health 12:497, 1991.
7. Farrow JA, Deisher RW, Brown R, et al: Health and health needs of homeless and runaway youth. A position paper of the Society for Adolescent Medicine. J Adolesc health 13:717, 1992.
8. Johnston LD, O'Malley PM, Bachman JG: Monitoring the Future Study 1975–1995. University of Michigan, Institute for Social Research, National Institute on Drug Abuse, U.S. Department of Health and Human Services, NIH Publication No. 96-4139, 1996.
9. Klein JD, Slap GB, Elster AB, Cohn SE: Adolescents and access to health care. Bull NY Acad Med 70:219, 1993.
10. Lieu TA, Newacheck PW, McManus MA: Race, ethnicity and access to ambulatory care among US adolescents. Am J Public Health 83:960, 1993.
11. MacKenzie RG, Kipke MD: Substance use and abuse. Comprehensive Adolescent Health Care. St. Louis, MO: Quality Medical Publishing, 1992.

12. Martin AD, Hetrick ES: Designing an AIDS risk reduction program for gay teenagers: Problems and proposed solutions. In Ostrow D (ed): Biobehavioral Control of AIDS. New York, Irvington Publishers, 1987.
13. Martin AD, Hetrick ES: The stigmatization of the gay and lesbian adolescent. J Homosex 15:163, 1988.
14. Newacheck PW: Adolescents with special health needs: Prevalence, severity and access to health services. Pediatrics 84:872, 1989.
15. Newacheck PW, McManus MA, Brindis C: Financing health care for adolescents: Problems, prospects and proposals. J Adolesc Health 11:398, 1990.
16. Office of Technology Assessment: Adolescent Health: Summary and Policy Options, vol. I. Washington, DC, United States Congress, 1991.
17. Savin-Williams RC: Gay and lesbian adolescents. In Bozett FW, Sussman MB (eds): Homosexuality and Family Relations. Binghamton, NY, Harrington Park Press, 1990.
18. Savin-Williams RC, Lenhart RE: AIDS prevention among gay and lesbian youth: Psychosocial stress and health care intervention guidelines. In Ostrow DG (ed): Behavioral Aspects of AIDS. New York, NY, Plenum Publishing, 1990.
19. Society for Adolescent Medicine: Access to health care for adolescents. J Adolesc Health 13:162, 1992.
20. U.S. Bureau of the Census: Statistical Abstract of the United States, 1994. Washington, DC, U.S. Bureau of the Census, 1994.

CHAPTER 2

Lesbian and Gay Adolescents— Identity Development

We are not only lesbian and gay. We are also white, black, Latino, sons, daughters, brothers, students, friends. Providers need to understand that we are more than our sexual identity.

—*Juan, age 19*

Lesbian and gay adolescents represent all racial and ethnic groups, all socioeconomic levels and religious denominations. They live in large cities, small towns, and rural communities. They are members of single-parent, two-parent, blended, and foster families. They are student leaders, athletes, and active members of civic groups as well as school dropouts and street youth. For the most part, lesbian and gay adolescents are indistinguishable from their heterosexual peers—in fact, most are invisible.

Homosexuality and Sexual Orientation

As defined by the American Academy of Pediatrics, "homosexuality is the persistent sexual and emotional attraction to members of one's own gender and is part of the continuum of sexual expression."[1] Homosexuality has been reported in most societies throughout recorded history.[40,45] During the 1930s and 1940s, Kinsey's landmark research found that many people were neither exclusively heterosexual nor homosexual throughout their lives; instead, human sexuality was far more fluid and diverse.[24,25] Kinsey identified a spectrum of human sexual behavior that ranged from sexual attraction and behaviors with the opposite sex (heterosexuality) to both sexes (bisexuality) to the same sex (homosexuality). This pattern of physical behavior and sexual attraction is called *sexual orientation.*

Sexual orientation is likely determined by early childhood; recent studies have suggested it may be biologically based, although environmental factors may also contribute.[40] Although the origin of homosexuality remains unclear, the majority of experts believe that sexual orientation is not a conscious choice.[1] In addition, negative experiences such as sexual abuse or dysfunctional parenting are not shown to influence sexual orientation.[40,45] And although the prevalence of homosexuality has not been established, a sizeable proportion of men and women report same-sex experiences.

Kinsey's studies showed that 1 out of 3 men (37%) and 1 out of 10 women (13%) had at least one homosexual experience resulting in orgasm; 4% of women and 10% of men were exclusively homosexual for at least 3 years. Among all adults surveyed, 4% of men and 2% of women were exclusively homosexual (Fig. 2.1).[24,25] Similar results were found in follow-up studies by the Kinsey Institute in 1970 and by the National Opinion Research Center in 1988, while a study of 16- to 19-year-olds found that 6% of adolescent females and 17% of males reported at least one homosexual experience.[2,33]

Kinsey has been criticized for not using a probability sample (a method of randomly selecting part of the population so that each person has a known chance or probability of being selected). However, his study clearly showed the rationale for

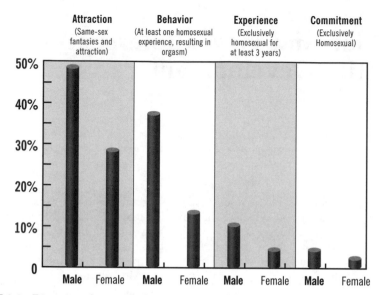

FIGURE 2.1 Diversity of sexual behavior and experience (Kinsey): homosexual attraction, behavior, and identity. (From Kinsey AC, Pomeroy WB, Martin CE: Sexual Behavior in the Human Male. Philadelphia, WB Saunders, 1948, and from Kinsey AC, Pomeroy WB, Martin CE, Gebbard PH: Sexual Behavior in the Human Female. Philadelphia, WB Saunders, 1953.

considering attraction *and* behavior in research on sexuality. More recent large-scale studies that used representative samples found lower, but still substantial, rates of same-sex behavior and desire. In an international study, same-sex behavior or attraction was reported by as many as 21% of men and 18% of women in the United States, with 6.2% of American men and 3.6% of women reporting same-sex behavior since age 15.[43] Another recent U.S. study found that 9% of men and 4% of women had engaged in same-sex behavior since puberty, with higher rates found in urban areas that have organized lesbian and gay communities.[26]

Because the repercussions of disclosing one's homosexual orientation can be extremely negative, including loss of job, loss of family and friends, victimization, and violence, many lesbians and gay men share their sexual identities only with other gay people.[18,32,52] However, this limits awareness of the diversity of human sexuality, while perpetuating a false assumption among providers that all patients are heterosexual. For example, if only 2% of the nation's estimated 40 million youth, ages 13–24, are lesbian or gay, at least 800,000 lesbian and gay youth are currently receiving or will need health services in the near future.

Identity Development

During adolescence, males and females begin to consolidate adult identity (Table 2.1). Identity is a complex integration of cognitive, emotional, and social factors that make up a person's sense of self. These include gender (personal sense of being male or female), sex roles (social and cultural expectations of masculinity and femininity), personality (individual traits and disposition), and sexual orientation (sexual attractions and behaviors).

TABLE 2.1. Identity

Identity is comprised of gender identity, sex (or gender) role, sexual orientation and personality. Consolidating adult identity is a primary developmental task of adolescence.

Gender identity	Personal sense of being male or female, established by age 3.
Sex roles	Social and cultural expectations, attitudes (e.g., stereotypes) and beliefs of male and female behavior, usually established between ages 3–7.
Sexual orientation	Pattern of physical behavior and emotional-erotic attraction to others, believed to be established by early childhood.
Homosexuality	Same-sex attraction
Heterosexuality	Opposite-sex attraction
Bisexuality	Attraction to both sexes

Lesbian and gay adolescents and adults frequently describe a sense of feeling "different" from early childhood.[41,45] As they age and develop cognitively, many lesbian and gay youth begin to understand the nature of their difference and society's negative reaction to it. In identifying and learning to manage stigma, lesbian and gay adolescents face additional, highly complex challenges and tasks. Unlike their heterosexual peers, lesbian and gay adolescents are the only social minority who must learn to manage a stigmatized identity without active support and modeling from parents and family. Children and adolescents stigmatized because of race and ethnicity learn coping behaviors and survival skills from parents, families, and cultural groups that provide nurturance and support against intolerance and discrimination.[28] This support creates a buffer against hostility and humiliation experienced within the larger society, while providing the framework for building self-esteem and a positive sense of self. Even with positive parental support, minority adolescents and adults struggle with the powerful sequelae of stigma that have significant impact on health and mental health. Ethnic minority youth who are lesbian or gay face additional stressors and developmental tasks in integrating their sexual with their ethnic and racial identities; as a result, they often feel dually or triply stigmatized.[13,15,31]

Understanding the concept of lesbian/gay identity requires an awareness of adolescent sexual behavior and knowledge of both the common coping mechanisms for managing a stigmatized identity and the process of identity development in lesbian and gay youth. Same-sex behavior is more common among adolescents than adults; however, few adolescents are likely to label themselves as lesbian or gay.[41] They not only are fearful of rejection and discrimination, but also may feel uncertain or may be unaware of their sexual orientation. In a representative survey of 1,067 adolescents, for example, only 1 youth self-identified as gay, yet 5% reported having engaged in homosexual activity.[39] A large-scale study of Minnesota junior and senior high school students found that although more than 88% described themselves as predominantly heterosexual and 1% said they were either bisexual or predominantly homosexual, more than 10% were unsure of their sexual orientation.[37] However, uncertainty declined with age, from 25.9% of 12-year-old students to 5% of 18-year-old students. Older adolescents were more likely than younger peers to report homosexual identities,

TABLE 2.2. Factors Contributing to Identity Confusion in Lesbian and Gay Youth

Cognitive dissonance	Lack of opportunity for socialization with gay peers
Lack of role models	or positive exploration of sexual identity
Inability to identify with stereotypes	Attraction to the opposite sex

TABLE 2.3.   Average Age (Years) Event Occurs

Behavior/Identity	Adults* (Retrospective Studies)		Adolescents† (Prospective Studies)	
	Males	Females	Males	Females
First awareness of homosexual attraction	13	14–16	9	10
First homosexual experience	15	20	13	15
Self-identification as lesbian or gay	19–21	21–23	16	16

* From Troiden RR: Homosexual identity development. J Adolesc Health 9:105, 1988.
† From Herdt G, Boxer A: Children of Horizons, 2nd ed. Boston, Beacon Press, 1996.

attractions, and behaviors. Although more than half of students surveyed (52%) reported having some heterosexual experience, only 1% reported homosexual experience; however, homosexually active students were more likely to have been heterosexually active as well.

Adolescence is a time of exploration and experimentation; as such, sexual activity does not necessarily reflect either present or future sexual orientation.[2,41] Confusion about sexual identity is not uncommon in adolescents. Many youth engage in same-sex behavior; attractions or behaviors do not mean that an adolescent is lesbian or gay. Moreover, sexual activity is a *behavior*, whereas sexual orientation is a component of *identity*. Many teens experience a broad range of sexual behaviors that are incorporated into an evolving sexual identity, consolidated over a period of time.[41]

Providers should avoid overly interpreting the significance of adolescent sexual behavior in relation to sexual identity. For example,

• Many lesbian and gay adolescents are not sexually experienced.
• Many lesbian and gay adolescents may have heterosexual experiences.
• Heterosexual adolescents may have homosexual experiences.
• Some adolescents may self-identify as lesbian or gay without ever having had homosexual (or heterosexual) experiences.[39]

Identity development and consolidation depend on many factors, including individual maturity and experience, access to reliable information, availability of supportive adult role models, and sophistication or knowledge of peers. Although some adolescents may consolidate identity at an early age, others may not until early adulthood or even later. Increased access to information and wider availability of support services for lesbian and gay youth, particularly in urban areas, likely have contributed to greater self-awareness of sexual identity at earlier ages.

Studies of adolescent sexual orientation show that the age of "coming out" or self-identification as lesbian or gay has been dropping steadily (Table 2.3).[3,16,35] Access to a supportive lesbian and gay community provides adolescents with increased access to positive role models and opportunities for self-affirmation and socialization that were not available to previous generations. Unlike older lesbians and gay men whose survival often depended on separating their social, professional, and emotional lives, today's generation of lesbian, gay, and bisexual youth has an opportunity to live fully integrated lives. However, self-identification as lesbian or gay at younger ages also means greater stress, more negative social pressure, and greater need for support, particularly from nonjudgmental and informed providers who can offer appropriate guidance, health education, and referrals.[5] The need for support is particularly critical to avoid isolation when adolescents begin to question their sexual identity (Table 2.4).

TABLE 2.4. Isolation Experienced by Lesbian and Gay Youth

Social	Feel alone in every social situation (with family, peers, in school, church, synagogue). Feel they have no one to talk to. Fearful of discovery, they continue to hide.
Emotional	Feel they must be vigilant at all times, increasing their emotional distance. Feel separated affectionally and emotionally from others, especially from family Fearful that friendships will be misunderstood by same-sex friends or may give away their secret.
Cognitive	Lack accurate information about homosexuality, including appropriate role models. Base their information on other lesbians and gay males, including future life options, on crude stereotypes.

From Martin AD, Hetrick ES: Designing an AIDS risk reduction program for gay teenagers: Problems and proposed solutions. In Ostrow D (ed): Biobehavioral Control of AIDS. New York, Irvington Publishers, 1987.

Coming Out: Developmental Model

Coming out—acknowledging one's lesbian or gay identity—is an interactive, ongoing process through which lesbians and gay men "recognize their sexual [orientation] and choose to integrate this knowledge into their personal and social lives."[7] Several models of identity development have been proposed to describe the coming out process; almost all were based on retrospective descriptions of earlier experiences recalled by adults.[41] Nearly all models (1) recognize the impact of stigma, which affects both the formation and expression of homosexual identity; (2) unfold over a period of time; (3) involve increasing acceptance of a "homosexual" identity; and (4) include disclosure to non-gay persons.[48]

A four-stage model proposed by Troiden,[49] commonly used by adolescent medicine specialists, is included to help providers understand the coming out process; however, these stages are not fixed, and individual development may vary (Table 2.5).

Stage I. Before puberty, children experience feelings of being "different" from peers. Differences are based on gender-neutral or atypical gender-role choices or behaviors rather than awareness of sexuality. For example, girls may be more interested in sports, and boys might show greater interest in solitary activities, such as music or reading, and less interest in sports than their heterosexual peers. Such feelings can result in an early sense of social isolation.

Stage II. After puberty, adolescents become increasingly aware of sexual thoughts and feelings. By early to mid-adolescence, most lesbians and gay males have experienced both homosexual and heterosexual arousal.[39] They also have internalized widespread misconceptions about homosexuality (e.g., "gay males are effeminate," "lesbians hate men"). However, the need to hide inhibits many young people from asking questions and blocks access to other gay people. Inability to identify with widespread stereotypes and lack of access to openly gay adult role models, who can foster healthy, integrated lives, result in *identity confusion* and cognitive dissonance— a sense that what one feels or perceives is out of step with the perceptions of others. Lack of opportunity for socialization with lesbian and gay peers increases social isolation and constricts key aspects of development; when heterosexual peers are developing communication and self-disclosure skills that enhance ability to interact and form intimate relationships, lesbian and gay youth are learning how to hide core aspects of identity.

Stage III. Although adolescents are increasingly self-identifying at younger ages,

TABLE 2.5.   Stages of Lesbian/Gay Identity Development

Stage I: Sensitization	Before puberty, children experience feelings of being "different" from peers, based on gender-neutral or atypical gender role choices or behaviors. Few see themselves as sexually different before age 12.
Stage II: Identity confusion	After puberty, adolescents become aware of same-sex thoughts and feelings. Negative stereotypes of homosexuality lead to *cognitive dissonance* and confusion as adolescents struggle to make sense of their emerging identity. Lack of accurate information about homosexuality or positive lesbian/gay role models increases isolation and confusion; adolescents respond by developing coping behaviors and usually hide their sexual identity or may adopt a bisexual identity.
Stage III: Identity assumption	During mid-to-late adolescence or early adulthood, youth begin to self-identify and disclose their identity (come out) to other gay people. Over a period of several years, they interact with lesbian and gay peers; positive experiences strengthen self-esteem and dispel negative stereotypes. Access to an organized lesbian/gay community provides opportunities for socialization and for developing relationships and finding positive role models. Youth learn a variety of strategies to manage their stigmatized identity.
Stage IV: Commitment	Self-acceptance generally culminates with incorporating sexual identity into all aspects of one's life, usually during adulthood. Sexual identity is shared increasingly with non-gay friends and close family members. However, not all lesbians and gay males consolidate identity; integration depends on various factors, including access to support and positive role models, personal strengths and vulnerabilities, and experiences with discrimination.

From Troiden RR: The formation of homosexual identities. J Homosex 17:42, 1989.

many lesbians and gay males begin to self-identify and disclose their identity or *come out* to other gay people during late adolescence or early adulthood (Table 2.6). Access to a well-defined community of supportive social, recreational, and religious activities, including health, mental health, and career-related services, helps to dispel negative stereotypes and provides a broader range of life choices in such areas as education, occupation, and relationships. Interaction also provides support for managing stigma, learning how to deal with discrimination, violence, and other negative experiences that routinely occur within mainstream society.

During this stage, most adolescents try to hide their lesbian or gay identity

TABLE 2.6.   Definitions

Come out	v.	1. Recognize, acknowledge same-sex feelings; 2. Disclose lesbian/gay identity to others. (Shortened form of *coming out of the closet*.)
In the closet *Closeted*	n. adj.	1. Pass as heterosexual; 2. Unresolved sexual identity.
Homophobia	n.	1. Irrational fear, hatred, prejudice or negative attitudes towards homosexuals or homosexuality, felt or expressed by a person or group; 2. Institutionalized fear, hatred, prejudice or negative attitudes towards homosexuals or homosexuality that result in invisibility, discrimination, neglect or mistreatment.
Heterosexism	n.	1. Denial, denigration and stigmatization of non-heterosexual identity, behavior, relationships or community; often expressed in subtler forms than homophobia (e.g., absence of support and neglect rather than overt prejudice).
Anti-gay violence	n.	1. Bias-related violence and crimes committed against lesbians and gay males; includes physical assault, abuse, rape, vandalism, terrorism and murder. (Such crimes are now reportable under the federal Hate Crimes Statistics Act.)

through various coping strategies and behaviors, *passing* as heterosexual in most or all of their interactions. Passing is facilitated by a pervasive lack of awareness that gay people exist, particularly lesbian and gay adolescents. Other coping strategies include denying same-sex feelings, trying to avoid situations that might confirm sexual identity, trying to change sexual orientation by dating or engaging in heterosexual activity, using alcohol or drugs to repress same-sex feelings or behaviors, or trying to rationalize behavior as being only temporary (a phase or stage). As they acknowledge their lesbian/gay identity, many adolescents increasingly seek out accurate information and support.

Lesbian and gay youth who lack adequate support or who remain unaware of positive options for living integrated, productive lives may develop maladaptive coping behaviors that persist into adulthood. By continuing to separate their sexual and social identities, they are at increased risk for serious health and mental health problems, including substance abuse, depression, suicide, and HIV/AIDS.

Stage IV. Self-acceptance generally culminates with incorporating sexual identity into all aspects of one's life. Commitment is symbolized by entering a same-sex primary relationship and by disclosure to heterosexual peers. As lesbians and gay males more thoroughly integrate sexual identity, disclosure is normalized: information is shared appropriate to the context of various situations and activities. As with other stages of identity development, prior experiences, access to resources and information, the availability of support, and personal vulnerabilities and resilience determine the degree of identity integration that occurs.

More recent theorists contend that staged models, such as Troiden's, are too linear and fail to account for other aspects of identity such as gender, race, and ethnicity.[29] Moreover, they caution that widespread disclosure should not be construed as the only measure of integrated identity. Many factors such as legal and economic realities, racial/ethnic group membership, geographic area, family situation, and support systems determine the extent to which disclosure may be possible.[10] Providers should use this model (see Table 2.5) as a guide for the basic process of identity development, realizing that each individual is unique and development may be affected and shaped by many factors.

Identity Development in Ethnic and Racial Minorities

Although lesbians and gay males are members of all racial, ethnic, and socioeconomic groups, most models of homosexual identity development are based on the experiences of middle and upper-middle class white lesbians and gay men.[14,31] For providers, this information is particularly important since a greater proportion of ethnic minority youth than white youth obtains health care services in community-based public health settings. Moreover, ethnic minority youth face additional stressors and challenges in consolidating sexual, racial, and ethnic identities.

Within each cultural and ethnic group, sexuality holds different meanings, and lesbian/gay identity is shaped by various factors. These include attitudes, values, and beliefs about sexuality, stereotypes about gender and sex roles, responsibilities for childbearing, religious values, degree of acculturation or assimilation into mainstream society, and the importance of family and ethnic communities in providing acceptance and support.[14,31]

For members of ethnic minority groups, race and ethnicity form core components of identity; together with gender and sex roles (also culturally based), they frame an evolving sense of self (Fig. 2.2). By the time an adolescent becomes aware that same-

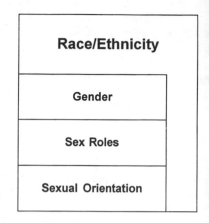

FIGURE 2.2.   Identity components of ethnic minority lesbians and gay men.

sex feelings and behaviors may signal homosexual orientation, primary identity—race/ethnicity—is well established.[20] In a society that discriminates on the basis of race and ethnicity, strong connections with family and ethnic community are essential for survival.[31,41] However, support is rarely available for an adolescent's homosexual identity. For many ethnic groups, being lesbian or gay may represent rejection of one's ethnic heritage.[4,14,47] Most ethnic minority groups consider homosexuality to be a "Western" or white phenomenon;[4,8,20] only among some American Indian tribes is homosexuality acknowledged in language and tribal history as part of a third-gender cultural tradition, although acceptance has largely been replaced by more negative mainstream attitudes.[21,46,51] Unlike racial stereotypes that are positively reframed by the family and ethnic community, negative cultural perceptions of homosexuality are reinforced; within ethnic minority communities, as with mainstream culture, homophobia is generally high.[14,15,31]

Ethnic minority lesbian and gay youth are required to manage more than one stigmatized identity, which increases their level of vulnerability and stress.[14] To meet their emotional, educational, and practical needs, they must learn to interact with three very separate communities that have different and often conflicting values.[31] These

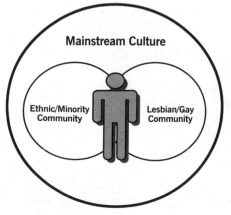

FIGURE 2.3.   Ethnic minority lesbians and gay males are required to interact with 3 separate cultures, which have different and often conflicting values. This interaction increases stress and vulnerability, particularly during adolescence when identity is formed.

TABLE 2.7. Ethnic Minority Lesbians and Gay Males: Challenges to Integrating Identity

	Ethnic Community	Lesbian/Gay Community	Mainstream Society
Positive	Acceptance/validation of ethnic identity	Acceptance/validation of lesbian/gay identity	National identity
	Family and community support	Access to community support	Access to multiple social and cultural groups
	Buffer for racism and discrimination experienced in mainstream society and lesbian/gay community	Access to information and lesbian/gay resources (e.g., organizations, health services, etc.)	Access to resources (e.g., education, employment, health and mental health services)
Negative	Denial of homosexuality	Racism and discrimination	Racism and discrimination
	Homophobia		Homophobia
	Rejection based on sexual orientation	Rejection based on ethnic identity	Rejection based on ethnic identity and sexual orientation
	Invisibility	Invisibility	Invisibility

include the ethnic community, the predominantly white lesbian and gay community, and mainstream society (Fig. 2.3). Each community provides access to important resources, but all devalue part of the youth's identity. Balancing the needs and demands of three separate worlds often requires lesbian/gay ethnic minorities to choose or prioritize allegiances, which results in prioritizing or suppressing (rather than integrating) key aspects of identity.[31]

In a mainstream society that is predominantly (83%) white, ethnic minority lesbian and gay people constitute a minority within a minority, in which both their ethnic and sexual identities are devalued and discriminated against (Table 2.7). They face similar challenges within the predominantly white, organized lesbian/gay community, which reflects many of the values of mainstream society, including racism. Since most ethnic communities are not large enough to support self-sustaining lesbian/gay subcultures, access to lesbian/gay resources, institutions, and services requires interaction with the broader lesbian/gay community; however, the only community that validates lesbian/gay identity often ignores, devalues, or discriminates on the basis of race and ethnicity.[4,8,14,20,31] Similarly, identifying as openly gay may jeopardize acceptance by the family and ethnic community. Because ethnic minority communities provide essential emotional and practical support, lesbian and gay youth are particularly vulnerable to rejection. As a result, many continue to hide.[47]

In general, lesbian and gay people of color are less visible than their white counterparts. Cultural expectations related to marriage and childbearing suggest higher levels of bisexuality and encourage less public acknowledgment of lesbian/gay identity, although relevant research is limited; studies of ethnic minority lesbians show higher rates of childbearing, particularly among African-American and Native American lesbians, than among white lesbians.[15] For providers, cultural and behavioral differences have implications for history taking, assessment, and diagnostic work-ups as well as for access to prenatal and reproductive care. The unique stressors of managing multiple levels of stigma, including race, ethnicity, homosexuality, and gender, require additional sensitivity and knowledge of appropriate community resources.

Bisexuality

Bisexuality has emerged more recently as a separate cultural identity from lesbian, gay, and heterosexual identity, and understanding of bisexual identity and its development is still evolving. Bisexuals are attracted to both the same and the opposite sex and have relationships with heterosexual and homosexual partners (though less often at the same time).[50] In addition to individual identity, *bisexuality* also refers to behavior and often represents an aspect of lesbian or gay identity development (many lesbian or gay adults and adolescents describe bisexuality as a stage of identity development prior to identifying as lesbian or gay).

A few researchers have explored bisexual identity development,[11,23,38,50] and findings suggest a different developmental pattern than for lesbians and gay males. Although studies show a broad range of behaviors, for most persons who identify as bisexual, this identity appears to be added after heterosexual identity,[50] and self-labeling generally occurs at a later age than for lesbians and gay males (mid-to-late 20s).[50] In addition, many people may engage in bisexual behavior (sexual activity with same- and opposite-sex partners) without self-identifying as bisexual.[50]

Although bisexuality is common among lesbian and gay adolescents who are exploring their sexual orientation, most research on bisexuality has been conducted retrospectively in adults. And although bisexual youth are included in research featured in this guide, studies cited here predominantly focus on lesbian and gay youth and young adults. Research is still evolving on bisexual identity, particularly among adolescents.* Although bisexual youth may not be mentioned consistently throughout this guide, providers should assume that the same treatment approaches and concerns generally apply to caring for adolescents who identify as bisexual as they do to lesbian or gay youth, or to those who are questioning sexual identity.

Experiences with Disclosure: Families, Friends, and Others

A critical aspect of identity management for all lesbian and gay youth is learning to assess when and with whom they can safely disclose their lesbian or gay identity. Negative experiences related to disclosure make it imprudent or even rash to come out in many settings. For example, studies show that some lesbian and gay youth have been expelled from their homes after their sexual orientation was disclosed or inadvertently discovered.[9,19,28] Not surprisingly, most lesbian and gay adolescents are cautious in disclosing lesbian or gay identity to anyone.

Providers should be aware that the decision to disclose one's lesbian or gay identity, particularly to parents, may have long-term consequences. Most adolescents are dependent on their parents for financial and emotional support. Although coming out can reduce stress and increase communication and intimacy in relationships, disclosure during adolescence may result in abandonment, rejection, or violence when parents abruptly learn or discover that their child is lesbian or gay. Adolescents who are considering coming out to their parents should be encouraged to explore their reasons carefully before doing so. Even parents who try to be supportive need time, access to accurate information, and an opportunity to process what for most will be a distressing and guilt-provoking experience.

Nevertheless, disclosure plays an important role in identity development and psy-

---

*The limited prospective research on sexual orientation development in adolescents shows several patterns of bisexual behavior: many lesbian and gay youth have heterosexual experiences before identifying as lesbian or gay; some may identify as "bisexual" for a period of time, while consolidating a lesbian or gay identity, perceiving "bisexual" as a less stigmatizing label; while others who have same-sex experiences as adolescents and predominantly heterosexual experiences as young adults may later report both opposite-sex and same-sex experiences.

chological adjustment, decreasing isolation while teaching and reinforcing identity management skills. An understanding of common disclosure patterns can help providers to assess available support, family dynamics and resource needs (Fig. 2.4). This understanding is particularly important given the isolation many adolescents experience during early stages of coming out and the correlation between isolation and suicide. Loneliness and social isolation are described as the principal causes of suicidal behaviors and suicidal potential.[39] Moreover, studies consistently show disproportionately high rates of attempted suicide among lesbian and gay youth.[5] Attempts have occurred more frequently among closeted youth and during the period immediately after self-labeling as lesbian or gay—periods when isolation is more extreme.[36,42]

When disclosure is voluntary, lesbians and gay males usually come out first to those they perceive as less threatening (emotionally, physically, and economically). Since friends are identified as their most important source of emotional support, lesbian and gay adolescents usually tell their friends before coming out to family members. Although lesbian and gay friends are more likely confidants, many adolescents, particularly those who are younger, have no friends who are lesbian or gay. And rejection by heterosexual friends appears common. In one study, nearly all (93%) of gay male adolescents (ages 15–19) said that friends were their most important source of help for problems or worries; however, 41% said they had lost friends after disclosing their gay identity.[34] In a 14-city survey, nearly three-fourths of lesbian and gay youth first disclosed their sexual identity to friends, and nearly half (46%) lost a friend after coming out to her or him.[6] The importance of these relationships in providing basic emotional support for lesbian and gay youth makes their loss especially painful.

Results of a national survey of adults suggest that most lesbians and gay men wait an average of 4½ years after knowing they are gay before telling others. However, initial disclosure may not include family members or coworkers: depending on

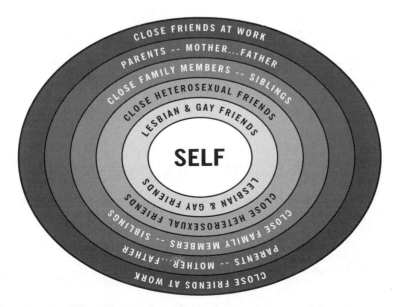

FIGURE 2.4. Sexual orientation: common disclosure patterns.

geographic area, 23–40% had *not* told their families, and 37–59% had *not* told co-workers.[17] Disclosure to siblings or other close family members usually precedes coming out to parents. Furthermore, some lesbian and gay adults never tell their parents; just as many tell very few or none of their coworkers.

Disclosure patterns are similar among ethnic minority lesbians and gay males, although community pressure to conceal lesbian or gay identity generally results in lower visibility overall. Although these adolescents more likely will tell close friends, they usually perceive disclosure to parents, extended family, and the broader ethnic minority community as being too threatening.[4,8,22]

References

1. American Academy of Pediatrics: Homosexuality and adolescence. Pediatrics 92:631, 1993.
2. Bidwell RJ: Sexual orientation and gender identity. In Friedman SB, Fisher M, Schonberg SK (eds): Comprehensive Adolescent Health Care. St. Louis, MO, Quality Medical Publishing, 1992.
3. Boxer A, Herdt G: Children of Horizons, 2nd ed. Boston, Beacon Press, 1996.
4. Chan CS: Issues of identity development among Asian-American lesbians and gay men. J Counsel Dev 68:16, 1989.
5. D'Augelli AR: Lesbian, gay and bisexual development during adolescence and young adulthood. In Cabaj RP, Stein TS (eds): Textbook of Homosexuality and Mental Health. Washington, DC, American Psychiatric Press, 1996.
6. D'Augelli AR, Hershberger SL: Lesbian, gay and bisexual youth in community settings: Personal challenges and mental health problems. Am J Community Psychol 21:421, 1993.
7. deMonteflores C, Schultz S: Coming out: Similarities and differences for lesbians and gay men. J Soc Issues 34:59, 1978.
8. Espin OM: Issues of identity in the psychology of Latina lesbians. In Garnets L, Kimmel D (eds): Psychological Perspectives on Lesbian and Gay Male Experiences. New York, Columbia University Press, 1993.
9. Farrow JA, Deisher RW, Brown R: Introduction (Special issue on homeless and runaway youth). J Adolesc Health 12:497, 1991.
10. Fassinger RE: The hidden minority: Issues and challenges in working with lesbian women and gay men. The Counseling Psychologist 19:157, 1991.
11. Fox RC: Coming out bisexual: Identity, behavior and sexual orientation self-disclosure. Doctoral dissertation, California Institute of Integral Studies, 1993.
12. Futterman D, Casper V: Homosexuality: Challenges of treating lesbian and gay adolescents. In Hoekelman RA (ed): Primary Pediatric Care, 2nd ed. St. Louis, MO, Mosby, 1992.
13. Gock TS: Asian-pacific islander issues: Identity integration and pride. In Berzon B (ed): Positively Gay. Berkeley, CA, Celestial Arts, 1992.
14. Greene B: Ethnic minority lesbians and gay men: Mental health treatment issues. J Consult Clin Psychol 62:243, 1994.
15. Greene B: Lesbian women of color: Triple jeopardy. In Comas-Diaz L, Greene B (eds): Women of Color: Integrating Ethnic and Gender Identities in Psychotherapy. New York, Guilford Press, 1994.
16. Herdt G: Introduction: Gay and lesbian youth, emergent identities and cultural scenes at home and abroad. J Homosex 17:1, 1989.
16a. Herdt G, Boxer A: Children of Horizons, 2nd ed. Boston, Beacon Press, 1996.
17. Herek GM: Stigma, prejudice and violence against lesbians and gay men. In Gonsiorek JC, Weinrich JD (eds): Homosexuality: Research Implications for Public Policy. Newbury Park, CA, Sage Publications, 1991.
18. Herek G, Berril K: Hate Crimes: Confronting Violence Against Lesbians and Gay Men. Newbury Park, CA, Sage Publications, 1992.
19. Hetrick ES, Martin AD: Developmental issues and their resolution for gay and lesbian adolescents. J Homosex 13:25, 1987.
20. Icard L: Black gay men and conflicting social identities: Sexual orientation versus racial identity. J Soc Work and Hum Sexuality 4:83, 1986.
21. LaFromboise TD, Berman JS, Sohi BK: American indian women. In Comas-Diaz L, Greene B (eds): Women of Color: Integrating Ethnic and Gender Identities in Psychotherapy. New York, Guilford Press, 1994.
22. Loiacano DK: Gay identity issues among black Americans: Racism, homophobia and the need for validation. J Counsel Dev 68:21, 1989.

23. Klein F: The Bisexual Option, 2nd ed. Binghamton, NY, Harrington Park Press, 1993.
24. Kinsey AC, Pomeroy WB, Martin CE: Sexual Behavior in the Human Male. Philadelphia, WB Saunders, 1948.
25. Kinsey AC, Pomeroy WB, Martin CE, Gebbard PH: Sexual Behavior in the Human Female. Philadelphia, WB Saunders, 1953.
26. Laumann EO, Gagnon JH, Michael RT, Michaels S: The Social Organization of Sexuality: Sexual Practices in the United States. Chicago, University of Chicago Press, 1994.
27. Martin AD, Hetrick ES: Designing an AIDS risk reduction program for gay teenagers: Problems and proposed solutions. In Ostrow D (ed): Biobehavioral Control of AIDS. New York, Irvington Publishers, 1987.
28. Martin AD, Hetrick ES: The stigmatization of the gay and lesbian adolescent. J Homosex 15:163, 1988.
29. McCarn SR, Fassinger RE: Re-visioning sexual minority identity formation: A new model of lesbian identity and its implications for counseling and research. The Counseling Psychologist 24(3):508, 1996.
30. McWhirter BT: Loneliness: A review of current literature, with implications for counseling and research. J Counsel Dev 68:417, 1990.
31. Morales ES: Ethnic minority families and minority gays and lesbians. In Bozett FW, Sussman MB (eds): Homosexuality and Family Relations. Binghamton, NY, Harrington Park Press, 1990.
32. Pilkington NW, D'augelli A: Victimization of lesbian, gay and bisexual youth in community settings. J Community Psychol 23:34, 1995.
33. Rathus SA, Nevid JS, Fichner-Rathus L: Human Sexuality in a World of Diversity. Boston, Allyn and Bacon, 1993.
34. Remafedi G: Adolescent homosexuality: Psychosocial and medical implications. Pediatrics 79:331, 1987.
35. Remafedi G: Male homosexuality: The adolescent's perspective. Pediatrics 79:326, 1987.
36. Remafedi G, Farrow JA, Deisher RW: Risk factors for attempted suicide in gay and bisexual youth. Pediatrics 87:869, 1991.
37. Remafedi G, Resnick M, Blum R, Harris L: Demography of sexual orientation in adolescents. Pediatrics 89:714, 1991.
38. Rust PC: "Coming out" in the age of social constructionism: Sexual identity formation among lesbian and bisexual women. Gender and Society 7:50, 1993.
39. Savin-Williams RC: Gay and lesbian adolescents. In Bozett FW, Sussman MB (eds): Homosexuality and Family Relations. Binghamton, NY, Harrington Park Press, 1990.
40. Savin-Williams RC: Theoretical perspectives accounting for adolescent homosexuality. J Adolesc Health 9:95, 1988.
41. Savin-Williams RC, Lenhart RE: AIDS prevention among gay and lesbian youth: Psychosocial stress and health care intervention guidelines. In Ostrow DG (ed): Behavioral Aspects of AIDS. New York, Plenum Publishing, 1990.
42. Schneider SG, Farberow NL, Kruks GN: Suicidal behavior in adolescent and young adult gay men. Suicidal and Life-Threatening Behavior 19:381, 1989.
43. Sell RL, Wells J, Wypij D: The prevalence of homosexual behavior and attraction in the United States, the United Kingdom and France: Results of national population-based samples. Arch Sex Behav 24:235, 1995.
44. Spencer MB: Black children's ethnic identity formation: Risk and resilience of castelike minorities. In Phinney J, Rotheram MJ (eds): Children's Ethnic Socialization. Newbury Park, CA, Sage, 1987.
45. Sturdevant M, Remafedi G: Special health needs of homosexual youth. Adolescent Medicine: State of the Art Reviews. Philadelphia, Hanley & Belfus, 1992.
46. Tafoya T, Rowell R: Counseling gay and lesbian Native Americans. In Shernoff M, Scott W (eds): The Sourcebook on Lesbian/Gay Health Care. Washington, DC, National Lesbian and Gay Health Foundation, 1988.
47. Tremble B, Schneider M, Appathurai C: Growing up gay or lesbian in a multicultural context. J Homosex 17:253, 1989.
48. Troiden RR: Homosexual identity development. J Adolesc Health 9:105, 1988.
49. Troiden RR: The formation of homosexual identities. J Homosex 17:43, 1989.
50. Weinberg MS, Williams CJ, Pryor DW: Dual Attraction: Understanding Bisexuality. NY, Oxford University Press, 1994.
51. Williams WL: Persistence and change in the berdache tradition among contemporary Lakota Indians. J Homosex 11:191, 1986.
52. Woods J: The Corporate Closet: The Professional Lives of Gay Men in America. New York, Free Press, 1993.

CHAPTER 3

Experiences, Vulnerabilities, and Risks

> *When I was 12 years old and first dealing with my lesbian identity, I thought I was going crazy. So I tried to avoid people. I didn't look at them. I tried to hide. I was afraid they would know I was a lesbian or that I was attracted to them or think I was crazy. Information is the most important thing. If someone could have helped me understand what I was going through, it would have made a real difference in my life.*
>
> *—Michele, age 19*

Stigma and Prejudice: Impact on Health and Mental Health

A primary task of identity development for lesbian and gay adolescents is learning to manage a stigmatized identity. Although there are clear differences between sexual and racial identities, similar developmental tasks are required of ethnic and racial minorities who developmentally transform a stigmatized identity into a positive one.[10,17,19] For lesbian and gay youth who experience stigma related to sexual identity with the onset of same-sex feelings, this task is no less difficult. Moreover, stigma has social, behavioral, and health-related consequences. Internalized as self-hate and low self-esteem, stigma may be acted out behaviorally, increasing high-risk behaviors, such as unprotected sex and substance abuse, and intensifying psychological distress and risk for suicide. Although the vast majority of lesbian and gay adolescents grow up to lead healthy, productive lives, the experience of acknowledging same-sex feelings and integrating a positive lesbian/gay identity represents a significant developmental crisis for most individuals, regardless of age.

Lesbians and gay males who have integrated a positive identity show better psychological adjustment, greater satisfaction, and higher self-concept, with lower rates of depression or stress than gay people in conflict with their identity.[9,19,25,45,54,60] Nevertheless, identity development takes place over time, and integrating a positive identity requires access to supportive peers and adults, accurate information, and connection to a community in which acceptance and validation are provided.[33,34,60] Stigma does not change; however, the way one perceives and responds to its dehumanizing effects does.

Living with Stigma

Although stigma may be either visible or invisible, some health and social costs are surprisingly similar. Goffman's work on social stigma discusses the stress associated with managing stigmatized identity: *visible* stigma such as race requires a range of coping skills to respond to prejudice and discrimination, whereas *invisible* stigma such as undisclosed homosexuality requires careful monitoring of all interactions and an awareness that relationships are based on a lie that could be exposed at any time (Table 3.1).[2] For double and triple minorities—ethnic minority lesbians and gay

TABLE 3.1. Social Stigma and Perceived Minority Group Status: Impact of Visibility

Health and Social Impact	Visible*			Invisible†	
Experiences and Vulnerabilities	Ethnic and Racial Minorities (Heterosexual)	Stereotypical Lesbians and Gay Men (Ethnic Racial Minorities)	Stereotypical Lesbians and Gay Men (White)	Closeted Lesbians and Gay Men (Ethnic Racial Minorities)	Closeted Lesbians and Gay Men (White)
Racism	✓	✓		✓	
Sexism	✓	✓	✓	✓	✓
Discrimination (housing, employment, life choices, etc.)	✓	✓	✓	✓	
Violence	✓	✓	✓	✓	
Potential rejection by family, peers, religious organizations		✓	✓	✓	✓
Internalized homophobia— associated with negative mental health outcomes and high-risk behaviors		✓	✓	✓	✓
Stress related to hiding— associated with negative health and mental health outcomes				✓	✓

Based on Goffman's (1963) concept of stigmatized persons as either *discredited* (visible*) or *discreditable* (invisible†).

males—the stress is even greater since racism is a reality whether they are closeted or not, both within mainstream society and the broader lesbian/gay community.

For adolescents and adults, the stress of hiding one's identity can be extreme; even casual conversations must be monitored and screened. Fear of discovery restricts relationships and shapes behavior. Intimacy, for example, requires disclosure; anonymous sex may protect identity but increases risk for STDs and HIV. Although hiding may appear to protect closeted lesbians and gay males from discrimination, rejection, and loss of an accepted social identity, it isolates them from access to a supportive community, sensitive health and mental health services, and positive role models. Hiding is also associated with negative health and mental health outcomes, including substance abuse, suicide, depression, and high risk behaviors.[21,25,45]

However, not all gay people are invisible; some choose to integrate their social and work lives rather than pass as heterosexual, while others may have been "discovered" and exposed, or are assumed to be gay since they fit common stereotypes. Openly gay or stereotypical lesbians and gay males are at risk for discrimination, violence, rejection by family and peers, and the negative mental health and behavioral effects of internalized homophobia that range from low self-esteem to self-hate. Although internalized homophobia is buffered by access to a supportive community, positive experiences, and role models, its residual effect often remains as an underlying vulnerability.[45]

Providers should be aware of the multiple stressors that lesbian and gay youth routinely experience, which heighten vulnerability and increase health and mental health risks. Unlike their heterosexual peers, lesbian and gay adolescents consolidate identity against a backdrop of social disapproval, misconceptions, distorted stereo-types, and hostility. Support, access to accurate information, and appropriate referrals help counter negative experiences. Careful assessment of an adolescent's support system, coping behaviors, experiences, and attitudes about disclosure and knowledge of available community resources are important components of history taking for youth who may be lesbian or gay (*see* Chapter 10, adolescent interview).

Prejudice

In studying the effects of prejudice on socially oppressed groups, Gordon Allport describes the process of stereotyping and labeling that justifies negative attitudes and discrimination, and often leads to violence (Fig. 3.1).[2] Allport found that members of

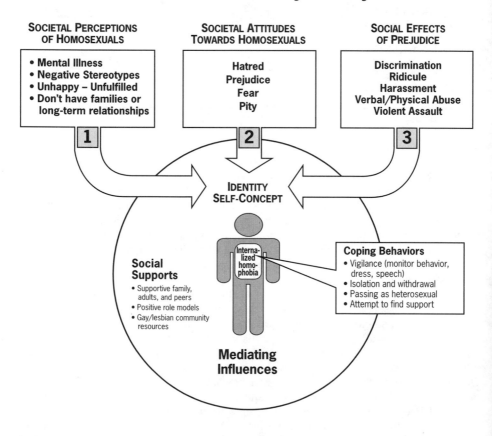

FIGURE 3.1. Widespread misconceptions and negative stereotypes are used to justify negative attitudes or homophobia, which leads to hostile behaviors, including discrimination, ostracism, and violence. These attitudes, stereotypes, and experiences are also internalized as low self-esteem or self-hate. Adolescents must develop a range of coping behaviors and seek external support to learn to manage stigma and prejudice.

victimized groups develop a series of coping strategies in response to prejudice; these include withdrawal and passivity, vigilance, self-hate, denial of membership in one's group or aggression against one's group, and expectations of rejection, discrimination, and violence. All are common coping responses to managing the stigma of a lesbian or gay identity, particularly in earlier stages of identity development. Providers working with lesbian and gay adolescents should understand the role of stigma in enhancing vulnerabilities and risks for various diseases and health problems.

On an ongoing basis, lesbian and gay adolescents are exposed to serious stressors that increase risk for a range of health problems; however, most are caused by stigma and oppression. As others have noted, Freud first pointed this out in 1903.[32] In its policy statement on "Homosexuality and Adolescence," the American Academy of Pediatrics concurs:

> The psychosocial problems of gay and lesbian adolescents are primarily the result of societal stigma, hostility, hatred and isolation. . . . These youths are severely hindered by societal stigmatization and prejudice, limited knowledge of human sexuality, a need for secrecy, a lack of opportunities for open socialization, and limited communication with healthy role models. Subjected to overt rejection and harassment at the hands of family members, peers, school officials, and others in the community, they may seek, but not find, understanding and acceptance by parents and others.
>
> Peers may engage in cruel name-calling, ostracize, or even physically abuse the identified individual. School and other community figures may resort to ridicule or open taunting, or they may fail to provide support. Such rejection may lead to isolation, runaway behavior, homelessness, domestic violence, depression, suicide, substance abuse and school or job failure. Heterosexual and/or homosexual promiscuity may occur, including involvement in prostitution (often in runaway youths) as a means to survive. Pediatricians should be aware of these risks and provide or refer youth for appropriate counseling.[3]

Social Disapproval, Discrimination, and Violence (Table 3.2)

Although negative attitudes toward lesbian and gay people are slowly changing and many "Americans are increasingly reluctant to condone discrimination on the basis of sexual orientation,"[28] discrimination persists in the lives of lesbians and gay males of all ages. Surveys of bias-related experience among adult lesbians and gay men show that during their lifetimes, more than half have experienced some kind of violence because of their sexual orientation.[5] Ethnic minority lesbian and gay males are more frequent victims.[6,35] Moreover, since the advent of AIDS, violence against lesbians and gay males has steadily increased.[30] Between 1985 and 1989, reported incidence of anti-gay violence grew by nearly 350%.[29] Still many crimes are not reported.

Although many providers may not be aware of the extensiveness of anti-gay

TABLE 3.2.   Victimization Experiences of Lesbian/Gay Youth, Ages 14–21*

Verbal abuse	80%	Chased/followed	30%
Threats of attack	44%	Physical assault	17%
Objects thrown	33%	Assault with a weapon	10%

* Results of 14-city study, 1993.
From D'Augelli AR, Hershberger SL: Lesbian, gay and bisexual youth in community settings: Personal challenges and mental health problems. Am J Commun Psychol 21:421, 1993.

violence, a report about bias crime sponsored by the National Institute of Justice found that "homosexuals are probably the most frequent victims."[30] At highest risk are lesbian and gay youth and young adults. Significant numbers report having been verbally, physically, or sexually assaulted and abused by family members and peers.[48] In studies conducted in 9 cities and 3 states, including Pennsylvania, Wisconsin, and Maine, one-third to one-half of lesbian and gay participants report being victimized in junior and senior high school.[48] A review of anti-gay violence on college campuses reveals that 55–72% of lesbians and gay males sampled reported verbal or physical abuse; 64% of abusers were peers, and 23% were faculty, staff, and administrators.[51] Among students surveyed at Yale University, more than 42% had been physically abused, and nearly 1 in 5 had been assaulted two or more times because of their sexual orientation.[27]

Studies show that although some youth are victimized at home, much abuse occurs in schools and other community settings.[48] Adolescents who are open about their sexual orientation, who are suspected of being lesbian or gay, or who behave in ways associated with lesbian or gay stereotypes are the most frequent victims.[48] Among adolescents receiving services at a New York City agency for lesbian and gay youth (of whom 84% were Black or Latino), 2 out of 5 had been physically assaulted, and more than three-fifths of gay-related violence occurred in their homes.[35]

Effects of Victimization

Fearful of discovery or further abuse, most lesbian and gay youth face the aftermath of victimization alone or with help from a few friends or a supportive adult, when available.[48] Typically, depression, anxiety, fear, low self-esteem, and self-blame follow victimization, together with a range of somatic symptoms (see Chapter 11 for discussion of sequelae). A more serious complication may be posttraumatic stress disorder. Those who are seriously hurt have no choice but to seek help from others, such as parents or teachers; doing so, however, may cause further victimization since having to reveal sexual orientation may lead to rejection, ostracism, violence, or being forced out of their homes.[48] An added threat for closeted gay youth who witness pervasive anti-gay abuse in school and community settings is the realization that this could happen to them; fear of discovery increases anxiety, thus reinforcing their sense of devaluation and isolation and encouraging them to hide.[40]

Moreover, witnessing bias-related discrimination and violence through the media, hearing reports of what happens to others, and having personal experiences with discrimination and abuse have a sobering impact on such key developmental tasks as career development and life choices. Mental health providers and youth service workers have observed for some time that lesbian and gay adolescents face restricted life choices as a result of prejudice, discrimination, and internalized homophobia.[7,22] For some lesbian and gay youth, school failure limits options early. Ridicule and physical abuse at school and inadequate support or disapproval at home may result in poor grades, truancy, or dropping out of school. In one study, for example, more than two-thirds of gay and bisexual males, ages 15–19, reported verbal or physical abuse at school related to their sexual orientation; of these, 28% dropped out. Four-fifths reported recent changes in school performance, and two-fifths acknowledged having been truant at least ten times during the previous year.[49]

Career development, which is intimately linked to self-concept and identity, is also affected. Believing they will never be accepted in mainstream society, some lesbian and gay youth abandon career or educational goals, and others may opt for stereotypic jobs. Although all adolescents are socialized to strive for common expectations and ideals, lesbian and gay youth soon realize that such goals are only relevant or achievable by their heterosexual peers.[52] In a study of sexual orientation and stress in the workplace, for example, nearly half of lesbians and gay men surveyed said that sexual orientation had influenced their choice of career.[63]

Runaways/"Throw-aways" and Institutionalized Youth

Rejection by family and friends and the cumulative effect of harassment, ridicule, and physical abuse cause some lesbian and gay youth to run away, whereas others may be forced out of their homes after parents discover their sexual orientation.[3,7,22,35] Although the actual number of lesbian/gay runaways and "throw-aways" is not known, some estimates suggest that 1 in 4 street youth may be lesbian or gay.[20] Local estimates are even higher. Agencies serving street youth in Los Angeles estimate that 25–35% of homeless youth are lesbian or gay, and in Seattle, 40% of homeless youth are estimated to be lesbian or gay.[36]

The stressors that lead lesbian and gay youth to leave home and school also increase the potential for exploitation. Without employable skills, some turn to prostitution, drug dealing, or other illicit activities for survival.[7,51] Others enter foster care, youth homes, and social service systems where they are at risk for further discrimination, neglect, harassment, and violence[37] (Fig. 2). A study of lesbian/gay youth in New York City's child welfare system, for example, showed that more than two-thirds (70%) had been victims of violence because of their sexual orientation, while more than half (56%) said they had stayed on the streets, at times, where they felt safer than living in group or foster homes.[38]

Like their heterosexual peers, homeless and runaway youth who are lesbian, gay or bisexual have multiple health and social problems, often resulting from abuse and

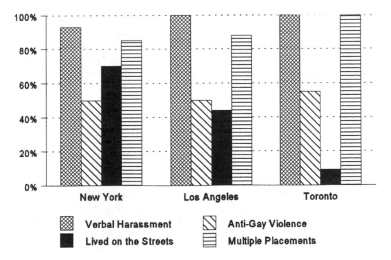

FIGURE 3.2. Lesbian/gay youth in foster care settings: experiences in three cities. (From Mallon G: We Don't Exactly Get the Welcome Wagon: The Experience of Gay and Lesbian Adolescents in North America's Child Welfare System. New York, Columbia University Press, in press, with permission.)

neglect. These include serious substance abuse and mental health problems, high risk for suicide, sexually transmitted diseases (including extremely high risk for HIV/ AIDS), pregnancy, and a range of untreated and chronic conditions.

Lesbian and gay youth may also become involved with the juvenile justice system as a result of substance abuse, prostitution, and running away. They may cycle in and out of institutions, where few will openly identify, fearful of further victimization and abuse from both peers and staff.

Providers' Attitudes and Perceptions of Lesbian and Gay Clients

Although the American Psychiatric Association removed homosexuality from its list of psychiatric disorders in 1973, negative attitudes persist and continue to affect the treatment provided to many gay people.[52] Beyond health services, lesbian and gay adolescents are at risk for discrimination and inappropriate or compromised care in mental health, foster care, detention facilities, and a range of community settings.[22,24,38] As a result, many lesbian and gay clients are fearful of disclosing their sexual orientation to providers and believe that doing so will result in rejection, discrimination, or poor care.[24,47] Unfortunately, many studies confirm their fears.[8,53,57–59]

Research on provider training, attitudes, and perceptions of lesbian and gay clients further validates these fears, by demonstrating negative and homophobic attitudes among a sizeable proportion of providers in a variety of disciplines.[15,16,41,62] In a national survey of physician attitudes toward lesbian and gay patients, 9 out of 10 lesbian and gay physicians reported observing anti-gay bias in patient care.[53] More than two-thirds knew of lesbian and gay patients who had received poor care or who were denied care because of their sexual orientation. And although nearly all agreed that physician knowledge of a patient's sexual orientation was important to ensure that specific medical needs were addressed, two-thirds believed that patients who "come out" to providers will receive inferior care. Such bias extends to lesbian and gay providers as well. Among 711 lesbian and gay physicians responding to the survey, more than half had been discriminated against by medical peers, 1 in 3 had experienced economic discrimination, and 1 in 7 had been victims of violence because of their sexual orientation.[53]

Lesbian, Gay, and Bisexual Youth Speak Out on Their Health Care Needs and Experiences

In preparation for HRSA's 1994 Conference on the Primary Care Needs of Lesbian and Gay Adolescents, a series of focus groups was conducted with 64 lesbian, gay, and bisexual youth in 7 cities to discuss their experiences in receiving health, mental health, and HIV-related services. Participants included an equal number of males and females; 56% represented a broad range of ethnic and racial minorities, while 44% were white. Although some were as young as age 14, the median age was 18, and all were at least somewhat open about their sexual orientation. Adolescents were asked a series of questions about their experiences with primary care providers. Their responses have direct relevance to these issues.

While 9 out of 10 adolescents reported needing health care during the past five years, only 2 out of 3 were able to obtain care. Two-fifths said they generally tell providers about their sexual orientation, and only 1 out of 3 felt he or she could talk openly with providers. Four-fifths were sexually active, but only half of their providers had discussed STDs and sexual activity with them; and only 55% of providers had discussed

HIV. Although 61% had been tested for HIV, testing had been suggested by only 16% of primary care providers. Nearly half of adolescents reported that some primary care providers had been helpful in dealing with issues related to sexual orientation. However, more than three-quarters acknowledged that providers had assumed they were heterosexual.

Negative attitudes and perceptions and discriminatory care have life-long implications for lesbian and gay youth. During adolescence, attitudes about health, self-care, and help-seeking behaviors are formed. Negative or discriminatory experiences can undermine provider-client trust, cause lesbian/gay clients to withhold important information, avoid routine or preventive care, and delay seeking help until health problems are well advanced. Such behaviors are routinely observed in lesbian and gay clients of all age groups.[32,59]

By keeping sexual orientation secret, many lesbian and gay adolescents seek to protect themselves from potential abuse. However, this information is an important part of their medical histories that helps providers understand what types of tests may be indicated, what kinds of referrals may be appropriate, and what types of health prevention information are needed. Despite the relevance for treatment and care, few providers routinely ask clients about their sexual orientation. In a recent statewide survey of lesbians' perceptions of their primary care providers, only 1 out of 10 physicians inquired about the client's sexual orientation.[61] Although many providers claim that asking their clients about sexual orientation will make them uncomfortable, nearly all lesbians in the study who discussed this information with providers felt comfortable doing so. Similar findings related to lesbians' experience with gynecologic care show that while 41% had disclosed their sexual orientation to physicians, less than 1 in 10 had ever been asked about sexual orientation by physicians.[57]

Denial and Minimization

A common response among health and mental health providers to an adolescent's concerns that he or she might be lesbian or gay is to deny or minimize such concerns. This response is generally based on the misconception that homosexual behavior is merely a "phase" or "stage" that adolescents ultimately grow out of.[22,50] Some providers may fear that discussing same-sex concerns will actually encourage homosexuality or potentially "cause" an adolescent to "become" homosexual.[31] Although a larger proportion of adolescents is sexually active with same-sex partners than will ultimately consolidate adult homosexual identity, such fears are false.[22,52] When expressed or acted out by providers, they may undermine the client-provider relationship and result in increased anxiety, secrecy, and failure to share pertinent information.[22,52]

Health and Mental Health Concerns: An Overview

The medical needs and concerns of lesbian and gay youth are similar to those of heterosexual teens; however, denial and fear of discovery make lesbian/gay youth less likely to seek medical care or to acknowledge homosexual orientation or sexual activity.[7] Some concerns, such as substance abuse, are more common to vulnerable and stigmatized groups, and several studies suggest that lesbians and gay males are at high risk for substance abuse.[1] Other studies report different patterns of alcohol and drug use, including higher rates of alcohol-related problems and more widespread use of marijuana and cocaine than among heterosexuals.[42,56] More troublesome for lesbian and gay youth is use of alcohol and drugs to cope with stigma-related stress, which may heighten vulnerability for chemical dependency in later years.[44] Use of alcohol and drugs is also associated with high-risk sexual behaviors and HIV infection.

Like their heterosexual peers, lesbian and gay youth who are sexually active are at risk for sexually transmitted diseases, including HIV/AIDS. At particular risk are young gay and bisexual men, who constitute a second major wave of HIV infection; seroprevalence rates in this group range from 9.4% in a San Francisco sample (ages 17–22 years old) to a median of 30% among young gay men attending STD clinics nationwide.[11] Attempts to pass as heterosexual or to deny homosexual feelings or identity may result in bisexual behavior, which also increases risk for pregnancy.

Lesbian and gay youth, particularly those who are open or assumed to be gay, are more frequent victims of bias-related crime and assault than adults; the most frequent victims are ethnic minority lesbian and gay youth.[6] However, the reason for assault may be overlooked by providers rendering follow-up care. Hate crimes and anti-gay violence, in particular, have behavioral, psychological, and somatic sequelae, which heighten vulnerability and risk for health and mental health problems.[18] Without appropriate follow-up care, including accurate assessment and referral for needed counseling and support, survivors may internalize the assault and try to deny or minimize its impact, thus intensifying psychological or physical problems. Because adolescent victims of anti-gay violence are not likely to reveal why they were attacked, providers should consider this possibility and carefully assess follow-up counseling and support needs when treating youth who have been assaulted or raped.

Mental Health (Table 3.3)

Studies of lesbian and gay adolescents show broad use of counseling services, when services are available.[12] Nearly three-quarters (72%) of 15–19-year-old gay males in one study sought help from psychologists or psychiatrists;[49] nearly two-thirds (62%) of a national sample of lesbians, aged 17–24, reported use of mental health profes-

TABLE 3.3. Mental Health Concerns of Lesbian and Gay Youth

Mental Health Concerns	Males (18–25 years old)	Females (17–24 years old)
Coming out to parents	93%	—
Coming out to friends	63%	—
Relationship with family	60%	46%
Sadness/depression	63%	40%
Relationship with lover	—	29%
Anxiety	77%	26%
Personal growth	—	23%
Being lesbian or gay	—	22%
Concerns about AIDS	92%	27%*
Loneliness	—	21%
Alcohol use	22%	8%
Drug use	18%	6%

* 62% had other concerns (27% were related to infection).
From D'Augelli A: Gay men in college: Identity processes and adaptations. J College Student Dev 32:140, 1991; and Bradford J, Ryan C: The National Lesbian Health Care Survey: Final Report. Washington, DC, National Lesbian and Gay Health Foundation, 1987.

sionals, and 31% used nonprofessionals, such as peer counselors and support groups.[8] Reasons for seeking mental health services commonly include issues related to sexual orientation, family conflict, concerns with relationships, substance abuse, depression, and anxiety; referrals are also made for attempted suicide and conduct disorders.

Many though not all of these problems emerge as adolescents begin to confront the stigma of homosexuality and struggle with reframing negative myths and misconceptions, reconciling dreams and expectations of a socially accepted heterosexual identity with an emerging lesbian or gay identity. Without an awareness of positive options for relationships, education, and career, lesbian and gay youth have difficulty imagining satisfying, productive lives. Common psychological reactions to the stigma of being lesbian or gay include adjustment problems, impaired psychosocial development, family alienation, inadequate interpersonal relationships, alcohol and drug abuse, depression, suicidal ideation, and sexual acting out.[12] Lack of support and inaccurate information about homosexuality further compound these problems, particularly when providers misinterpret (and thus misdiagnose) psychological responses to an emerging lesbian or gay identity.

With appropriate support, including access to accurate information, assistance in developing positive coping and social skills, gradually exploring sexuality and enhancing the quality of interpersonal relationships, issues of sexual identity will ultimately resolve. Although the majority of adolescents are aware of their sexual feelings and some acknowledge sexual orientation during early adolescence, many do not consolidate sexual identity until their early 20s.[55] Thus, adolescence for many lesbian and gay youth is characterized by indecision, uncertainty, and vacillation between heterosexual, bisexual, or homosexual labels.[23] Negative experiences with exploring homosexual identity reinforce negative perceptions and internalized stereotypes, further delaying and complicating identity resolution.

Preexisting vulnerabilities engendered by dysfunctional or addicted parents, emotional deprivation, physical and sexual abuse, severe stress, and prejudice may inhibit development of a positive gay identity. Moreover, adolescents with such histories may comprise the majority of youth who attempt or complete suicide or who experience serious chemical dependency.[32] Regardless of prior trauma, however, the reported prevalence of suicidal ideation and attempted suicide among lesbian and gay youth is alarmingly high. Based on available research, reported suicide attempts among lesbian and gay youth range from 20–42%, compared with estimated rates of 8–13% among high school students in general.[31] These rates remain consistently high regardless of sample, geographic area, or time period.

Given the multiple stressors that lesbian and gay youth experience in the process of coming out, psychosocial assessment should be included as part of routine history taking; moreover, providers should be familiar with symptoms of depression and suicide and should periodically review psychosocial status during provision of primary care services (*see* Chapter 11 for assessment). As a result of wider access to information and increasing availability of support services for lesbian and gay youth, particularly in urban areas, adolescents are self-identifying as lesbian or gay at younger ages. Thus, providers are more likely to see increasing numbers of adolescents who raise issues about sexual orientation and who require nonjudgmental counseling and appropriate referrals.

Attempts to Reverse Sexual Orientation

Before Kinsey's groundbreaking study provided a framework for understanding sexual diversity, medical treatment of homosexuals focused on trying to change their sexual orientation. Based on the assumption that homosexuals were mentally ill, such attempts ranged from severe exercise and aversive conditioning to drug treatment, electroconvulsive shock, brain surgery, and hysterectomies.[26,46] Kinsey documented the broad range of human sexual behavior, and numerous studies have consistently shown no difference in psychological adjustment between homosexuals and heterosexuals.[23] The American Psychiatric Association removed homosexuality from its list of mental disorders more than twenty years ago; nevertheless, efforts to change sexual orientation persist.[31]

Generally unsuccessful over time, attempts to change sexual orientation raise many ethical concerns and often contribute to negative self-esteem and mental health problems.[22] Nevertheless, providers may be asked by parents or even by youth to assist in changing their sexual orientation. Experts in adolescent medicine recommend against such attempts, which are further cautioned against by the American Academy of Pediatrics:

> Therapy directed specifically at changing sexual orientation is contraindicated, since it can provoke guilt and anxiety while having little or no potential for achieving changes in sexual orientation.[3]

In addition, the American Psychiatric Association (APA) states that "there is no published scientific evidence supporting the efficacy of 'reparative therapy' [also known as conversion therapy] to change one's sexual orientation."[3]

> There are a few reports in the literature of efforts to use psychotherapeutic and counseling techniques to treat persons troubled by their homosexuality who desire to become heterosexual; however, results have not been conclusive, nor have they been replicated. There is no evidence that any treatment can change a homosexual person's deep seated sexual feelings for others of the same sex.[3]

Acknowledging the role of social disapproval and homophobia in sexual identity conflict, the APA further states that "any person who seeks conversion therapy may be doing so because of social bias that has resulted in internalized homophobia."[3]

References

1. Adger H: Problems of alcohol and other drug use and abuse in adolescents. J Adolesc Health Care 12:606, 1991.
2. Allport GW: The Nature of Prejudice. Reading, MA, Addison Wesley, 1954.
3. American Academy of Pediatrics: Homosexuality and adolescence. Pediatrics 92:631, 1993.
4. American Psychiatric Association: Gay and lesbian issues. Fact Sheet. Washington, DC, American Psychiatric Association, 1994.
5. Badgett L, Donnelly C, Kibbe J: Pervasive patterns of discrimination against lesbians and gay men: Evidence from surveys in the United States. Washington, DC, National Gay and Lesbian Task Force, 1992.
6. Berrill KT: Violence and victimization overview. In Herek GM, Berrill KT (eds): Hate Crimes: Confronting Violence Against Lesbians and Gay Men. Newbury Park, CA, Sage Publications, 1992.
7. Bidwell RJ: Sexual orientation and gender identity. In Friedman SB, Fisher M, Schonberg SK (eds): Comprehensive Adolescent Health Care. St Louis, MO, Quality Medical Publishing, 1992.
8. Bradford J, Ryan C: The National Lesbian Health Care Survey: Final Report. Washington, DC, National Lesbian and Gay Health Foundation, 1987.
9. Brooks VR: Minority Stress and Lesbian Women. Lexington, MA, Lexington Books, 1981.
10. Chan CS: Issues of identity development among Asian-American lesbians and gay men. J Counsel Dev 68:16, 1989.
11. Coates TJ, Faigle M, Stall RD: Does HIV prevention work for men who have sex with men? Report prepared for the Office of Technology Assessment. University of California, San Francisco, Center for AIDS Prevention Studies. February 1995.

12. Coleman E, Remafedi GP: Gay, lesbian and bisexual adolescents: A critical challenge to counselors. J Counsel Dev 68:36, 1989.
13. D'Augelli A: Gay men in college: Identity processes and adaptations. J College Student Dev 32:140, 1991.
14. D'Augelli AR, Hershberger SL: Lesbian, gay and bisexual youth in community settings: Personal challenges and mental health problems. Am J Community Psychol 21:421, 1993.
15. Douglas CJ, Kalman CM, Kalman TP: Homophobia among physicians and nurses: An empirical study. Hosp Community Psychiatry 36:1309, 1985.
16. Eliason MJ, Randall CE: Lesbian phobia in nursing. Western J Nurs Res 13:363, 1991.
17. Espin OM: Issues of identity in the psychology of latina lesbians. In Garnets L, Kimmel D (eds): Psychological Perspectives on Lesbian and Gay Male Experiences. New York:, Columbia University Press, 1993.
18. Garnets L, Herek GM, Levy B: Violence and victimization of lesbians and gay men: Mental health consequences. In Herek GM, Berrill KT (eds): Hate Crimes: Confronting Violence Against Lesbians and Gay Men. Newbury Park, CA, Sage Publications, 1992.
19. Garnets LD, Kimmel DC: Identity development and stigma management. In Garnets L, Kimmel D (eds): Psychological Perspectives on Lesbian and Gay Male Experiences. New York, Columbia University Press, 1993.
20. Gibson P: Gay male and lesbian youth suicide. In ADAMHA, Report of the Secretary's Task Force on Youth Suicide, vol 3. Washington, DC, US Government Printing Office, DHHS Pub. No. (ADM) 89-1623,1989:110–142.
21. Goffman E: Stigma: Notes on the Management of Spoiled Identity. Englewood Cliffs, NJ, Prentice-Hall, 1963.
22. Gonsiorek JC: Mental health issues of gay and lesbian adolescents. J Adolesc Health Care 9:114, 1988.
23. Gonsiorek JC: Results of psychological testing on homosexual populations. Am Behav Sci 25:385, 1982.
24. Gonsiorek JC: What health care professionals need to know about gay men and lesbians. In Jospe M, Niberding J, Cohen B (eds): Psychological Factors in Health Care. Lexington, MA, D.C. Heath, 1980.
25. Gonsiorek JC, Rudolph JR: Homosexual identity: Coming out and other developmental events. In Gonsiorek J, Weinrich J (eds): Homosexuality: Research Implications for Public Policy. Newbury Park, CA, Sage Publications, 1991.
26. Haldeman DC: The practice and ethics of sexual orientation conversion therapy. J Consult Clin Psychol 62:221, 1994.
27. Herek GM: Documenting prejudice against lesbians and gay men on campus: The Yale sexual orientation study. J Homosex 25:18, 1993.
28. Herek GM: Stigma, prejudice and violence against lesbians and gay men. In Gonsiorek JC, Weinrich JD: Homosexuality: Research Implications for Public Policy. Newbury Park, CA, Sage Publications, 1991.
29. Herek GM. Why are hate crimes against lesbians and gays on the rise? The Advocate, Nov 5, 1991.
30. Herek G, Berrill K: Hate Crimes: Confronting Violence Against Lesbians and Gay Men. Newbury Park, CA, Sage Publications, 1992.
31. Hershberger SL, D'Augelli AR: The impact of victimization on the mental health and suicidality of lesbian, gay and bisexual, youth. Developmental Psychol 31:65, 1995.
32. Hetrick ES, Martin AD: Developmental issues and their resolution for gay and lesbian adolescents. J Homosex 13:25, 1987.
33. Hooker E: The homosexual community. Proceedings of the XIV International Congress of Applied Psychology. Copenhagen, Munksgaard, 1961.
34. Hooker E: The adjustment of the male overt homosexual. J Projective Tech 2:18, 1957.
35. Hunter J: Violence against lesbian and gay male youths. In Herek GM, Berrill KT (eds): Hate Crimes: Confronting Violence Against Lesbians and Gay Men. Newbury Park, CA, Sage Publications, 1992.
36. Kruks GP: Gay and lesbian homeless/street youth: Special issues and concerns. J Adolesc Health 12: 515, 1991.
37. Mallon G: Gay and no place to go: Assessing the needs of gay and lesbian adolescents in out-of-home care settings. Child Welfare 71:547, 1992.
38. Mallon GP: The experience of gay and lesbian adolescents in New York City's child welfare system. In Siskind A, Kunreuther F (eds): Report and Recommendations of a Joint Task Force of New York City's Child Welfare Administration and the Council of Family and Child Caring Agencies. New York, 1994.
39. Mallon G: We Don't Exactly Get the Welcome Wagon: The Experience of Gay and Lesbian Adolescents in North America's Child Welfare System. New York, Columbia University Press, in press.

40. Martin AD, Hetrick ES The stigmatization of the gay and lesbian adolescent. J Homosex 15:163, 1988.
41. Matthews WC, Booth MW, Turner JD, Kessler L: Physicians' attitudes toward homosexuality—Survey of a California county medical society. West J Med 144:106, 1986.
42. McKirnan DJ, Peterson PL: Alcohol and drug use among homosexual men and women: Epidemiology and population characteristics. Addict Behav 14:545, 1989.
43. McKirnan DJ, Peterson P: Chicago survey documents anti-gay bias (social issues survey). Windy City Times. March 12, 1987.
44. McKirnan DJ, Peterson PL: Stress expectancies and vulnerability to substance abuse: A test of a model among homosexual men. J Abnorm Psychol 97:461, 1988.
45. Meyer I: Minority stress and mental health in gay men. J Health Soc Behav 36:38, 1995.
46. Murphy TF: Redirecting sexual orientation: Techniques and justifications. J Sex Res 29:501.
47. Paroski PA: Health care delivery and the concerns of gay and lesbian adolescents. J Adolesc Health Care 8:188, 1987.
48. Pilkington NW, D'Augelli A: Victimization of lesbian, gay and bisexual youth in community settings. J Community Psychol 23:34, 1995.
49. Remafedi G: Adolescent homosexuality: Psychosocial and medical implications. Pediatrics 79:331, 1987.
50. Savin-Williams RC: Gay and lesbian adolescents. In Bozett FW, Sussman MB (eds): Homosexuality and Family Relations. Binghamton, NY, Harrington Park Press, 1990.
51. Savin-Williams RC: Verbal and physical abuse as stressors in the lives of lesbian, gay male and bisexual youths: Associations with school problems, running away, substance abuse, prostitution and suicide. J Consult Clinical Psychol 62:261, 1994.
52. Savin-Williams RC, Lenhart RE: AIDS prevention among gay and lesbian youth: Psychosocial stress and health care intervention guidelines. In Ostrow DG (ed): Behavioral Aspects of AIDS. New York, Plenum Publishing, 1990.
53. Schatz B, O'Hanlan K: Anti-gay discrimination in medicine: Results of a national survey of lesbian, gay and bisexual physicians. San Francisco, American Association of Physicians for Human Rights, 1994.
54. Schmitt JP, Kurdek LA: Personality correlates of positive identity and relationship involvement in gay men. J Homosex 13:101, 1987.
55. Schneider M, Tremble B: Gay or straight? Working with the confused adolescent. J Soc Work and Hum Sexuality 4:71, 1986.
56. Skinner WF: The prevalence and demographic predictors of illicit and licit drug use among lesbians and gay men. AJPH 84:1307, 1994.
57. Smith EM, Johnson SR, Guenther SM: Health care attitudes and experiences during gynecologic care among lesbians and bisexuals. AJPH 75:1085, 1985.
58. Stevens PE: Lesbian health care research: A review of the literature from 1970 to 1990. Health Care for Women Int 13:91, 1990.
59. Stevens PE, Hall JM: Stigma, health beliefs and experiences with health care in lesbian women. Image: J Nurs Schol 20:69, 1988.
60. Weinberg MS, Williams CJ: Male Homosexuals: Their Problems and Adaptations. New York, Oxford University Press, 1974.
61. White J: Factors influencing health risk and health seeking behavior in lesbians. Paper presented at the Gay and Lesbian Medical Association Conference, 1995.
62. Wisniewski J, Toomey B. Are social workers homophobic? Soc Work 32:454, 1987.
63. Woods J: The Corporate Closet: The Professional Lives of Gay Men in America. New York: The Free Press, 1993.

CHAPTER 4

Confidentiality and Legal Issues

As with adults, confidentiality is a basic principle of adolescent health care; in addition, studies show that lack of confidentiality may cause adolescents to avoid or delay needed care.[4,8,10] Because health risks for adolescents are so compelling, health professional associations have supported confidential health services for adolescents for specific health care needs and as a general tenet of care for several decades. For example, the AMA recommended treatment of STDs in adolescents without parental notification as early as 1967.[2] More recently, a joint policy statement of the American Academy of Pediatrics, American Academy of Family Physicians, American College of Obstetricians and Gynecologists, and the National Medical Association states that although providers should encourage parental participation in an adolescent's care, "legal barriers and deference to parental involvement should not stand in the way of needed care."[1] Nevertheless, confusion over state laws that cover minor's consent to treatment and discomfort among some providers about supporting independent decision-making that may conflict with parental wishes increase barriers to care for many youth. Fear that confidentiality may not be protected becomes a further barrier to care, particularly for lesbian and gay youth who have not come out to their parents.

Consent to Treatment Laws

Historically, minors were not permitted to make their own treatment decisions since they were not allowed to sign legally binding contracts (e.g., physician-patient) and were assumed to lack the developmental capacity to make such decisions. However, studies have shown that adolescents, particularly those aged 14 years and above, are as competent as adults to make their own health care decisions,[6,7,11] including the ability to understand the risks and benefits of treatment and to give informed consent.[9] Moreover, since the 1960s, both the courts and state legislatures have created a range of exceptions that allow adolescents to consent to treatment without parental consent.[5]

In most states, adolescents 18 years of age or older are legally considered adults and can consent to treatment. Youth under 18 years old are considered minors; however, consent may be authorized according to their legal status (e.g., mature or emancipated) or for treatment of specific health concerns. Mature minors include youth who have the ability to understand the risks and benefits of treatment, thus enabling them to give informed consent. (Although only a few states have passed mature minor laws, this concept is recognized by courts in other states.[5]) Minors are considered to be legally emancipated if they are married, serve in the military, live independently, or support themselves financially; although not every state includes consent-to-care provisions for emancipated minors, the courts have recognized minors' rights to consent, even without specific state laws.[5]

Besides authorizing consent based on a minor's legal status, all states have laws that allow minors' consent to treatment (without parental consent) for specific health services, including emergency care, STDs (or venereal disease), and substance abuse services. In addition, most states cover contraceptive services and pregnancy, and laws also may include HIV testing and treatment, inpatient and outpatient mental health services, and treatment for rape and sexual assault.[5] Since minor consent-to-treatment laws differ from state to state and may be changed or amended as new issues (such as HIV) emerge, providers should become familiar with these statutes. Providers should also be aware that even though state laws may vary, no known cases have been reported in which physicians have been sued successfully for providing non-negligent treatment without parental consent to minors aged 15 years and older.[3]

Confidentiality

Virtually every health profession is bound by a code of ethics that mandates client confidentiality, which is also governed by state medical records laws, federal funding statutes, and the right to privacy. Nevertheless, fear of inappropriate disclosure prevents many adolescents from receiving needed care (Table 4.1), and many lack a basic understanding of their rights in the provider-client relationship. For example, a Massachusetts study of diverse high school populations found that more than half (54.7%) had never discussed confidentiality with their health providers, and only 1 in 3 was knowledgeable about the right to confidential care.[4]

Fear of inappropriate disclosure is a significant concern for lesbian and gay youth, who may experience discrimination, rejection, loss of critical relationships (e.g., family and close friends), compromised care, and ejection from their homes if confidentiality regarding their sexual identity is violated. In addition to assessing the capacity of referral sources to care for lesbian and gay youth, providers should review confidentiality procedures and ask how agencies manage confidentiality of HIV status and sexual orientation. Before referring lesbian and gay adolescents to other programs or practitioners, providers should discuss whether or not it is safe to disclose sexual identity, as well as how and under what circumstances they might do so.

During initial visits and as needed to reassure youth of the privacy of the physician-client relationship, providers should inform adolescents and parents about how confidentiality will be protected and when it will be breached (e.g., in situations of danger to self or others and of sexual abuse). Providers should be familiar with the requirements of state reporting laws, including confidentiality and "duty to warn" provisions, which call for notifying others when a client is at risk for harming self or others, and clearly understand their responsibilities in disclosing information that adolescents shared in confidence. Ideally, when sexual abuse has occurred, the youth may assist with reporting; however, lesbian and gay teens may also be at risk for unauthorized disclosure of sexual orientation when information which is relevant to reporting is later inappropriately disclosed by others.

Providers also should ensure that adolescents are fully informed about state reporting requirements for specific health concerns; for example, some states, such as Colorado, Iowa, and Michigan, allow disclosure of HIV testing and treatment to a

TABLE 4.1.　Likelihood of Adolescents Seeking Care for Specific Health Concerns

	With Parental Notification	Without Parental Notification
Depression	45%	57%
Birth control	19%	—
Drug use	17%	64%
STDs	15%	65%

From Marks A, Malizio J, Hoch J, et al: Assessment of health needs and willingness to utilize health care resources of adolescents in a suburban population. J Pediatr 102:456, 1983.

minor's parent or legal guardian (*see* Chapter 13 for additional information on HIV reporting).

References

1. American College of Obstetricians and Gynecologists: ACOG Statement of Policy: Confidentiality in Adolescent Health Care. Washington, DC, American College of Obstetricians and Gynecologists, 1988.
2. American Medical Association. Council on Long Range Planning and Development: AMA Policy Compendium. Chicago, American Medical Association, 1990.
3. American Medical Association. Council on Scientific Affairs: Confidential health services for adolescents. JAMA 269:1420, 1993.
4. Cheng TL, Savageau JA, Sattler AL, DeWitt TG: Confidentiality in health care: A survey of knowledge, perceptions and attitudes among high school students. JAMA 269:1404, 1993.
5. English, A: Legal and ethical concerns. In Friedman SB, Fisher M, Schonberg SK (ed): Comprehensive Adolescent Health Care. St. Louis, MO, Quality Medical Publishing, 1992.
6. Gittler J, Quigley-Rick M, Saks MJ: Adolescent Health Care Decision Making: The Law and Public Policy. New York, Carnegie Council on Adolescent Development. Report for the U.S. Congress Office of Technology Assessment, June 1990.
7. Kaser-Boyd N, Adelman HS, Taylor L, et al: Children's understanding of risks and benefits of psychotherapy. J Clin Child Psychol 15:165, 1986.
8. Marks A, Malizio J, Hoch J, et al: Assessment of health needs and willingness to utilize health care resources of adolescents in a suburban population. J Pediatr 102:456, 1983.
9. Morrissey JM, Hofmann AD, Thrope JC: Consent and Confidentiality in the Health Care of Children and Adolescents: A Legal Guide. New York, The Free Press, 1986.
10. Resnick MD, Blum RW, Hedin D: The appropriateness of health services for adolescents: Youth's opinions and attitudes. J Adolesc Health 2:137, 1980.
11. Weithorn LA, Campbell SB: The competency of children and adolescents to make informed treatment decisions. Child Dev 53:1589, 1982.

Part 2

Primary Care and Prevention

Like heterosexual adolescents, lesbian, gay, and bisexual youth require routine health maintenance and are at risk for a range of health concerns, including sexually transmitted diseases and HIV, pregnancy, substance abuse, and mental health concerns. In addition, lesbian and gay youth are also at risk for increased stress, anti-gay violence, and assault because of sexual orientation.

In many cases, providers may not be aware of an adolescent's sexual orientation. Some youth may be fearful of disclosure, while others are still exploring their identity. Regardless of sexual orientation, many adolescents experiment with same-sex behavior, putting themselves at risk for STDs and HIV without access to appropriate prevention information. By creating a nonjudgmental, supportive environment where adolescents feel safe to disclose health problems and concerns, providers can address the needs of *all* adolescents, including those who may be lesbian, gay, or bisexual. The provider's goal, as noted in the American Academy of Pediatrics' Statement on Homosexuality and Adolescence (see Appendix G), "is not to identify all gay and lesbian youths, but to create comfortable environments in which they may seek help and support for appropriate medical care while reserving the right to disclose their sexual identity when ready."[4]

Part 2 provides a comprehensive overview of health needs and concerns for adolescents who may be lesbian, gay, or bisexual, including guidelines for assessment, treatment, and prevention; a model client interview; information on working with families and anticipatory guidance, and a referral checklist for assessing the capacity of agencies and providers to care for lesbian and gay youth. Guidance for adolescents who are or may be HIV-infected, including protocols for clinical care and HIV counseling and testing, is provided in Part 3.

CHAPTER 5

Health Concerns of Lesbian and Gay Adolescents

I finally found a person who was there for me, who would listen to me. She told me she had never had any gay patients, but she knew an organization that could help me. She took me to the lesbian and gay center. I had never been there before. When you live with your family it's so hard to get services because you're not "out." If she hadn't helped me, I don't know how long it would have taken to find support.
—*Lesbian Youth*

Sexually Transmitted Diseases

After upper respiratory viral infections, sexually transmitted diseases (STDs) are the second most commonly diagnosed infectious diseases in adolescents. Sexually active adolescents are at particularly high risk for infection; nearly two-thirds (66%) of STDs occur in persons < 25 years old.[64] Younger adolescents, especially females, are least likely to be considered at risk or to be screened if they are asymptomatic.[48] Both lesbian and gay adolescents who are sexually active are at risk for STDs, and gay male youth are particularly vulnerable. Risk is heightened by prejudice and anti-gay violence, the need for secrecy, and the lack of supportive environments for open socialization, which promote anonymous sexual encounters and other high-risk behaviors.

Lesbians

Research on adults shows that most lesbians have been sexually active with men. However, risk for most STDs is substantially lower for lesbians who have sex only with other women. In fact, lesbians who are exclusively homosexual are the least likely group to contract bacterial sexually transmitted diseases.[9,62] Moreover, no gynecologic problems have been identified that are unique to lesbians or that occur more often in lesbians than in bisexual or heterosexual women.[62]

Although documentation is limited in lesbians, some STDs can be transmitted between women. For example, human papillomavirus (HPV),[45] bacterial vaginosis,[8] and trichomonas[41] have been reported in lesbians and their female partners. Rates of herpes and chlamydia, which have also been found in lesbians who have not had sex with men, appear to be lower than among heterosexual women.[45] In one study of lesbians and STDs, for example, the prevalence of herpes simplex type-2 was found to be 13%[45] compared with approximately 21% in heterosexual women. Cases of female-to-female transmission of HIV are extremely rare, although at least two instances have been reported.[22] (*See* Chapters 12 and 14 for information on HIV/AIDS.) Lack of penile–anal contact prevents transmission of many rectal/anal STDs that affect gay males or heterosexuals who engage in anal sex.

Lesbians who have sex with men are at risk for a range of STDs, including chlamydia, gonorrhea, herpes, syphilis, and HIV. Among heterosexually active lesbians, STDs may be overlooked by providers who assume that lesbians do not have

TABLE 5.1.   Adolescent Sexuality

Providers should

• Support and encourage awareness and acceptance among adults that sexuality is a part of adolescent development.
• Affirm family involvement with children's sexual education.
• Support innovative efforts to delay onset of coitus and affirm the importance of self-exploration and intimacy.
• Increase awareness of sexual abuse and provide services to adolescent victims.
• Improve reproductive health care of adolescents with disabilities and chronic illnesses.
• Support health care and enhance life options to meet the needs of heterosexual, gay, and lesbian youth.

From Society for Adolescent Medicine: Position statements on reproductive health care for adolescents. J Adolesc Health 12:657, 1991, with permission.

sex with men. Because viral infections (e.g., herpes, HPV, HIV) are lifelong, prevention and early diagnosis are particularly important for lesbian adolescents who may not understand their risks or may disregard prevention messages that do not specifically mention lesbians.

Since lack of gynecologic care is frequently reported, health guidance is essential for lesbian adolescents. In two separate studies, for example, 5% and 8% of lesbians had never received a Papanicolaou smear;[15,39] in the former, this includes 23% of 17–24-year-olds and 5% of lesbians > age 55.[15] Providers should be aware that fear of ridicule or lack of understanding (including misconceptions that gynecological care is only relevant for heterosexual women) inhibits lesbians from obtaining both routine screening and ongoing care. Thus, routine Pap smear guidelines should be followed for all adolescent females.

Like heterosexual teens, lesbians may experience menstrual difficulties. They may have concerns about sexual behavior, intimacy, and relationships as well as questions about sexual orientation and parenting.

Gay Males

Studies of STDs in gay men have shown the highest rates among sexually active males in the youngest age group.[54] Young gay males often report using sexual experiences as a way to learn about being gay.[50,54] However, unprotected intercourse puts them at very high risk for HIV and other sexually transmitted diseases (Table 5.3). Sexually transmitted infections and complications in gay men include urethritis,

TABLE 5.2.   Provision of Education and Treatment for Sexually Transmitted Diseases

• Adolescents should have access to education, counseling and health care services for prevention, screening, diagnosis, and treatment of STDs.
• Minors should have access to these services on their own consent.
• Education and testing for STDs should be integrated into the delivery of all adolescent health care services, including those providing contraceptive and prenatal care.
• Condoms and foam should be widely available, and teenagers should be instructed in their use and how to integrate them into sexual relationships.
• HIV-testing programs must include a continuum of counseling not limited to one pre- and post-test counseling session and be linked to medical and psychosocial services.
• Access to HIV/AIDS services must be expanded; new protocols for AIDS clinical trials need to include age-appropriateness assessments.

From Society for Adolescent Medicine: Position statements on reproductive health care for adolescents. J Adolesc Health 12:657, 1991.

TABLE 5.3.   Possible STDs in Gay Males

Chancroid	Hepatitis
Chlamydia	Herpes
Condyloma acuminata (venereal warts)	HIV
Gastrointestinal infections (bacterial,	Pediculosis
parasitic, viral)	Scabies
Gonorrhea	Syphilis

anogenital conditions, oropharyngeal conditions, gastrointestinal disease, hepatitis, herpes, and HIV disease.[9] (*See* Chapters 12 and 14 for information on HIV/AIDS.)

Urethritis in gay men is most commonly caused by gonorrhea and/or chlamydia. Sexually transmitted dermatologic conditions (scabies, pediculosis) are also relatively common, as are venereal warts (penile, anal, and rectal).[9] Ulcerative lesions caused by syphilis, herpes, or chancroid are less common in the United States. Syphilis may be missed if the chancre is painless and concealed in the rectum.[9] Similarly, anogenital herpes may appear atypical and may be confused with another STD (e.g., mature lesions may present as ulcers that look like syphilis).[64] HIV infection may also be associated with severe recurrent herpes.[23] Some STDs may also occur in the oropharynx. Gonorrhea is the most common; others include syphilis, herpes, and venereal warts.[26] Among gay men with anogenital gonorrhea, for example, 10–25% have positive pharyngeal cultures, and diagnosis can be made only by culture.[64] Anal inspection and culture should be routine components of any examination since anal infections (e.g., herpes, warts, gonorrhea) are treatable and are indicative of anal intercourse in persons who might not otherwise disclose sexual orientation or behavior.

Sexually active gay males who have unprotected intercourse are also at risk for a range of gastrointestinal diseases, generally grouped in three syndromes: proctitis, proctocolitis, and enteritis. These infections occur as a result of anal intercourse and oral contact, and are more likely than other STDs to "masquerade" as non-sexually transmitted illnesses.[64] Gonorrhea, chlamydia, herpes simplex, primary syphilis, and human papillomavirus (HPV) may cause proctitis, resulting in rectal pain, discharge, tenesmus, constipation, and fever. Proctocolitis is caused by intestinal bacteria (e.g., *shigella, salmonella*); symptoms include abdominal pain, bloody diarrhea, and fever. Enteritis is caused by several intestinal parasites, such as *Giardia* and *Entamoeba histolytica*, which may or may not be symptomatic (e.g., two studies of gay men showed rates of *E. histolytica* at 20–29%, but only half were symptomatic).[64] Symptoms include abdominal pain, diarrhea, bloating, and nausea.

Hepatitis A and B are readily transmitted sexually. Hepatitis C is predominantly transmitted via contact with blood (and less often through sexual contact). Cytomegalovirus (CMV), which appears to be transmitted sexually, is also prevalent in sexually active persons.[1]

Reproductive Health and Parenting

Lesbian and gay adolescents may have questions about parenting. Historically, many lesbians and gay men have had children, most often in marriages prior to coming out. Increasingly, many lesbians and gay men are choosing to parent, through donor insemination, adoption, or foster care as well as conception. Estimates suggest that 1–5 million lesbian mothers and 1–3 million gay fathers currently live in the United States, and that an additional 5,000–10,000 lesbians have borne children after coming

TABLE 5.4. Health Problems Associated with Sexual Abuse

Depression	HIV infection
Suicidal ideation and behavior	Sexual identity confusion
Substance abuse	Sexual dysfunction
Posttraumatic stress disorder	

out.[51] Since the late 1970s, researchers have studied the development of children of lesbian mothers and found no significant differences in gender identity, sex-role behavior, sexual orientation, or peer-adult relationships compared with children of heterosexual mothers.[51]

Although some lesbian teens may become pregnant because they and their male partners fail to use contraceptives, others may become pregnant out of choice or in an attempt to change or to hide sexual orientation. Providers should address reproductive and parenting concerns, provide information on available resources (e.g., articles, lesbian/gay youth organizations), and make appropriate referrals (see Appendix B for a list of community resources and references).

Trauma and Sexual Assault

Because adolescents are at high risk for violence, providers are likely to encounter youth who are victims of assault, including rape and sexual assault. Nearly half of all rape victims are adolescents.[5] Most reported crimes involve young women, but males are also victimized, and incidence in males is believed to be significantly underreported[24] (shame and fear of being perceived as gay contribute to underreporting). Prevalence studies suggest that 15–22% of women have been raped at some time in their lives,[42] whereas estimates of sexual abuse prior to age 18 range from 3–31% for males[30] and 28–36% for females (< 14 years old).[63] Comparable data are not available for lesbian and gay youth, although in one study, half of lesbians, ages 17–24, reported rape or sexual assault.[15] In a study of gay males, ages 15–19, 6% reported sexual assault, and an additional 6% reported sexual abuse by family members.[53] Among college students in one study, 11.8% of gay males and 30.6% of lesbians reported sexual assault (compared with rates of 3.6% and 17.8% in heterosexual males and females).[25]

Rates of sexual abuse are considerably higher among clinical samples of lesbians and gay men and heterosexuals who have had higher lifetime exposure to trauma. In a survey of sexual abuse victims who attended STD clinics, for example, 37% of gay men had been sexually abused as children or adolescents.[7] And in an outcome study of lesbians and gay men who had completed inpatient substance abuse treatment, 44% reported having been sexually abused (37% of males and 67% of females), with abstinence being much more likely among those who had not experienced abuse.[52] Prevalence of sexual abuse appears higher among gay males than heterosexual males,[29,40] although gay males may be more willing to report such abuse.[17] Social isolation heightens vulnerability, particularly as young gay males attempt to learn about homosexuality in environments where they may be exploited or abused. Research with sex offenders shows that many are attracted to effeminate, sexually immature boys.[34] Lack of secondary sex characteristics and stereotypically feminine behaviors may increase the likelihood of sexual abuse in males.[35,36]

Childhood sexual abuse has a range of psychological and behavioral consequences that increase risk for further victimization and disease. These include depression[6,14] posttraumatic stress disorder,[10,13] substance abuse,[24,65] suicidal ideation and behavior,[13,33] and risk for HIV infection.[7,65] Victims also experience sexual identity confusion, sexual dysfunction, and relationship problems, and they are more likely to engage in prostitution,[21,65] to seek counseling, or be hospitalized for psychiatric problems.[7]

In addition to risk for sexual abuse and assault, lesbian and gay adolescents are at high risk for specific bias-related crimes (anti-gay violence), including rape, physical attacks, verbal and physical abuse, and harassment because of sexual orientation (*see* Chapter 3). Victimization is a common experience, particularly for youth who are openly or stereotypically gay. Although the psychological, somatic, and behavioral sequelae are similar to those seen in non-bias-related victimization, anti-gay attacks heighten an adolescent's feelings of vulnerability, often intensify negative feelings about sexual orientation (internalized homophobia), and may cause the youth and others to perceive the act as punishment for being gay.[33] Family and peer support are important resources for recovering from trauma; in many cases, an adolescent victim may not have "come out" previously to parents or peers. Parents may react to the assault with anger and "blame the victim" if the adolescent's sexual orientation is initially disclosed as a result of the incident.

Eating Disorders

Although few data are available, eating disorders have been identified as a concern for young gay males.[37,59] In one study of male and female patients in an inpatient program for eating disorders, male patients were more likely to be gay.[37] In other studies of body image, eating disorders, and weight, gay men were found to be more dissatisfied with body image and appearance than heterosexual men[16,60] or women,[59] whereas lesbians appeared least concerned.[59] In providing care for gay adolescents, providers should be aware that eating disorders may be more common than in heterosexual males and consider this possibility when screening or making a diagnosis. Data are not currently available on obesity rates in lesbians and gay males.

Substance Abuse

Alcohol and other kinds of drug abuse are the leading causes of disability among adolescents and young adults. Alcohol alone accounts for more than half of all motor vehicle fatalities in youth, ages 15–24, and is associated with some 40% of all homicides and suicides in this age group each year.[44] Moreover, the United States has the highest rate of drug abuse among industrialized countries.[3] Since the 1960s, alcohol and drug use have become endemic among teens (Table 5.5).

Nine out of 10 high school seniors have used alcohol and consider themselves "drinkers," while 43% have used marijuana.[27] And although cigarette use has decreased among adults, an additional 600,000 adolescents, ages 14–17, began smoking cigarettes between 1985 and 1989. If they continue to smoke regularly, half will die from smoking-related diseases.[19] Stimulants, such as cocaine and amphetamines, are the fourth type of drug most frequently used by adolescents; smokable forms of "crack" and "ice" are accessible, affordable, and highly addictive. Inhalants, such as toluene (in glue and paint thinner) and halogenated hydrocarbons (in solvents and paper correction fluid), are often the first drugs used by younger adolescents. Polydrug abuse (simultaneous use of more than one drug, such as alcohol and marijuana) is common practice among 75–95% of youth who use substances.[27] In addition to pre-

TABLE 5.5. Alcohol and Other Drug Use—Adolescents, Grades 9–12
(Youth Risk Behavior Surveillance—1993)

Drug Used	Ever Used	Past 30 Days	Current Use	Episodic Heavy Drinking Past 30 Days
Alcohol	80.9%	48%	—	30%
Tobacco	69.5%	30.5%	24.7%	
Marijuana	32.8%	17.7%	14.1%	
Cocaine	4.9%	1.9%	2.2%	
Crack	2.6%	—	—	
Steroids	2.2%	—	—	
Injection Drugs	1.4%	—	—	

From Centers for Disease Control: Youth risk behavior surveillance—U.S. 1993. MMWR 44:1, 1995.

mature death and diseases, including mental and emotional impairments, alcohol abuse and drug abuse contribute substantially to escalating violence and crime.

Substance abuse also increases risk for STDs, including HIV. Many adolescents report using alcohol before having intercourse (more than half who drink before sex report having 5 or more drinks), which impairs judgment and increases potential for high-risk behaviors.[31] Use of crack cocaine is highly predictive of HIV infection since crack users often exchange sex for drugs or money to buy drugs. In a cohort of adolescents with HIV, for example, two-thirds of girls and more than half of boys used crack; of these, 86% and 80%, respectively, exchanged sex for money, drugs, food, and shelter (survival sex).[32]

Rates of substance use and abuse vary among and within racial/ethnic groups. Highest rates are seen in Native American youth, particularly reservation youth, followed by whites, Hispanics, African-Americans, and Asians. Similar rates are found in both urban and rural youth, with higher rates in school drop-outs. The most frequently used drugs are used consistently by adolescents across racial and ethnic groups.[49]

Substance Abuse in Lesbians and Gay Males

Although substance abuse has been identified as a health concern for adult lesbians and gay men, limited information is available on substance use (and abuse) among lesbian and gay adolescents. Moreover, inadequate research (nonrepresentative samples, poor comparison groups, and inconsistent measures of alcohol and drug dependence) has made it difficult to determine prevalence of substance use and abuse.[38] Early studies of lesbians and gay men showed high rates of chemical dependency; however, many of these studies had limited samples, included few women, and recruited participants from bars, where a higher proportion of substance abusers are likely to be found.[2,18] More recent studies, which include larger and more diverse samples, have shown differences among lesbian, gay, and heterosexual adults. In one study of 3,400 lesbians and gay men, fewer lesbians and gay men abstained from alcohol use and fewer gender differences were seen between lesbians and gay men in use of alcohol than among heterosexual men and women; lesbians and gay men were twice as likely to be moderate drinkers and about as likely to be heavy drinkers as heterosexuals.[46,47] However, lesbians and gay men also reported rates of alcohol problems nearly twice as high as those reported for heterosexuals (23% vs. 12%). And unlike among heterosexual men and women, these problems did not decrease with age. Instead, use in lesbians increased with age—a finding seen in other studies.[15a,57]

Information about substance use reported by lesbian and gay youth is minimal. Some studies of urban gay youth show high rates of alcohol and drug use,[53,56] while others do not.[11,12,15] Findings from a national lesbian survey, with a cohort of young lesbians, ages 17–24, showed rates of lifetime use that are comparable to rates among heterosexual women, but higher rates of drug use overall. One out of 3 smoked daily; 13% were concerned about use of alcohol, and 5.9% and 2.4%, respectively, were concerned about marijuana and cocaine use.[15]

Before an organized lesbian and gay community was developed, access to other gay people was mediated by bars, which enabled lesbians and gay men, generally living in secrecy, to meet and socialize. However, restricting socialization to bars fostered substance use and abuse and likely contributed to high rates of use reported in many early studies.[28,43,58] During the past 20 years, the development of an extensive network of social and professional groups increasingly has provided an alternate social system to support basic needs for recognition, affiliation, and intimacy. More recently, similar support groups are being developed for lesbian and gay youth, particularly in urban areas. These organizations offer important referral and educational resources for primary care providers working with lesbian and gay adolescents. Moreover, programs for lesbian and gay youth often include social and mental health services as well as access to knowledgeable health providers and addiction specialists. (*See* Appendix B for a list of referral organizations and professional resources.)

Lesbian and gay youth use alcohol and drugs for many of the same reasons as heterosexuals: to experiment and assert independence, to relieve tension, to increase feelings of self-esteem and adequacy, and to self-medicate for underlying depression or other mood disorder. However, vulnerability is enhanced by social isolation and the need to hide sexual orientation. For these youth, substance use may be motivated by the attempt to manage stigma and shame, to deny same-sex feelings, or to defend against ridicule and anti-gay violence. Unless providers conduct a thorough medical and social history and are open to the reality that all adolescents are not heterosexual, underlying needs for emotional and practical support will often be missed, and these adolescents will remain at continued risk for chemical dependency, relapse following treatment, and the myriad complications of addictive disease.

References

1. Abadalian SE, Remafedi G: Sexually transmitted diseases in young homosexual men. Sem Pediatr Infect Dis 4:122, 1993.
2. Abbot LA: Alcohol use in lesbians: Review and research agenda. J Addiction [in press].
3. Alderman EM, Schonberg SK, Cohen MI: The pediatrician's role in the diagnosis and management of substance abuse. Pediatr Rev 13:314, 1992.
4. American Academy of Pediatrics: Homosexuality and adolescence. Pediatrics 92:631, 1993.
5. American Academy of Pediatrics: Rape and the adolescent. Pediatrics 81:595, 1988.
6. Atkeson BM, Calhoun KS, Resick PA, Ellis S: Victims of rape: Repeated assessment of depressive symptoms. J Consult Clin Psychol 50:96, 1982.
7. Bartholow BN, Doll LS, Joy D, et al: Emotional, behavioral and HIV risks associated with sexual abuse among adult homosexual and bisexual men. Child Abuse Negl 18:747, 1994.
8. Berger BJ, et al: Bacterial vaginosis in lesbians: A sexually transmitted disease. Clin Infect Dis 21: 1402, 1995.
9. Bidwell RJ: Sexual orientation and gender identity. In Friedman SN, Fisher M, Schonberg SK (eds): Comprehensive Adolescent Health Care. St Louis, MO, Quality Medical Publishing, 1992.
10. Blake-White J, Kline CM: Treating the dissociative process in adult victims of childhood incest. Soc Casework 66:394, 1985.

11. Boxer A: Life course transitions of gay and lesbian youth: Sexual identity development and parent-child relationships. Doctoral dissertation, University of Chicago, 1990.
12. Boxer A: Personal communication, July 17, 1996.
13. Briere J, Evans D, Runtz M, Wall T: Symptomatology in men who were molested as children: A comparison study. Am J Orthopsychiatry 58:457, 1988.
14. Briere J, Runtz M: Post-sexual abuse trauma: Data and implications for clinical practice. J Interpers Violence 2:367, 1987.
15. Bradford JB, Ryan CC: The National Lesbian Health Care Survey: Final Report. Washington, DC, National Lesbian and Gay Health Foundation, 1987.
15a. Bradford J, Ryan C, Rothblum ED: National lesbian health care survey: Implications for mental health care. J Consult Clin Psychol 62:228, 1994.
16. Brand PA, Rothblum ED, Solomon LJ: A comparison of lesbians, gay men and heterosexuals on weight and restrained eating. Int J Eat Disord 11:253, 1992.
17. Brown L: Personal communication, February 15, 1997.
18. Cabaj RP: AIDS and chemical dependency: Special issues and treatment barriers for gay and bisexual men. J Psychoactive Drugs 21:387, 1989.
19. Centers for Disease Control: Trends in smoking initiation among adolescents and young adults—United States, 1980-1989. MMWR 44:521, 1995.
20. Centers for Disease Control: Youth risk behavior surveillance—U.S. 1993. MMWR 44:1, 1995.
21. Coleman E: The development of male prostitution activity among gay and bisexual adolescents. J Homosex 18:131, 1989.
22. Chu SY, Buehler JW, Fleming PL, Berkelman RL: Epidemiology of reported cases of AIDS in lesbians, United States 9980-89. Am J Public Health 80:1380, 1990.
23. Corey L, Spear PG: Infection with Herpes simplex viruses—II. N Engl J Med 314:749–757, 1986.
24. Dimock PT. Adult males sexually abused as children. J Interpers Violence 3:203, 1988.
25. Duncan D: Prevalence of sexual assault victimization among heterosexual and gay/lesbian university students. Psychol Rep 66:65, 1990.
26. Eng T, Butler W (eds): The Hidden Epidemic: Confronting Sexually Transmitted Diseases. Institute of Medicine. Committee on Prevention and Control of STDs. Washington, DC, National Academy Press, 1997.
27. Farrow JA: Adolescent chemical dependency. Med Clin North Am 74:1265, 1990.
28. Fifield LH, DeCrescenzo TA, Latham JD: On My Way to Nowhere: Alienated, Isolated, Drunk. An Analysis of Gay Alcohol Abuse and an Evaluation of Alcoholism Rehabilitation Services for the Los Angeles Gay Community. Los Angeles, CA, Gay Community Services Center and Office of Alcohol Abuse and Alcoholism, Los Angeles County, 1975.
29. Finkelhor D: Child Sexual Abuse: New Theory and Research. New York, The Free Press, 1984.
30. Finkelhor D: The sexual abuse of children: Current research reviewed. Psychiatr Ann 17:233, 1987.
31. Fortenberry JD: Adolescent substance use and sexually transmitted diseases risk: A review. J Adolesc Health 16:304, 1995.
32. Futterman D, Hein K, Ruben N, Dell R, Shaffer N: HIV-infected adolescents: The first 50 patients in a New York City program. Pediatrics 91:730, 1993.
33. Garnets L, Herek GM, Levy B: Violence and victimization of lesbians and gay men: Mental health consequences. In Herek G, Berrill K (eds): Hate Crimes: Confronting Violence Against Lesbians and Gay Men. Newbury Park, CA, Sage Publications, 1992.
34. Groth AN, Birnbaum HJ: Adult sexual orientation and attraction to underage persons. Arch Sex Behav 7:175, 1987.
35. Harry J: Sexual orientation, a destiny. J Homosex 10:111, 1985.
36. Harry J: Parental physical abuse and sexual orientation in males. Arch Sex Behav 18:251, 1989.
37. Herzog DB, Norman DK, Gordon C, Pepose M: Sexual conflict and eating disorders in 27 males. Am J Psychiatry 141:989, 1984.
38. Hughes TL, Wilsnack SC: Research on lesbians and alcohol: Gaps and implications. Alcohol Health Res World 18:202, 1994.
39. Johnson SR, Guenther SM, Laube DW, Keettel WC: Factors influencing lesbian gynecologic care: A preliminary study. Am J Obstetrics and Gynecology 140:20, 1981.
40. Johnson R, Shrier D: Sexual victimization of boys. J Adolesc Health Care 6:372, 1985.
41. Kellock DJ, O'Mahony CP: Sexually acquired metronidazole-resistant trichmoniasis in a lesbian couple. Genitourin Med 72:60, 1996.
42. Koss MP, Gidycz CJ, Wisniewski N: The scope of rape: Incidence and prevalence of sexual aggression and victimization in a national sample of higher education students. J Consult Clin Psychol 55:162, 1987.

43. Lohrenz LJ, Connelly JC, Coyne L, Spare DE: Alcohol problems in several midwestern communities. J Studies Alcohol 39:1959, 1978.
44. MacKenzie RG, Kipke MD: Substance use and abuse. In Friedman SB, Fisher M, Schonberg SK (eds): Comprehensive Adolescent Health Care. St Louis, MO, Quality Medical Publishing, 1992.
45. Marrazzo JM, Stine K, Handsfield HH, Koutsky LA: Epidemiology of STD and cervical neoplasia among lesbian and bisexual women. Abstracts of the National Lesbian and Gay Health Association conference, Seattle, WA, July 1996.
46. McKirnan DJ, Peterson PL: Alcohol and drug use among homosexual men and women: Epidemiology and population characteristics. Addict Behav 14:545, 1989.
47. McKirnan DJ, Peterson PL: Psychosocial and cultural factors in alcohol and drug abuse: An analysis of a homosexual community. Addict Behav 14:555, 1989.
48. Mosher WD, Aral SO: Testing for sexually transmitted diseases among women of reproductive age: United States, 1988. Family Plann Perspec 23:216, 1991.
49. Oetting ER, Beauvais F: Adolescent drug use: Findings of national and local surveys. J Consult Clin Psychol 58:385, 1990.
50. Paroski PA: Health care delivery and the concerns of gay and lesbian adolescents. J Adolesc Health Care 8:188, 1987.
51. Patterson CJ: Children of lesbian and gay parents. Child Dev 63:1025, 1992.
52. Ratner EF, Kosten TK, McLellan AT: Treatment outcome of Pride Institute patients. Unpublished paper, 1991.
53. Remafedi G: Adolescent homosexuality: Psychosocial and medical implications. Pediatrics 79:331, 1987.
54. Remafedi G: Sexually transmitted diseases in young homosexual men. Sem Ped Infect Dis 4:122, 1993.
55. Remafedi G, Farrow JA, Deisher RW: Risk factors for attempted suicide in gay and bisexual youth. Pediatrics 87:869, 1991.
56. Rotheram-Borus MJ, Rosario M, Meyer-Bahlburg H et al: Sexual and substance use acts of gay and bisexual male adolescents in New York City. J Sex Res 31:47, 1994.
57. Skinner WF: The prevalence and demographic predictors of illicit and licit drug use among lesbians and gay men. Am J Public Health 84:1307, 1994.
58. Saghir MT, Robbins E: Male and Female Homosexuality: A Comprehensive Investigation. Baltimore, Williams & Wilkins, 1973.
59. Siever MD: Sexual orientation and gender as factors in socioculturally acquired vulnerability to body dissatisfaction and eating disorders. J Consult Clin Psychol 62:252, 1994.
60. Silberstein LR, Mishkind ME, Striegel-Moore RH, Timko C, Rodin J: Men and their bodies: A comparison of homosexual and heterosexual men. Psychosom Med 51:337, 1989.
61. Society for Adolescent Medicine: Position statements on reproductive health care for adolescents. J Adolesc Health 12:657, 1991.
62. White J, Levinson W: Primary care of lesbian patients. J Gen Intern Med 8:41, 1993.
63. Wyatt GE, Peters SD: Issues in the definition of child sexual abuse in prevalence research. Child Abuse Negl 10:231, 1986.
64. Zenilman J: Sexually transmitted diseases in homosexual adolescents. J Adolesc Health 9:129, 1988.
65. Zierler S, Feingold L, Laufer D, et al: Adult survivors of childhood sexual abuse and subsequent risk of HIV infection. Am J Public Health 81:572, 1991.

CHAPTER 6

Transgendered Youth

Cross-gender (transgendered) behavior has been documented throughout history in a broad variety of cultures.[5,11] Some non-Western societies, including many Native American tribes, have accepted and institutionalized cross-gendered persons, often as a third sex.[6,12] In modern Western societies, however, transgendered people are generally even more reviled than lesbians and gay men. Although the majority are heterosexual, anyone who exhibits gender-atypical behavior is considered to be homosexual. Thus, many transgendered people seek acceptance and support within the lesbian and gay community, where gender norms are more inclusive.[8]

Transgender covers a broad range of gender-nonconforming identities and behaviors, including transsexuals (preoperative, postoperative, and persons who are not interested in sex reassignment surgery), transvestites, male and female impersonators, and "gender benders"* (persons who overtly challenge gender norms for cultural or political reasons). Transgendered persons may be heterosexual, homosexual, bisexual, or asexual (Table 6.1).

Transgendered people face significant discrimination in employment, housing, and access to health care. Fearing ridicule and rejection, many avoid mainstream health services or seek gay-sensitive providers, who are seen as more accepting and knowledgeable about their health concerns. Many live outside of mainstream society. Since gender-atypical behavior is much less accepted in boys than girls, transgendered males become frequent targets of verbal and physical abuse. Without support at home, they may drop out of school, run away, and often end up on the streets, where they are at risk for drug use, prostitution, and HIV. Many are virtually unemployable because of gender nonconforming appearance, lack of education, or job skills.[10]

Providers may be more familiar with the terms *transsexual* or *transvestite*, which are used to describe persons who feel trapped in the wrong body or who cross-dress in opposite-gender clothes. The revised Diagnostic and Statistical Manual of Mental Disorders (DSM-IV)[1] has dropped use of "transsexual" and clustered persons with gender dysphoria (discomfort and distress with one's anatomic gender and role) under the category of Gender Identity Disorder (GID), which includes a range of gender-related disorders.

Criteria for gender identity disorder include having (1) a strong and persistent cross-gender identification and (2) a persistent (long-term) discomfort with one's anatomical gender.[1] Transsexuals are further categorized under primary transsexualism (emerging in early childhood) or secondary transsexualism (emerging during or after puberty). The actual incidence of transsexualism is unknown; estimates of 1 in 30,000 males and 1 in 100,000 females[2] are based on persons who have presented at gender identity clinics. However, only a minority actually requests services at such clinics, and for a variety of reasons, most do not seek sex reassignment surgery.[7] With increasing availability of support groups and advocacy organizations, transgendered people have become more visible and active in identifying their health and service needs. Access to support (including nonjudgmental providers) and to positive role models is

---

*Gender bending is increasingly common in popular culture: gender-bending celebrities include basketball star Dennis Rodman and rock stars David Bowie, Boy George, and k.d. lang.

TABLE 6.1.   Transgender Identity

Transgender covers a broad range of gender-nonconforming identities and behaviors. Transgendered persons may be heterosexual, homosexual, bisexual, or asexual. Providers should *not* assume that all transgendered people experience gender dysphoria.

Transgendered persons include the following:

Gender bender	Crossing the gender line in dress and behavior to make a political statement, to feel more comfortable, to express difference from conventional society (e.g., "queer" identity) or to provide entertainment (e.g., drag queens).
Transvestite	Cross-dressing (wear clothes of the opposite sex) for emotional comfort or erotic fulfillment.
Androgyne	Blending masculine and feminine characteristics for sense of emotional completeness.
Transsexual	Feeling "trapped in the wrong body"; anatomical gender does not match internal sense of being male or female.
Nonsurgical	Choosing to live as the opposite sex without sex reassignment surgery; may or may not use hormones to enhance development of secondary sex characteristics.
Pre- and post-operative	Choosing to have sex reassignment surgery; generally seeking assistance from gender identity clinics, which recommend counseling and living full-time for at least 1 year as the opposite sex before initiating surgery.

a key factor in self-acceptance, identity resolution, and living productive, satisfying lives.

Health/Mental Health Needs

Most information about transsexuals has been obtained from people who have sought counseling or services from gender identity clinics; of these, many report high rates of substance abuse, attempted suicide, and psychiatric problems.[10] Much less is known, however, about the nonclinical transsexual population, some of whom may present at community clinics or emergency rooms for a variety of health needs, including trauma from bias-related violence.

Among transsexuals who use hormones to develop desired female (or male) secondary sex characteristics (often in lieu of sex reassignment surgery), fear of judgmental or negative reactions from providers is so great that they may seek hormones on the street, putting themselves at risk for HIV infection from contaminated needles.[9] Improper use of sex hormones can cause other serious health complications, including thromboembolism, cardiovascular disease, hemorrhage, and hypertension.[3] Moreover, use during puberty can adversely affect growth and development.[4]

Although transsexualism is classified as a gender identity disorder in the DSM-III and DSM-IV (as gender dysphoric behavior), "it is harmful to treat adolescent transsexuals as disordered individuals."[3] Rather than attempting to change or "cure" transsexual youth, providers should offer counseling, support, and access to appropriate resources to help the adolescent clarify identity confusion (e.g., some youth mistakenly believe that being gay means engaging in cross-gendered behavior), resolve conflict, and determine whether treatment is appropriate (e.g., hormonal therapy following the growth spurt and/or eventual consideration of sex reassignment surgery). Since surgery is not an option during adolescence, hormonal therapy and ongoing counseling "may literally be lifesaving for many transsexual teens."[3] Moreover, lack of provider support, coupled with feelings of hopelessness, may actually contribute to the high suicide rate among transsexual teens.[3]

Regardless of sexual orientation, youth who suffer from gender identity disorder and experience severe distress with anatomic gender require ongoing counseling, anticipatory guidance, health education, and referrals to appropriate community support services.

References

1. American Psychiatric Association: Diagnostic and Statistical Manual of Mental Disorders, 4th ed. Washington, DC, American Psychiatric Association, 1994.
2. American Psychiatric Association: Diagnostic and Statistical Manual of Mental Disorders, 3rd ed. Washington, DC, American Psychiatric Association, 1987.
3. Bidwell RJ: Sexual orientation and gender identity. In Friedman SB, Fisher M, Schonberg SK (eds): Comprehensive Adolescent Health Care. St Louis, MO, Quality Medical Publishing, 1992.
4. Boxer A: Does "nonjudgmental" care include prescribing hormones?: A commentary. In Blustein J, Dubler N, Levine C (eds): The Adolescent "Alone": Decision Making in Health Care. New York: Cambridge University Press, 1998.
5. Bullough VI: Transsexualism in history. Arch Sex Behav 4:561, 1975.
6. Bullough VI, Bullough B: Cross-Dressing, Sex and Gender. Philadelphia, University of Pennsylvania Press, 1993.
7. Denny D: Introduction. In Denny D: Gender Dysphoria: A Guide to Research. New York, Garland Publishing, 1994.
8. Feinberg L: Transgender Warriors. Boston, Beacon Press, 1996.
9. Sbordone AJ: Transgenderism: Social and psychological issues in the treatment of HIV/AIDS, a case study. Paper presented at the National Lesbian and Gay Health Conference, New York, June 24, 1994.
10. Seil D: Transsexuals: The boundaries of sexual identity and gender. In Cabaj RP, Stein TS (eds): Textbook of Homosexuality and Mental Health. Washington, DC, American Psychiatric Press, 1996.
11. Steiner BW: From Sappho to Sand: Historical perspective on cross-dressing and cross gender. Can J Psychiatry 36:502, 1981.
12. Williams W: The Spirit and the Flesh: Sexual Diversity in American Indian Culture. Boston, Beacon Press, 1986.

CHAPTER 7

Special Populations

Lesbian and gay youth are represented in all populations of adolescents, within all social classes, and racial/ethnic groups, including youth with heightened vulnerabilities and frequently unmet needs. As with all adolescents, providers should not assume heterosexuality and should be familiar with community resources and appropriate referrals.

Disabled Adolescents

Lesbian and gay adolescents who are also disabled face additional barriers in meeting their informational, social, emotional, and health care needs. They encounter the same barriers as disabled heterosexual adolescents and adults in achieving maximum mobility, independence, and self-actualization. Moreover, they have the same needs as other lesbian and gay adolescents to understand and explore their sexuality, to struggle with coming out, to find supportive peers and adults, and to establish intimate relationships. But the denial and invisibility experienced by able-bodied lesbian and gay youth is amplified for them, and access to information about sexual orientation and intimacy is further restricted.

Providers often feel uncomfortable talking about sexuality with disabled persons and avoid raising or addressing these issues. Discomfort is increased when discussing sexual orientation. Among residents providing adolescent care, for example, 40% of primary care providers surveyed were not comfortable dealing with homosexuality, handicaps, and other chronic conditions, or rape.[9] However, taking a thorough medical history requires providers to address these and other sensitive issues that affect an adolescent's health status and risk profile. For example, data strongly suggest that children and adolescents with disabilities are at particular risk for physical abuse and sexual assault.[1] In a study of children with communication disabilities, nearly half (48%) had been sexually abused; moreover, males with disabilities are at greater risk for sexual abuse than males who are not disabled.[1] Sexual abuse victims are at increased risk for future victimization; however, early detection and treatment improves the prognosis for normal adult functioning. For disabled children and youth who are dependent on adults for care and mobility and who may have significant communication barriers, access to a sensitive provider who can identify and help address traumatic experiences helps restore trust and prevent more serious long-term sequelae.

Lesbian and gay youth who are visually or hearing impaired have more difficulty accessing appropriate information about sexual orientation, including referral sources and support groups, particularly if they are closeted and have no one they can ask for help. Health education information, such as HIV prevention, is rarely geared to meet their needs. Providers should be aware of community resources for disabled gay persons to help advocate for their clients and make appropriate referrals (*see* Appendix B).

Runaway/Homeless Adolescents

National prevalence studies show high rates of runaway and homeless youth. Figures range from 500,000 runaways (and 127,000 ''throwaways'') to 2 million adolescents living on the streets, with a fairly even distribution of males and females and a median age of 14–16 years.[8] Another 1.2 million run away from home each year; of these, approximately 1 in 4 becomes a street youth, who is dependent on the street for economic survival, recreation, and social support needs.[8] Estimates of lesbian and gay homeless youth vary, but youth service providers agree that rates are very high, ranging from 20–40% in various studies.[13,18,20] Because both males and females are often unlikely to disclose their sexual orientation, rates are probably under-reported.[12] Many are forced out of their homes because of sexual orientation.

Like other homeless and runaway youth, lesbian and gay youth who are homeless have multiple unmet health and social needs, often resulting from abuse and neglect. Serious physical abuse is reported by 60–75% of runaways, and the prevalence of sexual abuse is even higher.[8] Alcohol and drug abuse is pervasive and further increases risk for trauma and STDs, including HIV. In one study, for example, alcohol abuse was 6–8 times higher than among non-homeless youth, while drug abuse was 5 times higher among homeless adolescents.[17] Homeless youth are also significantly more likely to be diagnosed with an STD[11] and are among the highest risk groups for HIV infection.[7] Higher prevalences of mental health concerns are also reported. In one clinic, for example, 85% of homeless youth were diagnosed with depression, 20% had attempted suicide, 9% were actively suicidal, and 18% had a severe mental health problem.[21] As in the general population, suicide attempts appear to be higher among lesbian and gay homeless youth (53% vs. 32% according to one study).[12] Homeless youth are often victims of violence and are frequently involved in illegal activities for economic survival, including prostitution, drug-dealing, and theft.

Although approximately 3 out of 4 homeless youth remain in their original communities, few are knowledgeable about local health services.[8] Many have been exploited and victimized by adults and are reluctant to trust health care providers. They often seek emergency care at hospitals when untreated and chronic health conditions become too advanced to ignore.[6]

Adolescents Involved with Juvenile Corrections

Adolescents who are involved with juvenile courts and placed in correctional facilities have many of the same kinds of multiple health and social problems as runaway and homeless youth. Many are from dysfunctional and addicted families, and a high proportion has been sexually abused and exposed to considerable violence and victimization.[2] Health and mental health problems are often extensive, including high risk for sexually transmitted diseases and HIV infection.[3] Studies show high rates of depression, substance abuse, and attempted suicide.[2,4,15,16] Lesbian and gay youth in correctional facilities generally try to conceal sexual orientation to avoid further victimization; those who appear stereotypically gay are at risk for harassment, abuse, and violence. In a population with major underlying health and mental health needs, concerns related to sexual orientation are essentially ignored.

Adolescents with Severe Mental Illness

Severe mental illness (e.g., affective disorders, schizophrenia) affects thinking, feeling, and behavior in all aspects of an adolescent's life, including home, school, and relationships with peers and adults. Thus, adolescents with severe mental illness have a range of social, emotional, and clinical needs that require ongoing care, including accurate assessment and diagnosis, outpatient treatment, placement in inpatient and residential facilities or group homes, and advocacy to ensure appropriate treatment and services.

Like other youth, adolescents who are severely mentally ill experience age-appropriate strivings, such as the development of sexuality and identity. Because of impaired function, however, feelings may be acted out or expressed in ways that bring attention, clearly identify the youth as non-heterosexual, and result in treatment that focuses on sexual orientation rather than mental health problems.

Lesbian and gay adolescents with severe mental illness lack the level of support available in many communities for lesbian, gay, and bisexual youth. The dual stigma of homosexuality and mental illness further isolates and marginalizes them, while lack of accurate information and negative internalized stereotypes make it increasingly difficult to develop a more positive identity and to understand their risks. For example, a large proportion of severely mentally ill persons is already HIV-infected (4–22.9% of urban psychiatric patients in some studies),[5,19] and high-risk behavior is common in this population.[10,14] Continued high risk for HIV infection, particularly among gay male youth, makes specific health guidance and ongoing support for developing risk reduction skills essential for working with gay and lesbian youth with severe mental illness.

References

1. American Psychological Association: Violence and youth: Psychology's response. Washington, DC, American Psychological Association, 1993.
2. Brown RT: Health needs of incarcerated youth. Bull NY Acad Med 70:208, 1993.
3. Canterbury RJ, McGarvey EL, Sheldon-Keller AE, et al: Prevalence of HIV-related risk behaviors and STDs among incarcerated adolescents. J Adolesc Health 17:173, 1995.
4. Chiles JA, Miller ML, Cox GB: Depression in an adolescent delinquent population. Arch Gen Psychiatry 37:1179, 1980.
5. Cournos F, Empfield M, Horwath E, et al: HIV seroprevalence among patients admitted to two psychiatric hospitals. Am J Psychiatry 148:1225, 1991.
6. Deisher RW, Rodgers WM: The medical care of street youth. J Adolesc Health. 12:500, 1991.
7. Farrow JA, Deisher RW, Brown R: Introduction (Special issue on homeless and runaway youth). J Adolesc Health 12:497, 1991.
8. Farrow JA, Deisher RW, Brown R, Kulig JW, Kipke MD: Health and health needs of homeless and runaway youth. A position paper of the Society for Adolescent Medicine. J Adolesc Health 13:717, 1992.
9. Figueroa E, Kolasa KM, Horner RE, et al: Attitudes, knowledge and training of medical residents regarding adolescent health issues. J Adolesc Health 12:443, 1991.
10. Kalichman SC, Kelly JA, Johnson JR: Factors associated with risk for HIV infection among chronic mentally ill adults. Am J Psychiatry 151:221, 1994.
11. Kipke MD: HIV and substance abuse among homeless youth. Paper presented at the American Public Health Association conference, Atlanta, GA, 1991.
12. Kruks G: Gay and lesbian homeless/street youth: Special issues and concerns. J Adolesc Health 12: 515, 1991.
13. Los Angeles County Task Force on Runaway and Homeless Youth: Report and recommendations of the Task Force on runaway and homeless youth. Los Angeles, 1988.
14. McKinnon K, Cournos F, Sugden R, Guido JR, Herman R: The relative contributions of psychiatric symptoms and AIDS knowledge to HIV risk behaviors among people with severe mental illness. J Clin Psychiatry 57:506, 1996.
15. Miller ML, Chiles JA, Barnes VE: Suicide attempters within a delinquent population. J Consult Clin Psychol 50:491, 1982.
16. Mitchell J: Mental health problems in incarcerated delinquents. Paper presented at an American Medical Association Work Group on the Health Status of Incarcerated Youth, Chicago, IL, November 14, 1988.

17. Robertson MJ: Homeless youth: Patterns of alcohol use. A report to the National Institute on Alcohol Abuse and Alcoholism. Berkeley, CA, Alcohol Research Group, 1989.
18. Seattle Commission on Children and Youth: Report on Gay and Lesbian Youth in Seattle. Seattle, WA, Department of Human Resources, 1988.
19. Silberstein C, Galanter M, Marmor M, et al: HIV-1 among inner city dually diagnosed inpatients. Am J Drug Alcohol Abuse 20:101, 1994.
20. Stricof RL, Kennedy JT, Natell TC, et al: HIV seroprevalence in a facility for runaway and homeless adolescents. Am J Public Health 81:50, 1988.
21. Yates G, MacKenzie R, Pennbridge J, Cohen E: A risk profile comparison of runaway and non-runaway youth. Am J Public Health 78:820, 1988.

CHAPTER 8

Adolescent Mental Health Concerns

I'm a mental institution survivor. I was placed in an institution by my parents to fix something that wasn't broken—because I'm gay. I didn't go voluntarily. I needed more counseling when I got out than before I went in. Parents may come to you asking for help to institutionalize their child. If it's not necessary, please don't agree. It does much more damage than good.

—*Gay Youth*

Mental Health Concerns of Adolescents

Although moodiness, anxiety, and isolated symptoms of depression are far more common in adolescents than mental health disorders, pediatricians and other providers treating adolescents often miss mental health concerns and fail to make appropriate referrals.[65] This occurs despite the fact that early diagnosis and treatment of mental health problems improve long-term prognosis and help to prevent suicide. For example, 1 of 4 youth who commit suicide does so during a major depressive episode.[59] Approximately one-half to two-thirds of people who complete suicide sought medical care a month before their deaths (while 10–40% visited physicians during the week before their deaths).[1,13,38,44] However, less than one-third (30%) of adolescents who attempt or complete suicide have received previous mental health care.[60,64] Providers should screen routinely for major mental health problems, including depression, suicide, learning problems, and somatoform disorders, because these may also indicate underlying psychological problems or conflicts. Mentioning these concerns should not exclude or minimize the importance of other mental health problems that affect adolescents; however, depression, suicidal ideation, and somatoform disorders are associated with emotional conflict and stress, and may be indicators of internal stress in adolescents and adults who are struggling with sexual orientation issues.

Lesbian and gay adolescents experience the same mental health concerns that affect teens in general, with the addition of stress related to managing the stigma of homosexuality. Since most information about lesbian and gay adolescents is based on youth who receive mental health, medical care, or support services from lesbian/gay agencies, findings may reflect youth with greater psychological, physical, and social needs. Nevertheless, they provide important information about the needs of lesbian and gay youth who are more open, who more frequently self-identify as lesbian, gay, or bisexual at younger ages, and who may be more vulnerable.

Although available studies of lesbian and gay youth show high utilization rates of mental health and counseling services,[8,11] help seeking is also an adaptive response to coping with negative stereotypes and sanctions. Thus, lesbian and gay youth who seek care may actually be more resilient and have more effective coping skills than those who do not.

Depression

Depression is characterized by persistent sadness (dysphoric mood), lack of pleasure (anhedonia), and, in more serious cases, helplessness and hopelessness.[66] Prevalence studies show rates of 1–5% in general (nonclinical) adolescent populations,[67] with higher rates from self-reports. Females are more often diagnosed with depression, and family history of depression or substance abuse is a significant risk factor. Higher rates are seen in Native Americans and incarcerated teens, and rural youth may be at greater risk than urban or suburban teens.[37,67] Depression frequently occurs with other symptoms and disorders, such as anxiety and conduct and eating disorders; many youth who attempt suicide are depressed, and depressed mood, drug use, and suicide are strongly related.[37] Adolescent onset of clinical depression is considered a serious risk factor for adult depression and possibly other major mental disorders.[37] Since depressed youth are more likely to use mental health services and medical care,[37] providers should be alert for possible depression during routine screening and presentation of unrelated complaints.

Suicide (Table 8.1 and Fig. 8.1)

Suicide represents the second leading cause of death in youth aged 13–24[59] and the third leading cause in youth aged 15–19.[34] Every two hours another young person commits suicide.[6] Between 1952 and 1992, rates of suicide among adolescents and young adults nearly tripled. From 1980–1992, suicide increased by 28.3% in 15–19-year-olds and 120% in 10–14-year-olds.[10] For each death by suicide, as many as 60 additional attempts are made by older male teens, increasing to 600 attempts (per completed suicide) by younger female adolescents.[61] Like other primary causes of death among adolescents, suicide is preventable: appropriate identification, assessment, and treatment of mental illness by primary care providers is a key component in prevention. However, many suicide victims never received appropriate diagnosis or treatment.[7]

Between 6 and 13% of adolescents have reported at least one suicide attempt,[16] and a history of attempted suicide is a powerful predictor of suicide.[59] Thus, all suicidal behavior and ideation must be taken seriously. However, not all youth who attempt suicide go on to commit suicide.

Studies of completed suicides (psychological autopsies which screen records and interview friends and family after death) show that adolescent victims had higher rates of ideation and prior attempts.[9,63] More than half had depressive, aggressive, and antisocial symptoms[59] and up to half of all suicides were committed under the influence of alcohol and drugs. More than 90% of completed youth suicides had a psychiatric diagnoses, some of which may co-exist, such as conduct and mood disorders (particularly depression and bipolar illness), substance abuse, and psychoses.[6] However, not all were properly diagnosed until after their deaths. The combination of depression, substance abuse, and impulsivity is especially lethal.[6] Personality char-

TABLE 8.1. Risk Factors for Suicide

History of previous suicide attempt	Family history of suicide
Alcohol, drug abuse	Suicide of friend or peer
Psychiatric diagnosis, particularly depression and bipolar disorder	Sexual abuse
	Discipline and relationship problems
Anxiety, conduct, and personality disorders	Altered serotonin metabolism
	Firearm in the home

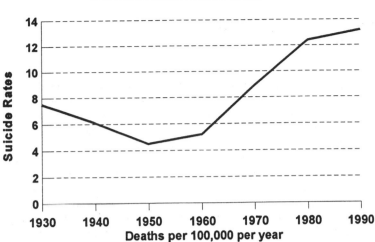

FIGURE 8.1.   Suicide rates in youth, ages 15–24: United States, 1930–1990. (From National Center for Health Statistics: Underlying Cause Mortality Files. Hyattsville, MD, National Center for Health Statistics, 1994.)

acteristics of suicidal adolescents include irritability, low frustration tolerance, poor self-concept, poor problem-solving skills, social isolation, sexual conflicts, rigidity, hostility, hopelessness, and helplessness.[59]

Suicidal behavior runs in families—an estimated 40% of adolescents who attempt suicide have family histories of suicidal behavior.[59] Such families also have increased incidence of affective and personality disorders. Studies suggest that suicide proneness, affective illness, and aggressive and impulsive tendencies may be genetically linked. Both physical and sexual abuse are more common in families with suicidal adolescents, in which youth are often the victims of such abuse. Suicide is often precipitated by life events that involve shame or humiliation; arrests, assaults, or disciplinary incidents at school are typical events that trigger suicide attempts in vulnerable youth.[6,59]

Somatic Disorders

Somatoform disorders—physical symptoms that lack an organic basis, which generally are not produced voluntarily—are assumed to be related to psychologic distress. Although overall prevalence is not known, physical complaints, such as headaches, chest and abdominal pain, commonly occur in 5–20% of adolescents; however, only 5–10% of the complaints have any organic basis.[4,36] Studies of somatic symptoms in adolescents and young adults show prevalence rates of 3–17%,[5,14,40] with females reporting more frequent symptoms than males and a significant correlation between high levels of anxiety and somatic complaints.[40] Risk factors for somatoform disorder include adolescence and external stressors.[32] Somatic complaints are also common responses to victimization, assault, sexual abuse, and rape.[3,15,27]

Mental Health Concerns of Lesbian and Gay Adolescents

Chronic Stress

A common theme identified in research and clinical reports about lesbian and gay youth is the experience of chronic stress from harassment (i.e., from verbal and physical abuse initiated by family members and peers). These reactions of peers and adults are associated with negative outcomes, such as school-related problems, running away from home, conflict with the law, substance abuse, prostitution, and suicide.[52] Like heterosexual male adolescents, gay and bisexual males are more likely to externalize stress, thus increasing their visibility and bringing themselves to the attention of service agencies and institutions.

In a study of stressful life events among minority gay and bisexual youth, emotional distress and multi-problem behaviors increased with the number of gay-related stressors (Table 8.2).[47] Gay-related stress included coming out to parents, other relatives, and friends; having sexual identity discovered; and being ridiculed because they were gay or bisexual. (The worst insult college-aged males can call each other is *fag* or *gay*;[39] the worst thing males can call females is *lesbian*.[51]) More than three-quarters had experienced at least one gay-related stressful event and an average of 6 non-gay-related stressors during the past 3 months (including problems with family and peers, moving, and major illness or injury). Gay-related stressors were associated with increasing depression; youth with higher self-esteem experienced less emotional distress, including depression and anxiety.[47]

The study confirmed what providers who work with gay youth have observed consistently: lesbian, gay, and bisexual youth experience chronic stress associated with their homosexuality. Coming out to others, having sexual orientation discovered by others, and being ridiculed because of homosexuality were the most stressful events.[49] Moreover, gay youth reported 3–5 times more negative non-gay-related stress than heterosexual peers.[48] As in other studies of stress related to sexual orientation, it appears that many non-gay-related stressful events (e.g., arguments with parents, problems at school) may actually be linked to sexual identity, thus compounding the stress experienced by lesbian, gay, and bisexual youth and increasing their vulnerability and need for support.[25,41]

Consistently, lesbian and gay youth report significant stress associated with school and related activities. Many describe harassment, verbal and physical abuse, and negative attitudes of both teachers and peers.[29,46,56] In one study of school coun-

TABLE 8.2. Gay-Related Stress Reported by Gay and Bisexual Adolescent Males

38%	Coming out to parents
28%	Coming out to siblings
50%	Coming out to friends
27%	Having sexual identity discovered by parents
33%	Having sexual identity discovered by other relatives
38%	Having sexual identity discovered by friends
50%	Being ridiculed because they were gay/bisexual*

* Most stressful event reported.
From Rosario M, Rotheram-Borus MJ, Reid H: Gay-related stress and its correlates among gay and bisexual male adolescents of predominantly black and hispanic background. J Commun Psychol, in press.

selors, two-thirds had negative attitudes about lesbian and gay youth;[56] in a study of prospective teachers, 8 in 10 had negative attitudes about homosexuality, while 42% ignored students' jokes about gay peers.[56] In surveys of lesbian/gay adolescents' experiences in high school, less than 1 of 5 could identify anyone who had been supportive in school,[68] and none reported positive perceptions of their experiences.[29]

Most frequently abused are youth who are transgendered—who do not or cannot meet traditional ("acceptable") cultural definitions of feminine and masculine behavior and thus deviate from typical gender behaviors and roles. Although these youth may be heterosexual, homosexual, or bisexual, their visibility often leads to scapegoating, harassment, and persistent verbal and physical abuse from peers.[53]

Lesbian and Gay Youth Talk About School

"The absolute lowest insult is to be called a fag. When kids want to really put another kid down, they call them a fag, whether or not they are gay."[29]

Lauren, 16

"The teachers would let harassment go on in the classroom. I would be called all kinds of names when I went to school. . . . One incident happened where my English teacher— we were talking about Oscar Wilde—we were fixing to read some of his books, and every time we read an author she would give us a biography on them. . . . What happened was she was giving out the biography, and she said back in those days they used to dress the guys up in dresses when they were little and bring them up like girls. . . . She said, in front of everybody, 'Maybe that's the reason he turned out that way—Isn't that right, Jennifer?' And she looked right at me, singled me out in front of the whole class."[29]

Jennifer, 20

"In sixth grade, I realized I was gay and came out to my parents. It wasn't a total acceptance on my part, or my parents' for that matter. But I realized I was gay and that it wasn't going to change. I basically dealt with it and accepted it. I would get up in the morning and say, 'I can't go to school. I can't go to school.' And my mother would say, 'You have to.' She'd always know what was the matter, but I don't think they realized the extent to which it was affecting me. Every day I had stomach aches. I lived in fear every day I got on that bus. I started walking to school because after a while, I wouldn't even take the bus anymore; it was just like my stomach was in knots. I had to live every day trying to avoid being harassed."[69]

Jaime, 20

"If someone would've been 'out' at my school, if the teachers wouldn't have been afraid to stop the 'fag' and 'dyke' jokes, if my human sexuality class had even mentioned homosexuality (especially in a positive light), if the school counselors would have been open to discussion of gay and lesbian issues, perhaps I wouldn't have grown up hating what I was and perhaps I wouldn't have attempted suicide."[50]

Kyallee, 19

Stressful experiences are cumulative. Although the majority of lesbian and gay youth learn to minimize the negative psychological effects of stigma, some are clearly more vulnerable. The negative impact of stigma coupled with earlier negative life experiences—child sexual abuse, chaotic family environments, addiction or family violence—increases vulnerability for a range of health and mental health problems.

Suicide in Lesbian and Gay Adolescents

Like most information about lesbian and gay youth, data about suicide have generally been gathered from youth who are open about sexual identity and who have sought health, mental health, or support services. Reported rates of attempted suicide and suicidal ideation* are generally very high in this population. Very little information is available on lesbian and gay youth who ultimately commit suicide. Of the two forensic community studies that have attempted to identify youth who may be lesbian and gay after their deaths, rates were much lower (between 2.5 and 5%).[43,62] However, trying to identify sexual orientation may be even more difficult after death since sexual identity unfolds over a period of years and fear of disclosure may have deepened isolation and prevented youth from discussing feelings of difference or same-sex attraction.

Studies of lesbian and gay youth that include information on suicidal ideation and attempts have been criticized for not being representative of all gay youth. What is clear, however, is that non-probability (non-random) studies of different populations of lesbian and gay youth conducted during the past 20 years in different settings and geographic areas, which include different racial and ethnic groups, have shown consistently that a significant proportion of lesbian and gay youth have attempted suicide, some multiple times.[8,11,23,41,42,54] Rates range from 20–42%, with higher percentages in youth who are homeless, runaways, and victims of sexual abuse or violence.

In a recent probability study of risk behaviors that included lesbian, gay, and bisexual youth (conducted by the Massachusetts Department of Education in 59 randomly selected high schools in 1995), lesbian, gay, and bisexual students and those who reported same-sex experiences were four times more likely than heterosexual students to have attempted suicide (Table 8.3).[30a] These findings are particularly important because they were obtained as a result of questions included in the CDC's Youth Risk Behavior Survey (YRBS), an ongoing survey of the leading causes of morbidity and mortality in youth in the United States. Although these questions were included only in one state and results are based on combining youth who identified as lesbian, gay, or bisexual with youth who engaged in same-sex behavior but did not self-identify as gay (4.4% of all students), they provide compelling evidence that these youth are at greater risk for suicide than their heterosexual peers. And unlike earlier non-probability studies of lesbian and gay youth, results are also generalizable to other Massachusetts high school students.

TABLE 8.3. Suicide Risk and School Safety—Massachusetts Youth Risk Behavior Survey, 1995

Reported Behaviors	Lesbian/Gay/Bisexual* Students (%)	Other Students (%)
Attempted suicide in the past year	36.5	8.9
Skipped school in the past month because they felt unsafe en route to, or at school	20.1	4.5
Were threatened/injured with a weapon at school in the past year	28.8	6.7

* Includes both lesbian, gay, and bisexual students and those who have had same-sex experiences. Results are statistically significant and accurate to within plus or minus 3%.

---

*Although people may have occasional thoughts of suicide, particularly during stressful experiences, suicidal *ideation* refers to persistent, intrusive thoughts of suicide and self harm.

Studies of gay and bisexual suicide attempters show that they were more likely to have self-identified as gay or bisexual and come out to others at younger ages,[25,42] to have friends and relatives who attempted or committed suicide,[25,42] and to have been rejected because of their sexual orientation.[54] Minority gay and bisexual youth were more likely to have dropped out of school, to have been ejected from their homes, and to have experienced a higher number of gay-related stressors than non-attempters.[25] Extensive pressure to conform to gender norms and behavior is perceived as a primary stressor for lesbian youth. In one of the few studies to assess suicide in both lesbian and gay youth, lesbians were more than twice as likely to have attempted suicide and to use more lethal means.[23]

Nearly half of gay and bisexual youth in one study reported family problems as the precipitating event.[42] One out of 3 suicide attempts was related to conflict over sexual identity. Three out of 4 attempts followed self-labeling as gay or bisexual. Cross-gendered youth (feminine gender-role behaviors) and those who used drugs had a 3-times higher risk for suicide. Youth who attempted suicide resembled actual suicide victims in terms of substance abuse, high levels of family dysfunction, and antisocial behaviors.[42]

Do Gay Youth Comprise Up to 30% of Completed Suicides?

Providers may wonder about a much repeated statistic that "gay youth are 2–3 times more likely to attempt suicide than other young people . . . and may comprise up to 30% of completed youth suicides" each year.[18] Although this information has been reported in many articles and texts about lesbian and gay youth, it is not based on an actual study but rather on a review of non-probability (non-random) studies and agency reports of lesbian and gay adolescents and adults conducted between 1972 and 1986. The review was done by Paul Gibson, a clinical social worker, as one of 50 papers or studies commissioned by the Secretary's Task Force on Youth Suicide, which was established in 1985 in response to growing rates of youth suicide and concluded its work in 1987. Although Gibson's paper accurately summarized many problems and experiences of lesbian and gay youth, his comparison of very different studies and diverse lesbian and gay populations resulted in an average that, while misapplied, has been consistently used to demonstrate the vulnerability of lesbian and gay adolescents for suicide.

In addition to being used to advocate for services and appropriate research on lesbian and gay youth, these conclusions have also been used to minimize or undermine such efforts, since they have been criticized for not being scientific or for being based on nonrepresentative studies that cannot be accurately compared. The controversy over scientific measurement tends to cloud the issue of vulnerability and risk, however, and to obscure repeated findings of suicidal ideation and attempts reported in many different studies in different populations of lesbian and gay youth over a period of years.[8,11,23,41,42,45,54] Providers should not allow definitional and measurement problems related to suicide to distract from the real issues of careful risk assessment for all adolescents, including those who self-identify as lesbian, gay, or bisexual.

Measuring Suicide Risk in Gay Populations

Increasingly, researchers are developing more accurate methods for studying hidden populations, including lesbian and gay youth and adults. An intriguing recent attempt assessed risk for suicide and depression among male twins (one of whom was gay and the other heterosexual) using the Vietnam Era Twins (VET) study, a data set or "registry" of pairs of twins who served in the military from 1965–1975.[24] The VET was established initially to study combat-related issues, including post-traumatic stress disorder, depression, long-term health, and substance use; 10 major studies have been conducted on the data set during the past decade. Using pairs of twins allows researchers to control for many variables that affect outcome, including environmental and genetic factors.

In the current study of sexual orientation and risk for suicide and depression, 103 pairs of twins (one of whom reported same-sex partners and one heterosexual) were assessed to determine their level of risk. While no increased risk of depression (major depressive episode) was seen in males with same-sex partners compared with heterosexuals, substantial risk and greater lifetime prevalence of suicidal behavior was seen in twins who reported same-sex partners after age 18 (after controlling for other risk factors, including chemical dependency and socioeconomic status).[24] Although these findings do not represent gay men, in general (as well as adolescents or lesbians), they are based on a controlled sample that increases their validity and offers compelling evidence that stressors related to being gay increase risk for suicidal behavior.

In a soon-to-be released study assessing risk in adolescents—the Youth Risk Behavior Survey, sponsored by the Centers for Disease Control and Prevention—questions on sexual orientation were added to the 1995 survey by the Massachusetts Department of Education. Findings showed that youth who had same-sex experiences (including self-identified lesbian, gay, and bisexual youth) were four times more likely than their heterosexual peers to have attempted suicide during the past year.[30a] These findings are particularly important because they are based on a random sample of youth in 59 high schools, and they corroborate earlier results of non-probability studies of lesbian, gay, and bisexual youth. Other studies related to suicide and lesbian and gay populations will ultimately provide additional information on vulnerability and risk. In the interim, providers should follow guidelines for assessing risk in all adolescents (see interview, Fig. 10.2), and carefully assess level of support, stage of coming out, and adjustment in adolescents who are lesbian, gay, or bisexual.

Gender Identity Disorder

Although some youth may genuinely suffer from gender identity disorder (GID)—a strong, persistent (long-term) discomfort with anatomic gender coupled with persistent cross-gender identification—others may confuse pervasive stereotypes of lesbian or gay people (e.g., effeminate males, masculinized females) with sexual orientation as they struggle to express their emerging lesbian/gay identities and connect with other gay people. Once exposed to the diversity of lesbian/gay lives, cross-dressing behavior and feelings of gender dysphoria, which are not related to core gender identity, generally resolve.[26]* Other youth may exhibit gender nonconforming behavior ("gender bending") as an act of defiance,[26] as a way of poking fun at conventional society or celebrating their membership in the lesbian/gay or, more recently, "queer" community.†

Providers should be cautious in assuming that gender-atypical youth are gender dysphoric or suffer from gender identity disorder. For example, gender-atypical behavior (which may be interpreted as GID when observed in male children) is con-

---

* Hetrick and Martin found this to be more common among Black and Hispanic youth.[26]
† Since the early 1900s, lesbian and gay identities have evolved from the concept of *invert* to *homosexual* (living a secret half-life, unconnected to a larger community), to *lesbian and gay* (having access to an extensive, open community), to *queer* (merging and celebrating difference and consciously violating gender rules in an attempt to transcend them).[12,22] Providers should be aware that lesbian, gay, bisexual, and transgendered youth may self-identify as "queer" rather than using more conventional terms such as lesbian, gay, etc. Providers should not assume that use of the term *queer* connotes self-deprecation, low self-esteem, or gender dysphoria.

gruen with gay male identity in adulthood without evidence of gender identity disorder.[58] More rigid role expectations for male children and adolescents makes gender nonconformity much more difficult for them and their parents than for girls, whose "tomboy" behaviors are generally more accepted. During puberty, however, rigid role expectations among peers cause increased distress for both gender nonconforming males and females, although adjustment is easier for females.[58]

Providers should also be aware that lesbian, gay, and transgendered youth are at risk for misdiagnoses of gender identity disorder, inappropriate treatment, and involuntary institutionalization, which includes use of behavioral conditioning and aversive treatment aimed at changing their sexual orientation and enforcing socially-sanctioned behavioral changes.[33] This occurs in spite of the American Psychiatric Association's determination in 1973 that homosexuality is not a mental illness, the American Academy of Pediatrics' warning that reparative therapy aimed at changing sexual orientation is contraindicated,[2] and the fact that use of involuntary aversive treatment is a clear violation of ethical standards. In addition, treatment aimed at enforcing strict gender codes which are contrary to one's core identity will likely result in harmful, potentially long-term iatrogenic disorders.

December 11, 1995

My name is R. I am 16, and I was in _____ Psychiatric Hospital last year. In my experience, _____ is not a good place to be gay. They say that it is okay, "if that is really your sexual preference and not a symptom of your mental illness." But they spent the entire time, at least for my time there, in trying to convince me that I actually wasn't a lesbian.

I know that I may have been confused at some time or at least when I first came out. But by the time I got [there] I was very much not confused at all. My parents are conservative and didn't want me to be gay, which is one of the main reasons I was sent there. My doctor wanted me to be straight, and he didn't even try to hide that from me. He portrayed gay people as confused, unhappy, mentally unstable, and never able to have children or be in a family. I know that this was not true in reality; I knew that gay people could be happy. When I would say this to my doctor, he would just change the subject.

I was told not just by my doctor, but also my nurse, that my homosexuality was a symptoms of mental illness, Borderline Personality Disorder. I was told that to get out I would first have to accept that I was mentally ill, and that would mean saying that I wasn't gay—it was just a symptom. I would not do this, and so I was harassed. The staff said that I would be sent to [another hospital] and would spend the rest of my life in a hospital. I was crying about this, and the staff was saying, "Go on cry; you have no one anymore. Your mother doesn't want a lesbian for a daughter. Who would? You've brought this on yourself." I became very depressed and started to think of suicide. After I got out I tried to kill myself.

(One of 300 notarized testimonies collected by the Stop Abuse Network, San Francisco, 100 of which were from institutionalized lesbian and gay youth.)

Compared with their heterosexual peers, lesbians and gay men less frequently conform to rigid gender expectations; moreover, they are more likely to create new patterns of behavior and to explore androgynous roles (e.g., greater autonomy and equality in relationships).[17,28] Many report having felt more comfortable in nontraditional or atypical gender roles as children and adolescents, to varying degrees. The lesbian and gay community encompasses a broad range of roles and identities and provides positive models of self-actualization for youth and young adults. Rather than attempting to repress or eliminate nonconforming behaviors that stand little chance of success and greater chance of causing harm, providers should encourage parents to obtain appropriate support and assist youth in understanding their emerging identities and to obtain needed counseling and community referrals.

Treatment Issues: Psychiatric Hospitalization

Like heterosexual youth who suffer from major psychiatric disorders that require inpatient treatment, some lesbian, gay, and bisexual adolescents may be hospitalized for severe mental health disorders. Historically however, providers in inpatient facilities have ignored issues related to sexuality; when sexual orientation is addressed, it can become an inappropriate focus of treatment.[19] This tendency is particularly problematic for youth since "it is not uncommon to find mental health staff who still believe that homosexuality is a form of psychopathology."[31] Moreover, coming out precipitates an emotional crisis that may resemble severe psychiatric disorders;[19] reactions may be especially intense for ethnic minority youth who struggle to manage multiple identities and allegiances.[20] Adolescents who are hospitalized because of symptoms related to their sexual orientation may encounter psychiatric providers who view such conflict as pathological.[31]

Treatment facilities that normally deal with very disturbed, acting-out youth may be overwhelmed by having a lesbian or gay adolescent in the milieu.[19] As in foster care agencies and other institutional placements for adolescents, staff may tolerate or even support prejudice and abuse of lesbian and gay teens.[19,30] Some treatment facilities take these issues very seriously and have provided training on sexual orientation to staff, although this level of response is rare. When inpatient treatment is warranted, providers should assess the capacity of facilities to treat lesbian, gay, and bisexual adolescents, including inpatient providers' attitudes, therapeutic approaches, and experiences working with lesbian and gay patients (*see* referral assessment form, Fig. 10.2).

During the 1980s and early 1990s, inpatient psychiatric and substance abuse treatment programs for children and adolescents increased dramatically, along with inappropriate admissions, including placement for nonpsychiatric behavioral problems,[55,70] gender nonconforming behaviors, and lesbian/gay identity.[33] Since parental placement of minors qualifies as "voluntary" admission, adolescents may be hospitalized against their will without the benefit of routine procedural hearings or due process.[33,35] Variations in state law permit placement in states with few procedural safeguards (e.g., California state law allows access to a hearing, but Utah does not; juveniles institutionalized in Utah can be subject to reparative therapy and aversive treatment designed to change sexual orientation).[33]

The National Center for Lesbian Rights (NCLR) coordinates a legal advocacy program for lesbian, gay, and transgendered youth who have been institutionalized and subjected to involuntary aversive treatment for sexual orientation. NCLR has documented dozens of cases of adolescents who have been hospitalized and forced to undergo involuntary treatment, which includes intense behavior modification that punishes same-sex feelings and gender nonconforming behavior; attempted conditioning through hypnosis; "desensitization" treatment that associates same-sex arousal with repugnant images, use of a plethysmograph to deliver electric shocks through penile electrodes (to deter same-sex attraction); and use of isolation and excessive medication.[33,70] Although the increase of managed care services may limit unnecessary hospitalizations, lesbian and gay adolescents may still be hospitalized for diagnoses that focus on sexual orientation.

In addition to ensuring that inpatient treatment programs provide appropriate treatment and support for lesbian and gay youth *before* referrals are made, providers should assist families in managing crisis reactions to the news that their sons or daughters may be lesbian or gay.

References

1. Allebeck P, Allgulander C: Psychiatric diagnoses as predictors of suicide: A comparison of diagnoses at conscription and in psychiatric care in a cohort of 50,465 young men. Br J Psychiatry 157:339, 1990.
2. American Academy of Pediatrics: Homosexuality and adolescence. Pediatrics 92:631, 1993.
3. American Academy of Pediatrics: Rape and the adolescent. Pediatrics 81:595, 1988.
4. Apley J: The Child with Abdominal Pains. Oxford, Blackwell Scientific Publications, 1975.
5. Binder J, Dobler-Mikola A, Angst J: A prospective epidemiological study of psychosomatic and psychiatric syndromes in young adults. Psychother Psychosom 38:128, 1982.
6. Blumenthal SJ: Youth suicide: Risk factors, assessment and treatment of adolescent and young suicidal patients. Psychiatr Clin North Am 13:511, 1990.
7. Blumenthal SJ: Youth suicide: The physician's role in suicide prevention. JAMA 264:3194, 1990.
8. Bradford J, Ryan C, Rothblum ED: National lesbian health care survey: Implications for mental health care. J Consult Clin Psychol 62:228, 1994.
9. Brent DA, Perper JA, Moritz G, et al: Psychiatric risk factors for adolescent suicide: A case-control study. J Am Acad Child Adolesc Psychiatry 32:521, 1993.
10. Centers for Disease Control and Prevention: Suicide among children, adolescents and young adults— United States, 1980–1992. MMWR 44:289, 1995.
11. D'Augelli AR, Hershberger SL: Lesbian, gay and bisexual youth in community settings: Personal challenges and mental health problems. Am J Community Psychol 21:421, 1993.
12. DeLauretis T: Queer theory: Lesbian and gay sexualities—an introduction. Differences 3:iii, 1991.
13. Fingerhut LA, Kleinman JC: Suicide rates for young people. JAMA 259:356, 1988.
14. Freeman EW, Rickles K, Mudd EBH, et al: Self-reports of emotional distress in a sample of urban black high school students. Psychol Med 12:809, 1982.
15. Frieze IH, Hymer S, Greenberg MS: Describing the victims of crime and violence. In Kahn A (ed): Victims of Crime and Violence: Final Report of the APA Task Force on the Victims of Crime and Violence. Washington, DC, American Psychological Association, 1984.
16. Garland AF, Zigler E: Adolescent suicide prevention: Current research and social policy implications. Am Psychol 48:169, 1993.
17. Garnets LD, Kimmel DC: Lesbian and gay male dimensions in the psychological study of human diversity. In Garnets L, Jones JM, et al (eds): Psychological Perspectives on Human Diversity in America. Washington, DC, American Psychological Association, 1991.
18. Gibson P: Gay male and lesbian youth suicide. In Alcohol, Drug Abuse and Mental Health Administration: Report of the Secretary's Task Force on Youth Suicide. Vol. 3: Prevention and Interventions in Youth Suicide. DHHS Publ. No. (ADM) 89-1623. Washington, DC, U.S. Government Printing Office, 1989.
19. Gonsiorek JC: Mental health issues of gay and lesbian adolescents. J Adolesc Health Care 9:114, 1988.
20. Greene B: Ethnic minority lesbians and gay men: Mental health treatment issues. J Consult Clin Psychol 62:243, 1994.
21. Hammelman T: Gay and lesbian youth: Contributing factors to serious attempts or considerations of suicide. J Gay Lesbian Psychother 2:77, 1993.
22. Herdt G: "Coming out" as a right of passage: A Chicago study. In Herdt G (ed): Gay Culture in America. Boston, Beacon Press, 1992.
23. Herdt G, Boxer A: Children of Horizons: How Lesbian and Gay Teens Are Leading a New Way Out of the Closet, 2nd ed. Boston, Beacon Press, 1996.
24. Herrell RK: Depression and sexual orientation: A co-twin control study in adult males. Master's thesis, University of Illinois at Chicago, 1996.
25. Hershberger SL, D'Augelli AR: The impact of victimization on the mental health and suicidality of lesbian, gay and bisexual youths. Dev Psychol 31:65, 1995.
26. Hetrick ES, Martin AD: Developmental issues and their resolution for gay and lesbian adolescents. J Homosex 13:25, 1987.

27. Janoff-Bulman R, Frieze IH (eds): Reactions to victimization. J Soc Issues 39:1, 1983.
28. Kurdek LA, Schmitt JP: Interaction of sex role self concept with relationship quality and relationship beliefs in married, heterosexual co-habiting, gay and lesbian relationships. J Pers Soc Psychol 51: 365, 1986.
29. Malinsky KP: Learning to be invisible: A qualitative study of lesbian students in Florida's public high schools. Doctoral dissertation, University of Sarasota, 1996.
30. Mallon G: Gay and no place to go: Assessing the needs of gay and lesbian adolescents in out-of-home care settings. Child Welfare 6:547, 1992.
30a. Massachusetts Department of Education: Massachusetts Youth Risk Behavior Survey, 1995 [unpublished data, 1997].
31. McDaniel JS, Cabaj RP, Purcell DW: Care across the spectrum of mental health settings. In Cabaj RP, Stein TS (eds): Textbook of Homosexuality and Mental Health. Washington, DC, American Psychiatric Press, 1996.
32. Mechanic D: Adolescent health and illness behavior: Review of the literature and a new hypothesis for the study of stress. J Hum Stress 9:4, 1983.
33. Molnar BE: Juveniles and psychiatric institutionalization: Toward a better system of due process and treatment review in the U.S. Health and Human Rights, [in press].
34. National Center for Health Statistics: Underlying Cause Mortality Files, U.S., 1991. Hyattsville, MD, National Center for Health Statistics, 1994.
35. Reference deleted.
36. Pantell RH, Goodman BW: Adolescent chest pain: A prospective study. Pediatrics 71:881, 1983.
37. Petersen AC, Compas BE, Brooks-Gunn J, et al: Depression in adolescence. Am Psychol 48:155, 1993.
38. Pfeffer CR, Klerman GL, Hurt SW, et al: Suicidal children grow up: Rates and psychosocial risk factors for suicide attempts during follow-up. J Am Acad Child Adolesc Psychiatr 32:106, 1993.
39. Preston K, Stanley K: "What's the worst thing . . . ?" Gender-directed insults. Sex Roles 17:209, 1987.
40. Rauste-Von Wright MR, Von Wright J: A longitudinal study of psychosomatic symptoms in health 11–18 year-old girls and boys. J Psychosom Res 25:525, 1981.
41. Remafedi G: Adolescent homosexuality: Psychosocial and medical implications. Pediatrics 79:331, 1987.
42. Remafedi G, Farrow JA, Deisher RW: Risk factors for attempted suicide in gay and bisexual youth. Pediatrics 87:869, 1991.
43. Rich CL, Fowler RC, Young D, Blenkush M: San Diego suicide study: Comparison of gay to straight males. Suicide Life-Threatening Behav 16:448, 1986.
44. Robins E, Murphy GE, Wilkinson RH Jr, et al: Some clinical considerations in the prevention of suicide based on a study of 134 successful suicides. Am J Public Health 49:888, 1959.
45. Roesler T, Deisher RW: Youthful male homosexuality. JAMA 219:1018, 1972.
46. Rofes E: Opening up the classroom closet: Responding to the educational needs of gay and lesbian youth. Harv Educ Rev 59:444, 1989.
47. Rosario M, Rotheram-Borus MJ, Reid H: Gay-related stress and its correlates among gay and bisexual male adolescents of predominantly black and hispanic background. J Comm Psychol 24:136, 1996.
48. Rotheram-Borus MJ, Hunter J, Rosario M: Suicidal behavior and gay-related stress among gay and bisexual male adolescents. J Adolesc Res 9:498, 1994.
49. Rotheram-Borus MJ, Rosario M, Koopman C: Minority youths at high risk: Gay males and runaways. In Colten ME, Gore S (eds): Adolescent Stress: Causes and Consequences. New York, Aldine de Gruyter, 1991.
50. Santanders K: Growing up as a lesbian [Internet data file].dalrympr@cs.colorado.edu (Producer). glb-youth-request@ucsd.edu (Distributor), January 12, 1995.
51. Sargent AG: Beyond Sex Roles. St. Paul, MN, West Publishing, 1977.
52. Savin-Williams RC: Verbal and physical abuse as stressors in the lives of lesbian, gay male and bisexual youths: Associations with school problems, running away, substance abuse, prostitution and suicide. J Consult Clin Psychol 62:261, 1994.
53. Savin-Williams RC, Cohen KM: Psychosocial outcomes of verbal and physical abuse among lesbian, gay and bisexual youths. In Savin-Williams RC, Cohen KM (eds): The Lives of Lesbians, Gays and Bisexuals: Developmental, Clinical and Cultural Issues. Fort Worth, TX, Harcourt-Brace Jovanovich, 1996.
54. Schneider SG, Faberow NL, Kruks GN: Suicidal behavior in adolescent and young adult gay men. Suicide Life-Threatening Behav 19:381, 1989.
55. Schwartz IM: Hospitalization of adolescents for psychiatric and substance abuse treatment. J Adolesc Health Care 10:473, 1989.
56. Sears J: Educators, homosexuality and homosexual students: Are personal feelings related to professional beliefs? J Homosex 22:29, 1991.

57. Sears J: Growing Up Gay in the South: Race, Gender and Journeys of the Spirit. NY, Haworth Press, 1991.
58. Seil D: Transsexuals: The boundaries of sexual identity and gender. In Cabaj RP, Stein TS (eds): Textbook of Homosexuality and Mental Health. Washington, DC, American Psychiatric Press, 1996.
59. Setterberg S: Suicidal behavior and suicide. In Friedman SB, Fisher M, Schonberg SK (eds): Comprehensive Adolescent Health Care. St. Louis, MO, Quality Medical Publishing, 1992.
60. Shaffer D: Suicide in childhood and early adolescence. J Child Psychol Psychiatry 15:275, 1974.
61. Shaffer D, Bacon K: A critical review of preventive intervention efforts in suicide, with particular reference to youth suicide. In Alcohol, Drug Abuse and Mental Health Administration: Report of the Secretary's Task Force on Youth Suicide. Vol. 3: Prevention and interventions in Youth Suicide. DHHS Publ No. (ADM) 89-1623. Washington, DC, U.S. Government Printing Office, 1989.
62. Shaffer D, Fisher P, Hicks R, et al: Sexual orientation in adolescents who commit suicide. Suicide Life-Threatening Behav 25:64, 1995.
63. Shaffer D, Garland A, Gould M, et al: Preventing teenage suicide: A critical review. J Am Acad Child Adolesc Psychiatry 27:675, 1988.
64. Slap GB, Vorters DF, Chaudhuri S, et al: Risk factors for attempted suicide during adolescence. Pediatrics 84:762, 1989.
65. Slap GB, Vorters MD, Khalid N: Adolescent suicide attempters: Do physicians recognize them? J Adolesc Med 13:286, 1992.
66. Society for Adolescent Medicine: Psychosocial screening. J Adolesc Health 13:52S, 1992.
67. Tancer NK, Shaffer D: Depression. In Friedman SB, Fisher M, Schonberg SK (eds): Comprehensive Adolescent Health Care. St. Louis, MO, Quality Medical Publishing, 1992.
68. Telljohann SK, Price JH: A qualitative examination of adolescent homosexuals' life experiences: Ramifications for secondary school personnel. J Homosex 26:41, 1993.
69. Walsh J: Profiles in Courage: Jamie Nabozny, URL: http://www.cyberspaces.com/outproud/oasis/ 9602/oasis-profiles. html, February 28, 1996.
70. Weithorn LA: Mental hospitalization of troublesome youth: An analysis of skyrocketing admission rates. Stanford Law Rev 40-773, 1988.

CHAPTER 9

Family Interventions and Anticipatory Guidance

Just as coming out precipitates an emotional crisis for individuals, disclosure of lesbian/gay identity to parents generally promotes a family crisis. Like adolescents or adults who self-identify as lesbian or gay, parents undergo a kind of multistage "coming out" process during which they grieve the loss of their child's heterosexual identity and ultimately reframe negative social sanctions and lost expectations into positive experiences of lesbian and gay lives. This process is lengthy and, for some parents, not achievable—they will never be able to accept their child as lesbian or gay.

Ultimately, however, most parents adapt to their child's new identity and incorporate their lesbian/gay child into conventional family life to varying degrees. All parents go through some process of adaptation to this new and, in most cases, disturbing disclosure; reactions are predictably more intense when parents accidentally discover their child's sexual orientation rather than have an opportunity for open and hopefully thoughtful discussion.

Most adolescents aspire to come out to their parents, but fear of rejection and other negative reactions holds many others back. Because adolescents are still dependent on their parents for emotional and financial support, providers should caution youth to carefully consider the consequences of coming out while they are still living at home and dependent on their parents' support. Adolescents may decide to come out to their parents for various reasons: to improve relationships;* to increase honesty and reduce the stress of passing and deception about their lives; to increase self-esteem, which is enhanced through coming out; for political reasons (to increase lesbian/gay visibility); and out of anger or to provoke confrontation.[6]

Need for Information and Support

After the initial shock of disclosure, which is often followed by denial, guilt, and various stages of grieving, parents begin to grapple with the stigma associated with homosexuality that their child (and now they) will experience (Fig. 9.1). In searching for information and understanding, they slowly confront and expose myths and misconceptions, learn about the broad support and extensive resources available through the lesbian and gay community, meet successful lesbian and gay role models, and fashion new expectations, hopes, and dreams for their lesbian/gay child.

However, acceptance takes time. Most parents of lesbian/gay children who participated in a national study compared learning of their child's homosexuality to mourning a death.[33] And in many ways, loss of their child's heterosexual identity is a death that needs to be grieved, since it includes the loss of parental expectations for (heterosexual) success, including marriage, family, and grandchildren.[4,6] With access to accurate information, however, parents develop a new understanding of the reality of lesbian and gay lives, which include options for positive long-term relationships, successful careers, and even parenting. At the same time, parents need information to

---

*Studies have shown that hiding sexual identity from parents increases distance in parent–child relationships[3,23,11] and causes feelings of alienation in parents.[34]

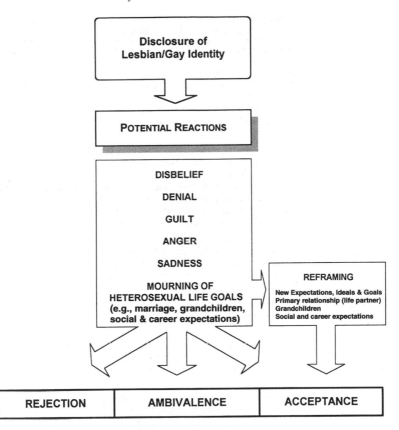

FIGURE 9.1. Parental/Family adaptation to disclosure of a child's lesbian or gay identity.

dispel outmoded, guilt-inducing psychoanalytic theories that have previously attributed homosexuality to unhappy childhoods and disturbed relationships with parents, including smothering, seductive mothers and cold, rejecting fathers.[12,26]

In a study of adolescent coming out and parental disclosure, parents' primary concerns were for their child's happiness and well-being.[6] After working through their initial distress, parents reported that it was not their child's homosexuality that bothered them, but the implications—discrimination, homophobia, and what would happen to their children in old age. Parents of gay males worried about AIDS.[6,33] Most reported improved relationships following disclosure; many described feelings of relief that their child's attempts at hiding his or her sexual identity (which they experienced as evasive or secretive) did not conceal something worse, such as drug use or drug dealing.[6]

Most information about the coming out experiences of adolescents and parents has focused on white, middle-class families. However, some researchers have suggested that coming out may be more difficult for ethnic minority lesbians and gay males;[16] moreover, disclosure jeopardizes family relationships and threatens their close-knit association with ethnic communities[28] (Table 9.1). For example, a study of the experiences of multicultural lesbian and gay teens found that coming out to parents

TABLE 9.1. Common Experiences and Attitudes about Homosexuality
among Ethnic Minorities*

Cultural and family values	Strongly interdependent family and extended family (that includes nonrelatives and friends) Structured interpretation of sex roles (ranging from greater flexibility in Native American and African American cultures to more sharply defined in Asian American culture) Importance of marriage and childbearing Importance of religion and spirituality Indirect response to conflict Lack of open discussion about sex (in Hispanic and Asian American cultures)
Cultural perceptions of homosexuality	Homosexuality is viewed as a "Western" or white phenomenon that "does not exist" in ethnic minority cultures Seen as rebellion or rejection of cultural heritage, or may be viewed as the result of too much assimilation by the mainstream culture Acceptance of third gender role among some American Indian tribes, which included homosexuality and bisexuality, was obscured during destruction of tribal culture
Experience of lesbian/gay identity	Feel pressure to choose between two communities (lesbian/gay or ethnic minority) Feel they cannot truly be themselves in either world since both communities reject or devalue a core part of their identities Feel most comfortable when they are able to express both ethnic and lesbian/gay identities
Family response to homosexuality	May cause major conflict in family if openly expressed May silently tolerate, rather than openly accept, so long as family member does not disclose
Experience with mainstream lesbian and gay community	Access to lesbian/gay community resources and activities provides essential support and decreases stress of hiding gay identity Racism, discrimination, stereotyping and invisibility are common experiences
Experience with ethnic community	Fear of rejection and stigma cause many to hide More are open with friends than family members; few are open with parents Coming out to family or other community members may jeopardize essential support for their ethnic identities or prevent them from serving their communities in leadership roles

* Synthesized from the following sources: 1, 7–10, 13, 14, 16–22, 24, 25, 27, 28, 35–39.

altered their relationships with their ethnic communities; to avoid shaming their families, some youth excluded themselves from cultural activities that were important in reinforcing their ethnic identity.[36] Among ethnic minority youth (and adults), fear of rejection and reluctance to be seen as rejecting traditional cultural roles that value marriage, child-bearing, and more rigid gender roles are primary reasons for not disclosing to parents.

Providers can assist families in dealing with the disclosure or discovery of an adolescent's lesbian or gay identity by providing individual or family counseling or mediation; providing accurate information, including written materials on lesbian and gay issues; and making referrals to family therapists and/or community support groups, such as Parents, Families, and Friends of Lesbians and Gays (PFLAG). PFLAG sponsors support groups and educational activities that provide accurate information about sexual orientation and assist parents and family members in dealing with their feelings and concerns. PFLAG chapters are located in cities throughout the country (*see* Appendix C for referral information). Parents have reported that contact with other parents of lesbian and gay children is extremely helpful in working through their distress and in debunking negative myths and misconceptions about homosexuality.

Counseling Parents and Adolescents— Anticipatory Guidance

Although providers may be more likely to work with adolescents who have not come out to their parents, they also may encounter situations in which parents are concerned or have discovered that an adolescent may be lesbian or gay. In such instances, both parents and adolescents require access to accurate information and support. In addition to family counseling by a health or mental health provider, resources are available to help parents deal with a child's homosexuality. (*See* Appendix B for referral information.)

Anticipatory guidance—providing information about adolescent development, needs, and challenges—is a way of making youth and parents aware of typical life events and changes that adolescents and families are likely to experience, and helping them anticipate responses and options to facilitate healthy development (Tables 9.2 and 9.3). An awareness of typical adolescent behaviors can help parents and youth to cope with multiple social, emotional, and developmental changes that seem overwhelming and frustrating at times.

During adolescence the struggle to establish independence and autonomy often conflicts with parental expectations. Communication patterns change, and adolescents spend less time with their families. They turn increasingly to peers for behavioral cues and standards. They experiment with risk-taking, including use of alcohol and drugs, explore their sexuality, and may appear moody or preoccupied. Providers can help adolescents and parents by telling them what to expect, encouraging and facilitating communication about issues of concern, and providing information about resources such as parent's groups, adolescent support groups, and reading lists.

Developmental tasks change and expand on the basis of an adolescent's age and level of maturity. Early adolescence (generally from age 10–13) is a time of rapid physical growth and sexual development. Young adolescents are frequently preoccupied with physical and emotional changes and begin to separate from parents and childhood experiences. Middle adolescence (age 14–17) is characterized by increasing separation from family, more conflict with parents, intense involvement with peers, and often sexual exploration. During late adolescence (roughly age 17 and above) adolescents focus on consolidating identity and making future career plans, and they often are involved in committed intimate relationships.

As adolescents struggle to self-identify and separate from their parents, conflicts increase, and communication may become more confrontational. Parents often have

TABLE 9.2. Anticipatory Guidance Topics for Discussion	**TABLE 9.3.** Adolescent Developmental Tasks
Health and nutrition	Development of increased cognitive ability (abstract thinking, introspection)
Safety and risk-taking	
Sexuality	Development of social skills (coping strategies, moral and ethical values, independence and autonomy)
Adolescent development	
Relationships	Development of psychosexual milestones (sexual identity, intimate relationships)
School and activities	
Future plans	Exploration of educational and vocational options

difficulty with an adolescent's excessive need for privacy and limited interaction with family as adolescents spend increasing amounts of time with peers. They may worry about risk-taking behaviors, moodiness, and lack of communication. Providers who have the confidence of both parent and adolescent can assist by helping to define problem behaviors and discussing ways to enhance communication and reduce conflict.[32] At times, behaviors may signal underlying problems that need to be addressed. These include decline in school performance; poor social skills and lack of close friends; symptoms of depression, such as sadness, social withdrawal, and chronic fatigue; weight loss or gain, which may indicate eating disorders; frequent accidents or self-destructive behavior; and suspicions of potential substance abuse or concerns about sexual behavior or identity.[15]

Such behaviors also may indicate conflict with sexual identity. When assessing the adolescent's underlying concern, providers should be sensitive to fears of disclosure, family, cultural and religious attitudes about sexuality, and other factors that may make youth reluctant to talk openly about their problems. Adolescents who are struggling with issues related to sexual identity should be assured that such feelings are normal and that many adolescents experience transitory same-sex attraction, which does not mean that they are gay. Providers should continue to offer reassurance and support and assess the adolescent's status during subsequent visits. If an adolescent feels that he or she is lesbian, gay, or bisexual, the provider should offer specific anticipatory guidance, counseling, and appropriate referrals to ensure emotional and social support.

Anticipatory Guidance for Lesbian/Gay Adolescents

Lesbian and gay adolescents and their families should receive the same kinds of anticipatory guidance as heterosexual youth, but other needs must be addressed as well (Table 9.4). For example, social isolation, lack of access to prevention information that discusses sexual orientation and stressors that affect lesbian and gay youth, and lack of positive role models or adequate social and emotional support require additional attention and counseling. Although these topics may seem overwhelming to providers who have had limited open interaction with lesbian and gay youth, many resources and materials are available (including continuing education courses) to increase the provider's knowledge and comfort in addressing such concerns. In many instances, introducing these topics or providing appropriate referrals or written materials may be all that is needed to help youth understand their relevance so that they can obtain appropriate information and support (see Appendices C and D for reference materials).

Identity Integration. Providers should talk with adolescents about their understanding of what it means to be lesbian or gay, explore their acceptance of myths and stereotypes about homosexuality, and share information about lesbian/gay identity development (*see* Chapter 2). Negative perceptions, including media depictions of homosexuality, fuel many misconceptions that affect self-esteem, shape behavior, and

TABLE 9.4.   Specific Topics for Anticipatory Guidance for Lesbian and Gay Adolescents

• Identity integration	• Discrimination and anti-gay violence
• Disclosure	• Social support (peers and adults)
• Sexual behavior and prevention	• Access to lesbian/gay community
• Substance use	• Career and vocational plans
• Mental health	

limit career options. For example, a study of lesbian and gay youth, ages 14–17, showed extensive acceptance of negative stereotypes: four-fifths (80%) believed that gay men were always effeminate and lesbians were always masculine (82%); half believed that all homosexuals were unhappy; nearly half believed that gay men dislike women, and more than one-third (37%) believed that lesbians dislike men. Most relied on television or ''word of mouth'' to learn about what it means to be lesbian or gay; only 16% had received this information from health care providers.[30] Lack of appropriate role models is a significant problem for lesbian and gay youth who turn to adults for modeling healthy behavior and relationships and for guidance about careers and life options. Support and acceptance are especially important from heterosexual adults because their validation helps to reframe the negative images and misperceptions that lesbian and gay youth have internalized. Providers can help by exposing myths and negative stereotypes, providing a reading list of materials written by lesbian and gay youth, and making referrals to gay youth groups and community services.

Disclosure. Adolescents need guidance about when and how to disclose sexual orientation to parents, friends, and others in their social network. Because lesbian and gay youth are at risk for rejection, discrimination, and violence if others (including parents) learn they are gay, providers should counsel them to consider disclosure very carefully. For example, some adolescents choose not to come out to others in high school, but disclose sexual orientation to parents and peers when they leave for college or begin to live on their own. Adolescents should be counseled to think about the consequences of disclosure and to take their time in sharing information which will have many repercussions.

Sexual Behavior and Prevention. Lesbian and gay youth should be counseled about sexual activity, which puts them at risk for STDs, HIV, and possible pregnancy. If they are sexually active, providers should counsel them about appropriate use of condoms, and avoiding risky sexual practices, such as using alcohol and drugs before and during sex, having multiple and/or anonymous partners, and having sex in unprotected areas, such as parks.

Providers should explain the difference between identity and behavior: people can be sexually active with same-sex partners without identifying as lesbian or gay. Similarly, people can identify as lesbian or gay without being sexually active. Some adolescents may become sexually active in an attempt to prove or disprove their sexual orientation. Providers should suggest alternatives to help youth explore sexual orientation (such as educational materials and support groups). Adolescents should clearly understand that they have other options than becoming sexually active to learn about their sexual identity.

Substance Use. Adolescents should be cautioned about substance use and the risk of chemical dependency. Use of alcohol and drugs to manage low self-esteem and isolation, shame, and negative internalized homophobia increases risk of addiction. The lack of supportive, age-appropriate activities for lesbian and gay youth restricts opportunities for normal socialization and interaction with peers. In rural communities and small towns, bars may be the only place for lesbians and gay males to socialize; this increases pressure to use alcohol and helps to normalize drug use and ''getting high.'' Providers should determine the availability of programs for lesbian and gay youth in the community, which provide a range of social, health, and support services, including supervised activities that encourage youth to seek socialization in drug-free environments.

Mental Health. Providers should counsel lesbian and gay adolescents about mental health stressors that affect gay youth, such as isolation, fear of discovery, ridicule, and harassment. Adolescents should understand that no psychological differences have been seen in studies of lesbians and gay men and their heterosexual peers. However, depression and thoughts about suicide have been reported by lesbian and gay youth, particularly those who have been sexually abused or who are experiencing problems with family, school, or peers. Although these feelings may be situational and transitory, adolescents should be encouraged to express their concerns to their provider and to share such feelings if they occur or persist.

Discrimination. Providers should caution lesbian and gay youth about their risks as targets of anti-gay violence and encourage them to socialize in groups and to seek appropriate counseling and follow-up care if they are victimized. Violence has many emotional and somatic effects, including self-blame and heightened vulnerability that increase risk for other health and mental health problems. Referral to support groups provides a buffer against stigma and discrimination while building self-esteem and positive coping skills.

Support System. Providers should assess the extent of an adolescent's support system, including peers and adults. Peer group interaction plays an important role in adolescent socialization and in separating from their family. Although peers are no less important to lesbian and gay youth (in one study, 93% of young gay males had identified friends as their most important source of help for problems or concerns), interactions are often restricted by the need to hide sexual orientation. In the same study, 42% reported losing friends when they came out to them.[31] Similarly, supportive adults play an important role in self-acceptance and social development.

Adolescents who are known or suspected to be lesbian or gay are often harassed by peers through behaviors that range from name-calling to rejection and physical abuse. Providers should explore negative experiences since peer rejection and ridicule are significant stressors that enhance vulnerability for depression, substance abuse, and suicide. Moreover, adolescents who are fearful of discovery are not likely to have told adults, including parents and teachers, which increases their isolation and need for support.

Parents also need support to deal with a parallel coming out process. Family counseling and support groups for parents of lesbian and gay children that encourage expression of feelings and experiences without fear of rejection provide accurate information about the reality of lesbian and gay lives and help parents to come to terms with their child's lesbian or gay identity.

Access to Gay Community. Access to the lesbian/gay community facilitates identity development and consolidation. Interaction with other lesbian and gay youth and adults helps an adolescent learn the broad range of diversity that living with an integrated lesbian/gay identity allows, including alternatives to stereotyped behaviors and options for committed, intimate relationships and for professional and occupational choices. Providers should be aware of lesbian and gay community resources and programs for lesbian and gay youth and make this information available. (For information about local services for lesbian, gay and bisexual youth, contact the resources listed in Appendix B).

Career Planning. Career planning is an important developmental task, although one that may be particularly difficult for lesbian and gay adolescents who lack positive models for occupational and vocational choices. Pervasive negative stereotypes may push lesbians and gay males into job choices with less security, lower pay, and fewer benefits, such as the food service and hospitality industries or the arts. A common misconception is that gay people have significantly higher salaries than heterosexuals.

TABLE 9.5. Occupational Perceptions of College Students Based on Gender
and Sexual Orientation

Stereotypes by Gender		Stereotypes by Sexual Orientation	
Appropriate Jobs for Men and Women[29]		Jobs Preferred by Gay Men and Lesbians[5]	
Male	Female	Male	Female
Lawyer	Elementary school teacher	Photographer	Auto mechanic
City planner	Dietician	Interior decorator	Plumber
Police officer	Social worker	Nurse	Truck driver
Mail carrier	Typist		
Truck driver	Librarian		

Lesbians and gay males actually earn less than heterosexuals with the same occupation, experience, and training.[2]*

Negative stereotypes about appropriate behavior and vocational options further limit choices (Table 9.5). For example, a study of college students that classified occupations by gender showed jobs typically held by men to include lawyer, city planner, mail carrier, or banker, whereas jobs for women included social worker, school teacher, dietician, or librarian.[29] When college students in another study were asked to identify the top jobs of interest to lesbians and gay men, biases were clearly evident: students believed that gay men would prefer photography, interior decorating, or nursing, and lesbians would choose auto mechanics, plumbing, or truck driving.[5] Although these stereotypes may seem ridiculous to many adults, they are routinely incorporated into the minds of children and, by the time they have reached adolescence, strongly influence self-concept, life choices, and goals. Providers can assist by exploring adolescents' interests and aspirations and helping them understand that sexual orientation should not limit their options.

Parenting. Providers should discuss parenting options with lesbian and gay youth. Contrary to stereotypes of childless gay people, many lesbians and gay men have had children, often in heterosexual marriages prior to coming out, and increasingly more lesbians and gay men are choosing to parent through donor insemination, adoption, foster care, and conception.

References

1. Atkinson DR, Morten G, Derald SW: Counseling American Minorities. Dubuque, IA, William C. Brown, 1983.
2. Badgett MVL: The wage effects of sexual orientation discrimination. Indust Labor Rel Rev 48:726, 1995.
3. Bell A, Weinberg M: Homosexualities. New York, Simon & Schuster, 1978.
4. Borhek MV: Helping gay and lesbian adolescents and their families: A mother's perspective. J Adolesc Health Care 9:123, 1988.
5. Botkin M, Daly J: Occupational development of lesbians and gays. Paper presented at the American College Student Personnel Association annual meeting, Chicago, 1987.

*According to an analysis of lesbians and gay men included in the General Survey (a nationally representative population survey), persons who engage in same-sex behavior earn less than their heterosexual peers who have similar occupations, levels of education, and experience. Average salaries for gay men were 11–27% less than those for their heterosexual peers, and lesbians had average earnings of 12–30% less than heterosexual women (differences for women were significantly less when selection control factors were included).[2]

6. Boxer AM, Cook JA, Herdt G: Double jeopardy: Identity transitions and parent-child relations among gay and lesbian youth. In Pillemer K, McCartney K (eds): Parent-Child Relations Throughout Life. Hillsdale, NY, Lawrence Erlbaum Associates, 1991.

7. Carballo-Diéguez A: Hispanic culture, gay male culture and AIDS: Counseling implications. J Counsel Dev 68:26, 1989.

8. Chan CS: Issues of identity development among Asian-American lesbians and gay men. J Counsel Dev 68:16, 1989.

9. Chan CS: Issues of sexual identity in an ethnic minority: The case of Chinese American lesbians, gay men and bisexual people. In D'Augelli A, Patterson C (eds): Lesbian, Gay and Bisexual Identities Over the Lifespan: Psychological Perspectives. NY, Oxford University Press, 1995.

10. Comas-Diaz L, Greene B (eds): Women of Color: Integrating Ethnic and Gender Identities in Psychotherapy. New York, Guilford Press, 1994.

11. Cramer DW, Roach AJ: Coming out to mom and dad: A study of gay males and their relationships with parents. J Homosex 15:79, 1988.

12. Drescher J: Psychoanalytic subjectivity and male homosexuality. In Cabaj RP, Stein TS (eds): Textbook of Homosexuality and Mental Health. Washington, DC, American Psychiatric Press, 1996.

13. Espin OM: Issues of identity in the psychology of latina lesbians. In Garnets L, Kimmel D, (eds): Psychological Perspectives on Lesbian and Gay Male Experiences. New York, Columbia University Press, 1993.

14. Gaw AC (ed): Culture, Ethnicity and Mental Illness. Washington, DC, American Psychiatric Press, 1993.

15. Green M: Anticipatory guidance for parents. In Friedman SB, Fisher S, Schonberg SK (eds): Comprehensive Adolescent Health Care. St Louis, MO, Quality Medical Publishing, 1992.

16. Greene B: Ethnic minority lesbians and gay men: Mental health treatment issues. J Consult Clin Psychol 62:243, 1994.

17. Greene B: Lesbian women of color: triple jeopardy. In Comas-Diaz L, Greene B, (eds): Women of Color: Integrating Ethnic and Gender Identities in Psychotherapy. New York:, Guilford Press, 1994.

18. Greene B: Sturdy bridges: The role of African-American mothers in the socialization of African-American children. Women and Therapy, 10:205, 1990.

19. Gock TS. Asian-pacific islander issues: Identity integration and pride. In Berzon B, (ed.): Positively Gay. Berkeley, CA, Celestial Arts, 1992.

20. Gutiérrez FJ, Dworkin SH: Gay, lesbian and African American: Managing the integration of identities. In Gutiérrez FJ, Dworkin SH (eds): Counseling Gay Men and Lesbians. Alexandria, VA: American Association of Counseling and Development.

21. Hidalgo HA, Hidalgo-Christensen E: The Puerto Rican lesbian and the Puerto Rican community. J Homosex 2:109, 1976/1977.

22. Icard L: Black gay men and conflicting social identities: Sexual orientation versus racial identity. J Soc Work and Hum Sexuality 4:83, 1986.

23. Jay K, Young A (eds): The Gay Report: Lesbians and Gay Men Speak Out About Their Sexual Experiences and Lifestyles. New York, Simon & Schuster, 1979.

24. LaFromboise TD, Berman JS, Sohi BK: American indian women. In Comas-Diaz L, Greene B (eds): Women of Color: Integrating Ethnic and Gender Identities in Psychotherapy. New York, Guilford Press, 1994.

25. Loiacano DK: Gay identity issues among black americans: Racism, homophobia and the need for validation. J Counsel Dev 68:21, 1989.

26. Magee M, Miller DC: Psychoanalytic views of female homosexuality. In Cabaj RP, Stein TS (eds): Textbook of Homosexuality and Mental Health. Washington, DC: American Psychiatric Press, 1996.

27. Manalansan MF: Double minorities: Latino, black and Asian men who have sex with men. In Cohen KM, Savin-Williams RC (eds): The Lives of Lesbians, Gays and Bisexuals. NY, Harcourt Brace, 1995.

28. Morales ES: Ethnic minority families and minority gays and lesbians. In Bozett FW, Sussman MB (eds): Homosexuality and Family Relations. Binghamton, NY, Harrington Park Press, 1990.

29. Panek PE, Rush MC, Greenawalt JP: Current sex stereotypes of twenty-five occupations. Psychol Rep 40:212, 1977.

30. Paroski PA: Health care delivery and the concerns of gay and lesbian adolescents. J Adolesc Health Care 8:188, 1987.

31. Remafedi G: Adolescent homosexuality: Psychosocial and medical implications. Pediatrics 79(3):331–337, 1987.

32. Robin AL: Communication Between parent and adolescent. In Friedman SB, Fisher M, Schonberg SK (eds): Comprehensive Adolescent Health Care. St. Louis, MO, Quality Medical Publishing, 1992.

33. Robinson B, Walters LH, Skeen P: Response of parents to learning that their child is homosexual and their concern over AIDS: A national study. J Homosex 18:59, 1989.
34. Strommen EF: "You're a what?": Family members' reactions to the disclosure of homosexuality. J Homosex 18:37, 1989.
35. Tafoya T, Rowell R:. Counseling gay and lesbian native Americans. In Shernoff M, Scott W, (eds): The Sourcebook on Lesbian/Gay Health Care. Washington, DC, National Lesbian and Gay Health Foundation, 1988.
36. Tremble B, Schneider M, Appathurai C: Growing up gay or lesbian in a multicultural context. J Homosex 17:253, 1989.
37. Williams W: The Spirit and the Flesh: Sexual Diversity in American Indian Culture. Boston, Beacon Press, 1986.
38. Williams WL: Persistence and change in the berdache tradition among contemporary Lakota Indians. J Homosex 11:191, 1986.
39. Wooden WS: Lifestyles and identity maintenance among gay Japanese-American males. Alternative Lifestyles 5:236, 1983.

CHAPTER 10

Medical Assessment, Treatment, and Prevention

Creating an environment in which lesbian and gay adolescents feel welcome increases the likelihood of open communication and trust. Even though adolescents may not disclose sexual orientation or discuss concerns about sexual identity during an initial visit, providers can let them know that these are safe topics to explore through visual cues such as posters, brochures, and books about sexuality in the office and waiting room. An excellent poster, "This is a Safe Place to Talk About . . . ,"[15] lets adolescents know that issues such as AIDS, substance use, and homosexuality can and should be talked about with the primary care provider (Fig. 10.1). Because most adolescents are uncomfortable picking up literature or showing an interest in materials that are visibly gay-related, an effective way to target lesbian and gay adolescents is to include information about lesbians and gay males, along with other client populations, in general literature such as clinic brochures.

Reading lists for parents and adolescents also should include books about sexuality and lesbian/gay issues. Books by and for lesbian and gay youth and their parents help to dispel myths and fears and provide important information about coming out, support, and referrals (*see* Appendix C for a list of resources). When adolescents are ready to discuss these concerns, they will have greater confidence that the provider is open and willing to listen.

Medical History

The initial interview and history taking provide an opportunity for the provider, parent(s), and adolescent to share key information and begin to build rapport and trust (Table 10.1). Regardless of an adolescent's sexual orientation, the provider can signal respect and inspire confidence by indicating that he or she is interested in the adolescent's needs and concerns and will provide a safe space in which to discuss them. Depending on the adolescent's age (younger teens and parents may initially be seen together), the provider may meet briefly with the parent(s) to elicit medical and psychosocial issues, then meet alone with the adolescent to complete the history and medical examination.

Providers should ensure that both the adolescent and parent(s) understand that information they share will not be disclosed, except in serious situations such as those involving suicidal feelings or sexual abuse. When confidentiality is openly discussed, adolescents are more willing to seek care for sensitive health concerns.[5] Describing the issues that comprise the context of care—health concerns, sexuality, health education and immunization, family and peer relationships, and school-based concerns—helps adolescents understand the kinds of information that they can share with providers and offers an option for potential guidance and support.

Health and risk behaviors are most accurately assessed in the full context of an adolescent's life (home, school, interests, activities, peers, relationships, and coping styles and behaviors). The medical interview is actually a dialogue with adolescents about their experiences, behaviors, and concerns; honesty is a cornerstone. Careful listening is just as important as active questioning, and includes sensitivity to topics that adolescents may avoid or to which they may react uncomfortably when introduced.

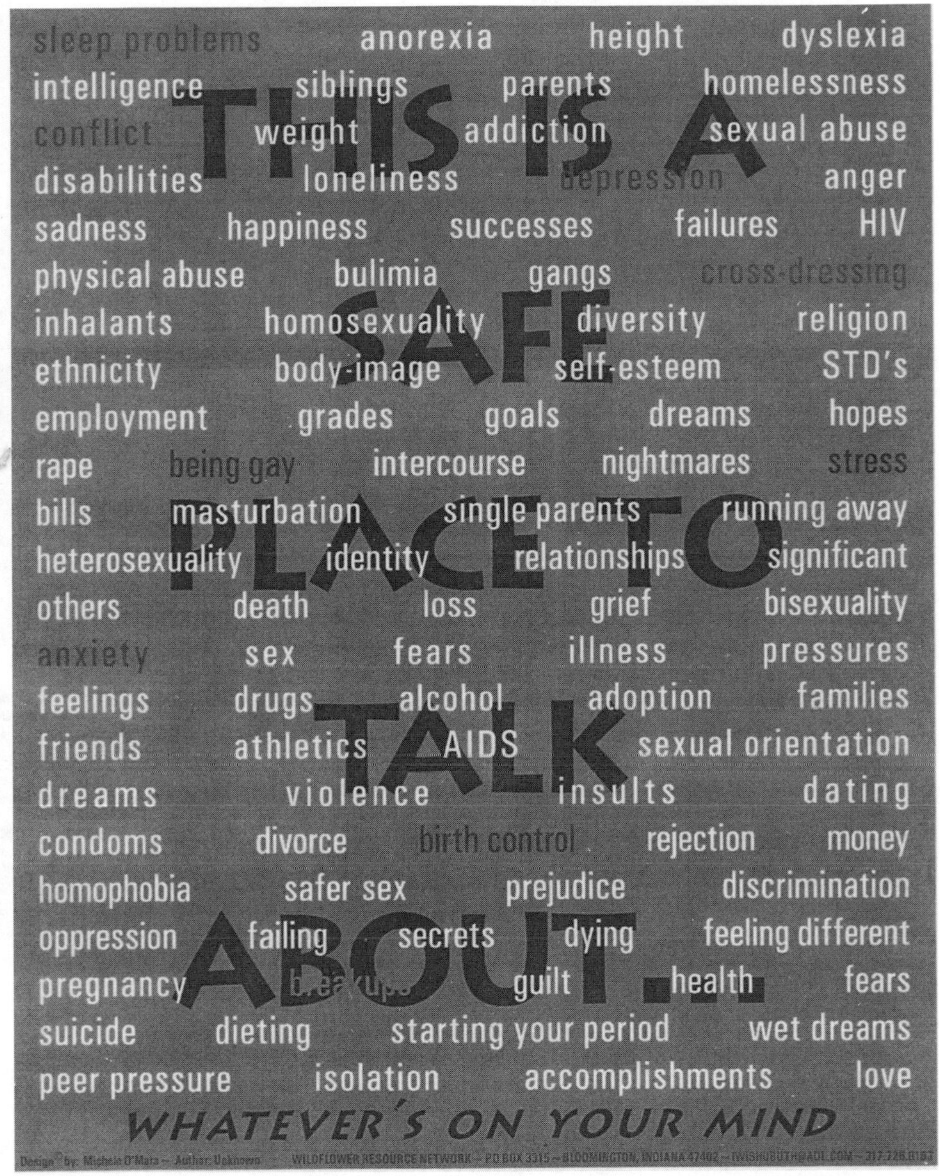

FIGURE 10.1   A useful poster for encouraging adolescents to discuss their concerns. (From Wildflower Resource Network, P.O. Box 3315, Bloomington, IN 47402, with permission.)

An excellent general assessment tool for adolescent interviews is the HEADS questionnaire, developed by staff at Children's Hospital of Los Angeles, which provides a basic overview of adolescent functioning and behavior.[13] The questions have been adapted for use with adolescents who are lesbian, gay, or bisexual or who are questioning sexual identity (Table 10.2).

Most lesbian or gay adolescents will not come out to providers during an initial interview. Sharing this information will take time and establishment of trust. Providers

TABLE 10.1.   Initial Visit

Discussion with adolescent and parent(s)
Introductions and discussion of physician–client relationship
Confidentiality
Situations requiring disclosure (e.g., suicidal ideation)
Medical history and concerns from parent
Session with adolescent (alone)
Range of issues that can be addressed:
Health problems and concerns
Home/family and peer relationships
School/vocational/career issues
Activities and interests
Sexual activity and identity
Substance use
Suicide, depression, and other mental health concerns
Complete physical exam
Appropriate lab tests
Immunizations
Referrals
Discussion with adolescent
Feedback to adolescent and parent(s)

can build rapport by not assuming that all youth are heterosexual and by responding nonjudgmentally to the adolescent's comments and concerns.

Physical Examination

As with all adolescents, lesbian and gay youth should receive yearly routine preventive health assessments, as recommended by the American Medical Association's *Guidelines for Adolescent Preventive Services.*[9] These visits should include health guidance information for parent(s) and adolescent, screening, and immunizations[10] (Tables 10.3 and 10.4). Adolescents should receive annual screening for hypertension; eating disorders; obesity; tobacco use; alcohol and drug use; sexual behavior (and STDs, if sexually active); depression/suicide risk; physical, sexual, and emotional abuse; learning problems; and tuberculosis (if exposed, incarcerated, living in a shelter, or in an area endemic for TB). Health guidance should include information about adolescent development, safety practices, diet and fitness, and healthy lifestyles (sexual behavior, smoking, alcohol, and drug use).

Providers should conduct a routine physical examination and laboratory screening, as indicated, which should include patient education about breast and testicular self-examination. Since lesbian adolescents who are sexually active may have sex with male partners, the possibility of pregnancy should be considered and testing provided if indicated. Lesbians who have male sexual partners should also be routinely screened for STDs, including trichomonas, gonorrhea, chlamydia, and syphilis. HIV counseling should be provided and voluntary testing offered; lesbians who have unprotected sex with bisexual men or gay male friends may be at increased risk for HIV infection, contrary to the myth that "lesbians don't get AIDS." By offering health guidance that applies to same-sex and opposite sex practices (such as the frequency of heterosexual intercourse among lesbians), providers can ensure that all clients receive appropriate prevention messages, whether or not sexual orientation is known.

Lesbian adolescents may have misconceptions about their risks for sexually transmitted diseases and may even assume that they cannot get pregnant. When discussing

TABLE 10.2. Adolescent Risk Profile Interview
(HEADS Assessment)*

H **Home**		Where do you live?
		Who do you live with?
		How much time do you spend at home?
		What do you and your family argue about?
		Can you go to your parents with problems?
		Have you ever run away from home?
E **Education**		What grade are you in?
		What grades are you getting? Have they changed?
		Have you ever failed any classes or been kept back a grade?
		Do you ever cut classes?
		Have you ever been teased or attacked at school?*
		Do you work after school or on weekends?
		What are your career/vocational goals?*
A **Activities**		What do you do for fun?
		What activities do you do during and after school?
		Are you active in sports? Do you exercise?
		Who do you do fun things with?
		Who are your friends?
		Who do you go to with problems?
		What do you do on weekends? Evenings?
	If appropriate:	Does anyone in your home/family know you are lesbian/gay/bisexual? Why/why not?*
		Do any of your friends know you're gay?*
		Do you have any gay friends? Are they your age, older?*
		Do you go anywhere to meet other gay people?
		Do you go to gay bars or clubs?*
		What do you know about local social and recreational organizations for lesbians and gay men?*
D **Drugs**		Do you drink coffee or tea?
		Do you smoke cigarettes? Have you ever smoked one?
		Have you ever tried alcohol? When? What kind and how often?
		Do any of your friends drink or use drugs?
		What drugs have you tried? Have you ever injected steroids or drugs?
		When? How often do you use them?
		How do you get money to pay for drugs?*
		Are drugs used or available in places where you hang out?*
S **Sexual Activity/ Identity**		Have you ever had sex unwillingly?
		How many sexual partners have you had?
		How old were you when you first had sex? How old was your partner?*
		Have you ever had sex with men? Women? Both?
		Do you think you might be lesbian, gay, or bisexual?*
		Do you think you need to have sex to find out if you're lesbian, gay, or bisexual?*
		Do you want to become pregnant?* Have you ever been pregnant?
		Have you ever had an infection as a result of having sex?
		Do you use condoms and/or another form of contraception for STD and HIV prevention?
		Have you ever traded sex for money, drugs, clothes, or a place to stay?
		Have you ever been tested for HIV? Do you think it would be a good idea to be tested?
S **Suicide/ Depression**		How do you feel today, on a scale of 0–10? (0 = very sad, 10 = very happy)
		Have you ever felt less than a 5? How long did that feeling last?*
		What made you feel that way?
		Does thinking you may be lesbian, gay or bisexual make you feel that way?*
		Did you every think about hurting yourself, that life wasn't worth living, or hope that when you went to sleep you wouldn't wake up?

* Adapted for use with adolescents who may be lesbian, gay, bisexual, or questioning sexual identity.
Adapted from Goldenring JM, Cohen EH: Getting into an adolescent's H.E.A.D.S. Contemp Pediatr 5:7, 1988.

TABLE 10.3.   Medical Assessment/Primary Care

Physical Examination
1. Height and weight with percentiles
2. Blood pressure and pulse
3. Eyes, ears, nose, mouth, teeth, and gums
4. Thyroid
5. Lymph nodes
6. Breasts
7. Heart, lungs, and abdomen
8. Back/spine
9. Tanner staging of pubertal development
      Breasts and pubic hair pattern for females
      Testicular volume and pubic hair pattern for males
10. Anogenital exam/inspection (in all)
      Testicular exam
      Anal exam, if indicated
      Pelvic exam, if symptomatic, sexually experienced or > 18 years
         a. Speculum and bimanual
11. Skin
12. Neuro and mental status exam

Patient education
1. Breast or testicular self-exam
2. Genital exam (internal and external)
3. Menstrual history
4. Guidance (parenting, injury prevention, diet and fitness, adolescent development
   and healthy lifestyles)

Laboratory screening
1. Hemoglobin or hematocrit (sickle cell screen, if indicated)
      (Consider CBC for youth with chronic illness, such as HIV)
2. Urine analysis
3. Liver function tests (SGOT, SGPT) for substance-using adolescents
4. Cholesterol screening, if indicated by obesity, other history
5. Pregnancy-related tests
      Serum hCG, if history or clinical exam indicative
      Rubella serology, before pregnancy
6. See STD screen, Table 4

Immunizations
1. dT
2. MMR
3. Hepatitis A, Hepatitis B (Prescreen sexually active gay male, homeless, and HIV+
      youth for exposure to hepatitis B with HepB sAg, cAb, sAb)
4. Influenza, yearly, for chronic illness (including HIV) and homeless youth
5. Varicella, if nonimmune

*Tuberculosis evaluation
1. Skin testing
2. Baseline chest x-ray if anergic or PPD+
3. Facilitating completion of evaluation

Vision testing and audiometry

Referral for dental care

Other referrals

---

* From Centers for Disease Control and Prevention: Essential components of a tuberculosis prevention and control program MMWR 44:1, 1995.
From Hoffman N, Ocepek D: Protocol for primary care of lesbian and gay adolescents. Conference on the Primary Care Needs of Lesbian and Gay Adolescents, Health Resources and Services Administration, Washington, DC, December 5–6, 1994.

TABLE 10.4. Sexual History and Screening

Sexual identity
1. Behavior
    Same sex and opposite sex partners
    Age of coitarche and age of partners
    Consensual and nonconsensual sex
    Types of sexual experience
        Outercourse
            a. Kissing
            b. Massage and petting
            c. Masturbation
        Intercourse
            a. Vaginal-penile
            b. Oral-genital, oral-anal
            c. Anal-genital
        Condom use (settings and
            partner type)
        Concurrent substance use
        Survival sex
2. Disclosure of sexual orientation
    Family
    Friends/partner(s)/roommates
    Classmates/co-workers
    Teachers/supervisors/counselors
    Role of health care provider

Sexually transmitted diseases
1. Screening
    Gonorrhea (triple site—genital, oral, anal)
    Chlamydia
        a. Cervical
        b. Urine sediment versus urethral swab
    Vaginal wet mount (candida, vaginosis, trichomoniasis), if indicated by history or exam
    Hepatitis B (HBV) prevaccination screen HepB sAg, cAb, sAb
        (Consider hepatitis C serology if HBV+ or partner has HCV)
    HIV antibody (consent and confidentiality)
    Human papillomavirus (HPV)/dysplasia
        a. Cervical Papanicolaou (Pap) smear
        b. *Consider anal Pap and anoscopy if perianal warts present*
    Syphilis
    Intestinal parasites, if clinically indicated, but not routine
2. Treatment issues
    Adherence
    Test of cure
    Partner issues
3. Prevention
    Readiness for sexual experience
    Risk reduction

Reproductive Health
1. Contraception
2. Pregnancy decision-making
3. Parenting skills

From Hoffman N, Ocepek D: Protocol for primary care of lesbian and gay adolescents. Conference on the Primary Care Needs of Lesbian and Gay Adolescents, Health Resources and Services Administration, Washington, DC, December 5–6, 1994.

birth control, providers should be aware that many lesbians have been alienated from health encounters as a result of intense pressure from providers who tried to determine their method of birth control.[11] Alienation occurs most frequently when providers assume that their clients are heterosexual. For lesbian adolescents who may not have come out to anyone, pressure to discuss such an emotionally charged topic may cause them to avoid medical care in the future.

An important part of health education and routine care is to help young lesbians understand adult female development and the need for periodic screening, including cervical cytology and Pap smear. Like all women, lesbians are at risk for breast and gynecologic malignancies, and specific risks such as family history, alcohol abuse, obesity, and smoking heighten susceptibility. As with all female adolescents, menstrual history should include age of onset, interval, duration, flow, and concurrent symptoms.

Gay male adolescents who are sexually active are at risk for STDs and HIV. They should receive regular screening with triple-site gonorrhea cultures (urethral, pharyngeal, and rectal); urethral chlamydia (antigen or culture) or urine test for leukocytes, or ligase chain reaction (LCR) for gonorrhea or chlamydia; and testing for syphilis and hepatitis B. If they have not been tested previously for HIV, voluntary testing should be offered, with appropriate counseling and linkages to support services (*see* Chapter 13 for guidelines). Anal inspection should include evaluation for fissures, venereal warts, hemorrhoids, herpes, or syphilis lesions. Anal inspection is important for all males because it may provide the first indications of anal intercourse, whether or not an adolescent discloses same-sex behavior. Anal Pap and anoscopy should be considered if anal warts are present.

All adolescents who are sexually active should be tested for hepatitis B immunity and, if susceptible, should receive a three-dose series of hepatitis B vaccine.[1]

Assessment of Sexual Readiness

Providers should help adolescents to assess their readiness for sexual activity, which includes discussing their underlying needs and motives. For example, some youth assume that they can confirm or change sexual orientation by engaging in sexual intercourse. Providers should explain that sexual identity evolves over time and is not immediately confirmed or changed by initiating intercourse. Adolescents have other options for exploring their identities, such as books and support groups, which allow them to access support and accurate information about sexual identity while learning important communication skills and safer sex practices.

Providers should encourage young adolescents to postpone sexual activity until they are older. For youth who are intent on sexual exploration, providers should discuss the range of safer sex options—explaining the continuum of sexual behaviors from "outercourse" (nonpenetrative massage, petting, and mutual masturbation) to the use of barriers (condoms and dental dams) when exchange of fluids is possible. Providers should clearly explain the risks of unprotected oral, anal, and vaginal intercourse; for example, adolescents may not realize that many STDs, such as gonorrhea, intestinal parasites, and hepatitis, are readily transmitted through oral sex unless condoms are used. Providers should demonstrate proper use of condoms, including female condoms.

Additional anticipatory guidance topics for lesbian and gay adolescents include the importance of developing trusting relationships with health/mental health providers and other adults, a discussion of predictable stressors in consolidating lesbian/gay identity, the need for support, and pros and cons of disclosing sexual orientation to family and friends (*see* Chapter 9 for anticipatory guidance information).

Treating Victims of Rape and Trauma

Lesbian and gay youth are at risk for anti-gay violence, including rape and physical assault. In such cases, sensitivity is required not only in treating physical trauma, collecting the necessary specimens (in cases of rape and assault), and managing prophylaxis of STDs, but also in interviewing and counseling youth who may be lesbian or gay but who have not divulged the biased nature of the attack. Rape is especially traumatizing for both males and females, although male rape and sexual abuse victims have additional concerns: some fear that having been sexually abused by a male might "make them gay," that they were victimized because they are gay, or that family and friends will assume they are gay because they were raped. Counseling is important for both family and adolescent. Recovery takes time, and talking about the experience is a crucial part of resolving the trauma. Adolescents who are lesbian or gay also need to talk about how the assault affects their self-esteem, evolving sexual identity, and sense of vulnerability in a homophobic society.

Providers should assess the adolescent's support system and connections, if any, to the organized lesbian and gay community. Decisions need to be made about bringing charges against the assailant, which can facilitate recovery for some people. The adolescent needs support to interact with the legal system and with law enforcement personnel who may be judgmental or dismissive. Referral to a supportive counselor who is knowledgeable about lesbian and gay community resources can help the youth obtain appropriate support. Increasingly, lesbian/gay anti-violence projects which provide victim advocacy and counseling are available in large cities (*see* Appendix B for referral information).

Treating Homeless and Runaway Youth

Homeless and runaway youth are at extremely high risk for poor health, tuberculosis, STDs, HIV, substance abuse, and mental health concerns, including suicide. Because they are transient and receive sporadic care, providers should maximize all health visits as important opportunities for providing essential prevention information. Although these youth may be sexually experienced, they also may lack basic information about sexuality and high-risk behaviors, including HIV prevention and proper use of condoms.

Prescriptions and advice should be simple because many youth will not return for follow-up and may discontinue medication early.[7] Linkages with other service systems can help to address their multiple needs for shelter, substance abuse treatment, mental health services, and vocational rehabilitation programs; however, many homeless youth are mobile, making continuity of care very difficult.

Substance Abuse

Annual visits should include screening for tobacco and substance use. Not all adolescents who use alcohol and drugs become dependent on them. Susceptibility is enhanced by external and internal factors, including genetic characteristics (for some forms of substance abuse), environmental influences (family and peers), and psychological factors (personal vulnerability).[20] Although peer use is a primary influence, particularly for white youth, family and cultural attitudes toward alcohol and drugs also are important contributing or protective factors. In addition, factors such as low self-esteem, behavioral problems, poor academic performance, deviance, and depression heighten overall risk. Adolescents who have been physically or sexually abused, runaway or homeless youth, and lesbian and gay youth are at increased risk for substance abuse.

Since dependency and complications increase with duration of use, childhood prevention and early identification of substance abuse are critical interventions for primary care providers. Among adult smokers, for example, the majority became addicted to tobacco during adolescence. For this reason, groups such as the American Academy of Pediatrics have recommended that physicians be able to identify behaviors associated with substance abuse and incorporate prevention and treatment into routine care.[2]

Adolescent substance abuse has been called the most frequently missed pediatric diagnosis.[17] Because substance use has also become a "nearly universal right of passage" for adolescents, it may be difficult for providers to assess problem use. Few will volunteer information about alcohol and drug use unless specifically asked. Adolescents with emerging or even advanced substance abuse problems are identified most likely through routine provision of care, history taking, and interviewing.[6] Risk assessment requires information about family and peer relationships, school performance, recreational activities, and psychological or psychiatric symptoms in addition to alcohol and drug use (Table 10.5). Questions about such issues should be incorporated into the medical interview and used to review an adolescent's risk status during follow-up visits.

Substance abuse in adolescents seems to occur in four stages (Table 10.6).[16] Since most adolescents use at least one drug (alcohol) and many try marijuana, providers should determine frequency of use and settings in which drugs are used to assess the youth's level of involvement, related risks, and potential for addiction. Determining an adolescent's motivation for drug use is essential for successful intervention. For example, if use is precipitated by underlying emotional pain or possible depression, counseling is indicated. Affective disorders (particularly depression), suicidal behavior, conduct and antisocial personality disorders, and eating disorders are frequently seen in conjunction with adolescent substance abuse.[16] Of adolescents admitted for inpatient substance abuse treatment, as many as 60–80% are diagnosed with depression.[16] Although comparable data are not available for lesbian and gay adolescents, an outcome study of inpatient treatment for chemically dependent lesbian and gay adults found that 37% had an untreated psychiatric illness, 66% reported serious depression or anxiety, 48% reported persistent suicidal ideation, and 32% had attempted suicide.[19] Although the level of severity may vary, providers should assess for these conditions when substance abuse is suspected.

Substances commonly abused by adolescents do not cause frequent illness, and medical complications of chronic alcoholism are not generally seen until adulthood.[6] In the diagnosis of substance abuse in adolescents, the most useful objective criteria are (1) quantity and frequency of use; (2) symptomatic behaviors, such as intoxication or blackouts; and (3) functional impairments, such as loss of control over drinking

TABLE 10.5.   Substance Abuse Risk Factors

Family history of alcohol and drug abuse	Deviance and lack of conformity
Dysfunctional and abusive family	Low self-esteem
Peer drug use	Depression
Behavioral problems	Physical and sexual abuse
Poor academic performance	

TABLE 10.6.   Stages of Adolescent Substance Use

Stages	Behaviors	Intervention Strategies
1. Experimentation	Experimental use of alcohol and cigarettes	Identify underlying motivation for use Provide education on health and social consequences Build self-esteem Encourage and reinforce substitute activity/behavior Provide possible skills training
2. Exploration	Social use with friends	Explore social context of use Identify specific risks (e.g., driving while intoxicated) Develop harm reduction strategies (e.g., designated driver) Clarify controlled use and indicators of problem use
3. Encapsulation	Persistent use during free time, possibly at school Active drug-seeking Interpersonal difficulties Possible juvenile court involvement	Determine whether abstinence is possible Provide counseling and assess degree of psychiatric problems Provide behavioral skills training in drug-free environment Potential residential or day-treatment program
4. Dependence	Deterioration of relationships Elevated depression Stealing to buy drugs Increased physical and psychological problems Drug use is fully normalized	Provide immediate treatment Possible referral for inpatient detoxification

From MacKenzie RG, Kipke MD: Substance use and abuse. In Friedman SB, Fisher M, Schonberg SK (eds): Comprehensive Adolescent Health Care. St. Louis, MO, Quality Medical Publishing, 1992.

and drugs, poor relationships with family, peers, and teachers, and juvenile court involvement.[16] Treatment is indicated if substance use interferes with any aspect of functioning, leads to negative consequences, and is uncontrolled or if withdrawal symptoms are evident.[16] For adolescents who are experimenting with alcohol and drugs (*see* Table 10.6, stages 1–2), providers should offer education about health and social consequences, identify immediate risks, such as driving while intoxicated, and help teens to determine problem behavior. If an adolescent's use has progressed to the stage where day-treatment or residential or inpatient programs are needed, the provider may seek consultation about treatment availability and appropriate placement.

Treatment

Substance abuse treatment options for adolescents include outpatient programs (intensive day-treatment), which care for 80% of adolescents who receive treatment for drug abuse, residential programs (non–hospital-based treatment in a community-like setting), and inpatient programs (short-term intensive hospital-based programs with a multidisciplinary staff).[16] However, access to adolescent treatment programs is generally limited on the basis of ability to pay; as a result, many adolescents receive treatment with adults. When referring any adolescent for treatment, providers should be familiar with a program's treatment philosophy and sensitivity to adolescent needs and to the needs of ethnic/racial minorities and lesbian and gay youth. For information about knowledgeable providers and help identifying appropriate referrals, providers should contact local lesbian and gay health programs or organizations such as the National Association of Lesbian and Gay Addiction Professionals (*see* Appendix B for resource information).

Finding the right contacts is particularly important in referrals of lesbian or gay adolescents since few treatment programs are knowledgeable about the needs of lesbian and gay clients, much less the needs of lesbian and gay youth, and many gay clients are fearful of disclosing sexual orientation in treatment and aftercare settings.[3] Lack of support for core aspects of identity (including racial/ethnic identity and sexual orientation) is a major barrier to successful recovery. Relapse is common in lesbian and gay substance abusers who have not been able to disclose sexual orientation and openly address issues related to stigma and shame. For example, more than half (53%) of lesbians and gay men admitted to the nation's only lesbian/gay inpatient treatment program reported having failed treatment when they they were unable to discuss issues related to sexual orientation.[19]

Lack of knowledge about the needs of lesbians and gay males is also common in outpatient and day-treatment programs. In a study of county-funded alcohol and drug treatment programs in San Francisco, more than half of treatment staff (56%) had no prior training on treatment needs of lesbian and gay clients and an equal number lacked knowledge of appropriate self-help/support referrals.[18] Similar problems persist in aftercare and Twelve Step programs (e.g., Alcoholics Anonymous [AA], Narcotics Anonymous [NA]).

In referrals of lesbian, gay, or bisexual adolescents for substance abuse treatment, it is important to help them to decide whether it is appropriate (i.e., safe) to disclose sexual orientation during treatment or aftercare. The decision may be contingent on the availability of family and peer support, as well as the level of anticipated or reported homophobia among clients and treatment staff. In many cases, an adolescent may not have come out to his or her parents, and the provider may be the primary advocate. If an adolescent cannot disclose his or her sexual orientation during treatment, these issues will need to be discussed in other settings. Self-acceptance, including dealing with sexual identity, is an integral task of recovery. Providers can assist by identifying gay-sensitive Twelve Step programs (e.g., through the central AA referral in their community) and gay-sensitive substance abuse treatment counselors for aftercare support.

Culturally Sensitive Treatment

Awareness of ethnic/cultural norms related to alcohol and drug use can help providers assess problem use in adolescents and anticipate support needs during treatment (Table 10.7). Substance abuse affects the entire family (and social) network; recovery requires the active participation of family members. Ethnic minority persons generally have large extended families. Sensitivity to cultural attitudes and beliefs is essential to engage families in treatment.[20] Several interventions have been developed for providing culturally sensitive substance abuse treatment; references are included in Appendix D. Although many providers may not offer outpatient treatment for substance abuse, they need to assist families in identifying appropriate treatment programs and serve

TABLE 10.7.   Components of Culturally Sensitive Intake/Interventions

Understand role of alcohol and drugs in family
Assess degree of ethnic identity and acculturation
Determine language preference
Assess adolescent's social network
Discuss previous treatment experience

From Delgado A: Alcoholism treatment for hispanic youth. J Drug Issues 18:59, 1988.

Assessing Community Referral Resources
For Sensitivity to Lesbian and Gay Adolescents

	Yes	No
Has the agency (provider) worked with lesbian and gay clients in the past?	___	___
If so, how often are lesbian and gay clients seen?	___	___
Rarely	___	___
Several times per year	___	___
Monthly	___	___
Weekly	___	___
Do any open lesbians or gay male staff work for the agency?	___	___
Does the agency routinely provide care for adolescents (ages 10–21)?	___	___
Is the agency (provider) supportive of lesbian and gay youth?	___	___
Describe treatment philosophy/approach to working with lesbian/gay youth.	___	___

_____

_____

_____

Are providers familiar with adolescent developmental needs?	___	___
Are providers familiar with the needs of lesbian and gay adolescents?	___	___
Has the agency sponsored special training or supported continuing education for staff on the needs of lesbian and gay clients?	___	___
Does the agency provide services to people with HIV/AIDS?	___	___
Are agency staff knowledgeable about HIV/AIDS?	___	___
Does the agency provide on-site HIV counseling and testing?	___	___

If counseling and testing is provided elsewhere, what kind of linkages are in place to ensure access to follow-up care?

_____

_____

_____

Does the agency have linkages to programs serving adolescents?	___	___
Does the agency have linkages to programs serving lesbian and gay youth?	___	___
Do agency policies include lesbian and gay clients?	___	___
Do agency brochures and outreach materials include lesbian and gay clients?	___	___

Comments:

_____

_____

_____

_____

_____

_____

_____

FIGURE 10.2. Referral checklist.

as advocates for chemically dependent youth. For ethnic minority youth who are lesbian, gay, or bisexual, knowledge of cultural norms can help providers to anticipate the unique stressors that treatment and recovery can precipitate and enable them to provide appropriate referrals and follow-up support (*see* Appendix B).

Regardless of ethnicity, treatment requires involving the entire family in assessment, family therapy, aftercare, and often in Al-Anon (Twelve Step self-help group for families of addicts and alcoholics). Substance abuse is frequently intergenerational; it is not unusual to uncover chemical dependency in a parent or other siblings once an adolescent's problem is disclosed.[14] Prevention and treatment of substance abuse in other family members will enhance the prognosis for recovery in adolescents.

Referrals

In many cases, providers will be required to make referrals to other agencies or health and mental health providers for a variety of services on behalf of lesbian and gay clients. These referrals may include chemical dependency treatment programs, inpatient or outpatient mental health services, specialty care, or support services. In some cases, agencies may be located in another geographic area, and providers may have little or no information about the agency's treatment approach, level of support, or quality of care for lesbian and gay clients.

Because many agencies have had limited experience serving adolescents, in general, and even more limited experience serving lesbian and gay youth, providers should assess the agency's capacity and level of support for lesbian and gay adolescents before making a referral. Many agencies and providers are still guided by outdated information based on inappropriate treatment philosophies, which continue to view homosexuality as pathologic or maladaptive. Such approaches are harmful to adults, and may be even more damaging to adolescents who have fewer resources and options and depend on adults for support. When lesbian and gay youth must be referred to agencies that lack appropriate support (e.g., no other options are available), providers should continue to serve as an advocate and ensure that appropriate care is provided.

Figure 10.2 (*see* previous page) provides a form to help providers assess the capacity and level of interest among referral sources (institutions, agencies, and individual providers) in serving lesbian and gay adolescents. Providers should adapt the form as required and use the information to help build a network of gay-sensitive and supportive agencies in their communities, sharing this information with colleagues and other agencies to expand available service options for lesbian and gay adolescents.

References

1. American Academy of Pediatrics: Homosexuality and adolescence. Pediatrics 92:631, 1993.
2. American Academy of Pediatrics: The role of the pediatrician in substance abuse counseling. Pediatrics 72:251, 1983.
3. Cabaj RP: AIDS and chemical dependency: Special issues and treatment barriers for gay and bisexual men. J Psychoactive Drugs 21:387, 1989.
4. Centers for Disease Control and Prevention: Essential components of a tuberculosis prevention and control program. MMWR 44:1, 1995.
5. Cheng T, Savageau JA, Sattler AL, DeWitt TG: Confidentiality in health care: A survey of knowledge, perceptions and attitudes among high school students. JAMA 269:1404, 1993.
6. Coupey SM, Schonberg SK: Drug, alcohol and tobacco abuse. In Hoekleman RA (ed): Primary Pediatric Care. St. Louis, MO, Mosby Year Book, 1992.
7. Deisher RW: Prostitution and pornography. In Friedman SB, Fisher M, Schonberg SK (eds): Comprehensive Adolescent Health Care. St. Louis, MO, Quality Medical Publishing, 1992.
8. Delgado M: Alcoholism treatment and hispanic youth. J Drug Issues 18:59,1988.
9. Elster AB, Kuznets NJ: AMA Guidelines for Adolescent Preventive Services (GAPS): Recommendations and Rationale. Baltimore, Williams & Wilkins, 1994.

10. Centers for Disease Control and Prevention: Immunization of adolescents. MMWR 45:1, 1996.
11. Futterman D, Casper V: Homosexuality: Challenges of treating lesbian and gay adolescents. In Hoe-kleman RA (ed): Primary Pediatric Care, 2nd ed. St. Louis, MO, Mosby Year Book, 1992.
12. Hoffman N, Ocepek D: Protocol for primary care of lesbian and gay adolescents. Conference on the Primary Care Needs of Lesbian and Gay Adolescents, Health Resources and Services Administration, Washington, DC, December 5–6, 1994.
13. Goldenring JM, Cohen EH: Getting into an adolescent's H.E.A.D.S. Contemp Pediatr 5:7, 1988.
14. Huberty DJ, Huberty CE, Flanagan-Hobday K, Blackmore G: Family issues in working with chemically dependent adolescents. Chem Dependency 34:507, 1987.
15. This is a safe place to talk about . . . , Wildflower Resource Network, P.O. Box 3315, Bloomington, IN 47402.
16. MacKenzie RG, Kipke MD: Substance use and abuse. In Friedman SB, Fisher M, Schonberg SK (eds.): Comprehensive Adolescent Health Care. St. Louis, MO, Quality Medical Publishing, 1992.
17. McDonald DI: Drugs, Drinking and Adolescents. Chicago, Year Book Medical Publishers, 1984.
18. Morales ES, Graves MA: Substance Abuse: Patterns and Barriers to Treatment for Gay Men and Lesbians in San Francisco. San Francisco, San Francisco Department of Public Health, Community Substance Abuse Services, 1983.
19. Ratner E: Treatment issues for chemically dependent lesbians and gay men. In Garnets L, Kimmel D (eds): Psychological Perspectives on Lesbian and Gay Male Experiences. New York, Columbia University Press, 1993.
20. Thurman PJ, Swaim R, Plested B: Intervention and treatment of ethnic minority substance abusers. In Aponte JF, Rivers RY, Wohl J (eds): Psychological Interventions and Cultural Diversity. Needham Heights, MA, Allyn and Bacon, 1995.

CHAPTER 11

Mental Health Assessment and Treatment

Many mental health providers I've gone to treat me like I'm a specimen. When they find out you're lesbian or gay, they focus on your sexuality as the basis of all your problems. They don't listen to what we say that's relevant to our problems. No matter what we tell them, they think it's our sexuality—being lesbian or gay—that's causing our problem. And we're not getting the help we really need.

—Gay Youth

Providers can identify mental health concerns and symptoms that require further review and follow-up during a routine clinical interview (*see* table 10.2). During a general discussion of events related to home, school, peers, substance use, and current stressful events, providers should be alert to the adolescent's manner of relating, speech and language, affect, and quality of thinking. Providers may further assess the youth's emotional state with questions that evaluate duration, severity, and frequency of distress whenever affect appears atypical, agitated, or depressed. Paying attention to the youth's emotional cues allows providers to build rapport, and encourages adolescents to share underlying concerns that may or may not have serious implications for their overall well-being (Table 11.1).

When identifying symptoms of depression, providers should also assess for anxiety, eating disorders, chemical dependency, victimization, and sexual abuse, which often underlie, mask, or occur in conjunction with depression. Among lesbians and gay males, depression is a common reaction to coming out, dealing with the stigma of homosexuality, and attempting to hide lesbian or gay identities. With appropriate support, however, depression related to sexual identity generally resolves; in fact, lesbian and gay youth who have come out and have accepted their identity report enhanced self-esteem.[10] A full protocol for mental health assessment is included in Appendix F.

Psychiatric History

Information about the adolescent's psychiatric history should be included in an initial assessment. Like heterosexual youth, lesbian, gay, and bisexual adolescents may suffer from mental disorders, some of which may be persistent and severe. Providers should ask adolescents about previous mental health counseling experiences in inpatient and outpatient settings, including interactions with counselors and mental health practitioners, helpful and harmful interventions, medication history, family psychiatric history, family attitudes, and perceptions of mental health services. This includes asking adolescents who have received mental health services to describe their experiences: Did they disclose their sexual identity? If so, how did mental health providers respond? Were attempts made to change sexual orientation ("reparative" therapy)? If so, what kinds? Adolescents who have been exposed to aversive therapies may be mistrustful of further counseling; however, follow-up mental health services

TABLE 11.1.   Mental Status

May include the following:

Current stressful life events	Speech and language
Physical appearance	Reading/writing
Sleep and appetite	Quality of thinking and perception
Manner of relating and relationships	Intelligence
Orientation to time, place, person	Memory
Current medical problems; medications	Fantasies and conflict(s)
Central nervous system functioning	Impulsivity and risk-taking
Emotional states/affects	Coping resources/defenses
General	Judgment and insight
Anxiety	Adaptive capacities
Depression	Positive attributes/resilience
Anger	
Other	

From Boxer A, Haas J: Protocol for mental health care of lesbian and gay adolescents. Conference on the Primary Care Needs of Lesbian and Gay Adolescents, Health Resources and Services Administration, Washington, DC, December 5 6, 1994.

are generally warranted to ''undo'' psychological damage caused by such ill-advised attempts.

Assessing Risk for Suicide

Since mood disorders, particularly depression, are associated with suicidal ideation and attempts, providers should carefully assess all adolescents who present with symptoms of depressed mood. Providers may feel uncomfortable asking adolescents about suicide; however, incorporating depression and suicide into the routine medical interview normalizes assessment and helps adolescents who are struggling with painful, generally unspoken feelings verbalize their distress. Just as asking appropriate questions about sexuality and sexual orientation embarrasses few youth, asking about suicide and self-destructive behavior is likely to cause more discomfort for providers than for clients. Concerns that asking about suicidal feelings or behaviors may encourage youth to contemplate or attempt suicide are unfounded.

If an adolescent displays some level of suicidal ideation during a routine clinical interview, providers should ask about the frequency, duration, and intensity of such thoughts and feelings (Table 11.2). Having a plan—actually thinking about how and under what circumstances he or she might commit suicide—signals a far more serious degree of intent. Adolescents who have attempted suicide in the past are at much higher risk for attempting and completing suicide. Providers should carefully assess the youth's emotional state, motivation, family and environmental circumstances, im-

TABLE 11.2.   Talking with Teens about Suicide

Have you ever felt so sad that you considered hurting yourself?
Have you ever thought about suicide?
How often—and how many times a day—do you think about suicide?
Have you thought about how you might hurt or try to kill yourself?
Do you have a plan for how you might kill yourself? What is it?
Are you considering doing this now?

TABLE 11.3. Evaluating Suicide Risk

1. Current/past suicidal actions/feelings/fantasies	6. Experiences/concepts of death
a. Methods	7. Depression and other predominant emotional
2. Concepts/intentions of outcome	states/affects
3. Life circumstances/situation at time of attempt	8. Family and environmental circumstances
4. Past experience/history of suicidality	9. Assessment of impulsivity
5. Motivations for suicidal behavior	10. Assessment of suicide within the peer network

From Boxer A, Haas J: Protocol for mental health care of lesbian and gay adolescents. Conference on the Primary Care Needs of Lesbian and Gay Adolescents, Health Resources and Services Administration, Washington, DC, December 5–6, 1994.

pulsivity, and suicidal behavior among peers (Table 11.3). If the adolescent's sexual orientation is unknown or has never been discussed, providers should ask about sexual identity. In one study, among gay and bisexual youth who had attempted suicide, the majority of attempts occurred after self-identification as gay or bisexual (1 of 3 attempts was related to conflicts about sexual identity).[13] Attempts were more frequent among youth who came out at younger ages, who were rejected because of their sexual orientation, who were transgendered, and who were ejected from their homes. Among lesbians, attempts occurred twice as often in victims of child sexual abuse, rape, and anti-gay violence.[7]

Adolescents who are actively suicidal should be placed in a safe environment immediately; youth who express suicidal thoughts and feelings should be referred for counseling with follow-up by the provider within the next few days.

Victimization and Abuse

Like heterosexual teens, lesbian and gay adolescents may be victims of physical or sexual abuse in or out of the home; they may experience traumatic events, including exposure to crime and violence. Lesbian and gay youth are also at risk for anti-gay violence and trauma related to sexual orientation. Reactions to victimization include posttraumatic stress disorder, sleep disturbances, anxiety, depression, nightmares, somaticization, suicidal ideation and attempts, and increased use of drugs. Like rape victims who rarely seek help immediately after the assault, lesbian and gay youth (particularly those who are not out to family and friends) may fear additional victimization if the cause of attack is revealed. Unless immediate treatment is required, some may hide their victimization or deny the cause; as with rape, however, recovery requires external support and time to work through the trauma and develop positive coping skills. The greater the trauma, the more time is needed for readjustment after assault. Many rape victims are negatively affected several years after the trauma; this is particularly true of victims who lack social support.[14] Moreover, vulnerability and negative reactions are heightened by social stigma, such as race and homosexuality.[9]

Lesbian and gay youth (and adults) who are victimized may blame themselves for the attack, which, in turn, may intensify internalized homophobia and feelings of self-hate. Reactions may be heightened or minimized depending on the individual's stage of coming out or degree of self-acceptance. Adolescents who have developed connections to the organized lesbian/gay community, who have positive identities and supportive networks, have a greater ability to buffer anti-gay victimization[8] (Table 11.4).

TABLE 11.4. Factors that Enhance Recovery from Victimization and Anti-Gay Violence

Strong support system
Access to supportive counseling
Opportunity to talk about the trauma over a period of time
Positive coping skills
Access to lesbian/gay community resources
Access to legal remedies (whether they choose this option or not)
Perceiving the attack as an act of prejudice rather than personal failure

Asking adolescents about their experiences with victimization and abuse (regardless of sexual orientation) can hasten recovery and potentially avert further abuse (since victimization may reinforce behaviors that attract exploitation). Because some adolescents feel deep shame and humiliation, they may be reluctant to reveal the biased nature of their attack; however, careful attention to emotional and somatic sequelae can help providers identify the problem and ensure appropriate support. Listening empathically to the adolescent's ordeal helps reduce alienation and encourages participation in follow-up counseling, which is important for recovery. Providers should assess the adolescent's reaction to and interpretation of the trauma, including the extent to which the youth equates victimization with his or her sexual identity, and evaluate coping skills, access to support, and involvement with lesbian and gay community networks. Because recovery requires separating the experience of victimization from a lesbian or gay identity, referral to a nonjudgmental counselor is essential for restoring a sense of self-worth and positive world view.

Psychological Reactions to "Coming Out"

Adolescents (and adults) who are struggling with sexual identity experience a range of intense feelings and psychological reactions. As with any emotional crisis, coming out is mediated by coping resources, underlying personality structure, and access to support. Once the crisis has passed, however, psychological distress clears, and what may appear on the surface as a moderate to severe psychiatric disorder resolves. Providers should reassure adolescents who question their sexual identity that such confusion is normal, while providing access to supportive counseling and community support services (including peer support and accurate information about being gay). When sexual identity does not resolve, underlying problems, such as sexual abuse or emotional trauma, need to be identified and addressed. Although coming out is a

TABLE 11.5. Assessing Adolescent Emotional States*

General Emotional Status	Anxiety
How do you feel most of the time these days?	What things make you nervous or anxious these days?
How do you feel now compared with the way you usually feel?	What is the most frightening thing that has ever happened to you?
What sorts of things make you happy these days?	What happens when you feel like that?
What sorts of things make you sad?	When you feel frightened/scared, does it bother you in other ways, (e.g., you cannot sleep, get headaches)?
What things do you enjoy doing most of all?	Do you ever feel nervous or scared for no reason you can
What was the happiest time of your life?	

* Adapt the questions to assess other emotional states, e.g., depression and anger, as required.

TABLE 11.6.　Diagnosing Clinical Depression

Major Depressive Disorder (MDD)	Dysthymic Disorder
Characterized by a marked change from previous functioning, including 5 or more of the following symptoms that persist for a least a 2-week period (at least one symptom must include depressed mood or loss of interest and pleasure):	*Chronic low level of depression (not as severe as MDD) characterized by depressed or irritable mood that persists for at least one year, without more than 2 symptom-free months, and includes at least 2 of the following symptoms:*
Depressed or irritable mood lasting most of the day	Poor appetite or overeating
Decreased interest in pleasurable activities	Sleeping problems
Changes in weight, including failure to gain during adolescence	Low energy or fatigue
Sleep problems	Low self-esteem
Psychomotor agitation or retardation	Poor concentration or difficulty making decisions
Fatigue or loss of energy	Feelings of hopelessness
Feelings of worthlessness or excessive guilt feelings	
Reduced concentration and decision-making ability	
Repeated suicidal ideation, attempts, or plans of suicide	

From American Psychiatric Association: Diagnostic and Statistical Manual of Mental Disorders, 4th ed. Washington, DC, American Psychiatric Association, 1994, with permission.

normal stage of lesbian/gay identity development, lesbian and gay youth are at risk for misdiagnoses, psychiatric labeling, and inappropriate treatment (including hospitalization) by uninformed or homophobic mental health practitioners.

At times, providers may need to advocate for youth to prevent inappropriate treatment; this is particularly important for youth with serious mental disorders that may be exacerbated by sexual identity crisis and whenever inpatient treatment is required. Because adolescents in many states lack the same legal safeguards as adults to protect against inappropriate psychiatric interventions, including hospitalization, providers should follow-up on psychiatric referrals and ensure that subsequent treatment does not violate appropriate standards of care. This includes assessing the capacity of psychiatric staff to work with lesbian and gay clients, particularly when placements are located in other states with minimal legal protections and poorly regulated facilities.

Providers should be aware of existing standards for adolescent psychiatric care to ensure appropriate placement and therapeutic interventions. According to standards issued by the American Academy of Child and Adolescent Psychiatry (AACAP) and endorsed by related professional associations, including the American Psychiatric Association (APA) and the National Association of Social Workers (NASW), criteria for medically supervised psychiatric residential placement or acute partial hospitalization for children and adolescents include the presence of a major psychiatric disorder that requires a supervised, structured, and supportive milieu (in addition to other criteria) to warrant such placement.[1] In addition to a DSM-IV diagnosis, which constitutes the basis for imminent risk, acute inpatient hospitalization requires all aspects of one of the following: (1) "severe and dangerous" risk for self-injury; (2) "high risk for recurrent and serious injury" to others; (3) acute and serious deterioration from ability to fulfill age-appropriate responsibilities "to the extent that behavior is so disordered or bizarre that it would be unsafe" to be treated in a lesser level of care; or (4) "imminent risk for acute medical status deterioration due to the presence and/or treatment of active psychiatric symptom(s)" that interfere with diagnosis or treatment of a serious and acute mental illness requiring inpatient medical care or requiring acute psychiatric interventions with a high probability of serious and acute deterioration of physical and/or medical health'' (*see* AACAP guidelines for full criteria[1]).

"Reparative" Therapy

Attempts to change sexual orientation from homosexual to heterosexual are rooted in the belief that homosexuality is pathologic or maladaptive. However, homosexuality was declassified as a mental illness more than 20 years ago by the American Psychiatric Association (APA), and no professional mental health associations support ''reparative'' therapy. In fact, the APA clearly states that ''there is no published scientific evidence supporting the efficacy of 'reparative therapy' ''; moreover, ''There is no evidence that any treatment can change a homosexual person's deep seated sexual feelings for others of the same sex.''[4]

**National Mental Health Provider Associations:
Policies on Lesbian and Gay Issues**

American Psychological Association (APA)

The APA urges all mental health professionals to take the lead in removing the stigma of mental illness that has long been associated with homosexual orientations.[5]
December 1973

The APA deplores all public and private discrimination against homosexuals in such areas as employment, housing, public accommodations, and licensing, and declares that no burden of proof of such judgement, capacity, or reliability shall be placed on these individuals greater than that imposed on any other persons. Further, the APA supports and urges the enactment of civil rights legislation at the local, state and federal level that would offer citizens who engage in acts of homosexuality the same protections now guaranteed to others on the basis of race, creed, color, etc. Further, the APA supports and urges the repeal of all discriminatory legislation singling out homosexual acts by consenting adults in private.[5]
January 1975

**American Psychological Association, National Association
of School Psychologists (NASP)**

The APA and NASP shall take a leadership role in promoting societal and familial attitudes and behaviors that affirm the dignity and rights, within educational environments, of all lesbian, gay, and bisexual youths, including those with physical or mental disabilities and from all ethnic/racial backgrounds and classes.

The APA and NASP support providing a safe and secure educational atmosphere in which all youths, including lesbian, gay, and bisexual youths, may obtain an education free from discrimination, harassment, violence, and abuse, and which promotes an understanding and acceptance of self.[5]
February 1993

American Psychiatric Association (APA)

The APA deplores all public and private discrimination against homosexuals in such areas as employment, housing, public accommodations, and licensing, and declares that no burden of proof of such judgement, capacity, or reliability shall be placed on homosexuals greater than that imposed on any other persons. Further, the APA supports and urges the enactment of civil rights legislation at the local, state and federal level that

would offer homosexual citizens the same protections now guaranteed to others on the basis of race, creed, color, etc.[4]
November 1973

National Association of Social Workers (NASW)
Social workers are guided by the NASW Code of Ethics which bans discrimination on the basis of sexual orientation. . . . NASW believes that nonjudgmental attitudes toward sexual orientation allow social workers to offer optimal support and services to lesbian and gay people. NASW affirms its commitment to work toward full social and legal acceptance of lesbian and gay people. The profession must also act to eliminate and prevent discriminatory statutes, policies, and actions that diminish the quality of life for lesbian and gay people and that force many to live their lives in the closet.[11]
August 1993

"Reparative" therapy ignores the impact of social stigma on the mental health of lesbians and gay men and focuses exclusively on homosexuality as the root cause of distress. However, major professional associations not only acknowledge the effect of internalized self-hate, but call for legal and social remedies, including "the enactment of civil rights legislation at local, state and national levels that would offer homosexual citizens the same protections now guaranteed to others on the basis of race, creed, color, etc." (American Psychiatric Association);[4] "the repeal of all discriminatory legislation singling out homosexual acts by consenting adults in private" (American Psychological Association);[5] and "the eliminat[ion] and prevent[ion] of discriminatory statutes, policies, and actions that diminish the quality of life for lesbian and gay people and that force many to live their lives in the closet" (National Association of Social Workers).[11]

**National Professional Associations:
Statements on "Reparative" or "Conversion" Therapy
for Lesbians and Gay Men**

American Academy of Pediatrics
The health care professional should explore each adolescent's perception of homosexuality, and any youth struggling with sexual orientation issues should be offered appropriate referrals to providers and programs that affirm the adolescent's intrinsic worth regardless of sexual identity. Providers who are unable to be objective because of religious or other personal convictions should refer patients to those who can.

Confusion about sexual orientation is not unusual during adolescence. Counseling may be helpful for young people who are uncertain about their sexual orientation or for those who are uncertain about how to express their sexuality and might profit from an attempt at clarification through a counseling or psychotherapeutic initiative. Therapy directed specifically at changing sexual orientation is contraindicated, since it can provoke guilt and anxiety while having little or no potential for achieving changes in orientation.[2]
October 1993

American Psychological Association
Societal ignorance and prejudice about same gender sexual orientation put some gay, lesbian, bisexual and questioning individuals at risk for presenting for "conversion" treatment due to family or social coercion and/or lack of information; children and youth experience significant pressure to conform with sexual norms, particularly from their

peers; [and] children and youth often lack adequate legal protection from coercive treatment.[5a]

Therefore . . . APA affirms the following principles with regard to treatments to alter sexual orientation: that homosexuality is not a mental disorder; that psychologists do not make false or deceptive statements concerning . . . the scientific or clinical basis for . . . their services; that psychologists obtain appropriate informed consent to therapy or related procedures [which] generally implies that the [client or patient] (1) has the capacity to consent, (2) has been informed of significant information concerning the procedure, (3) has freely and without undue influence expressed consent, and (4) consent has been appropriately documented.

The American Psychological Association opposes portrayals of lesbian, gay, and bisexual youth and adults as mentally ill due to their sexual orientation and supports the dissemination of accurate information about sexual orientation, and mental health, and appropriate interventions in order to counteract bias that is based in ignorance or unfounded beliefs about sexual orientation.
August 1997

American Psychiatric Association

There is no published scientific evidence supporting the efficacy of "reparative therapy" as a treatment to change one's sexual orientation. . . . There are few reports in the literature of efforts to use psychotherapeutic and counseling techniques to treat persons troubled by their homosexuality who desire to become heterosexual; however, results have not been conclusive, nor have they been replicated. There is no evidence that any treatment can change a homosexual person's deep seated sexual feelings for others of the same sex.

Clinical experience suggests that any person who seeks conversion therapy may be doing so because of social bias that has resulted in internalized homophobia, and that gay men and lesbians who have accepted their sexual orientation positively are better adjusted than those who have not done so.[4]
April 1993

National Association of Social Workers (NASW) National Committee on Lesbian and Gay Issues

Empirical research does not demonstrate that homosexuality is more likely than heterosexuality to be associated with psychopathology, or that sexual orientation (heterosexual or homosexual) can be changed through these so-called reparative therapies. If a client is uncomfortable about his/her sexual orientation, the sources of discomfort must be explored, but without a priori assumptions that same-sex attraction is dysfunctional.

The National Committee on Lesbian and Gay Issues (NCOLGI) believes that the use of reparative or conversion therapies by social workers violates the NASW policy statement on lesbian and gay issues, particularly with regard to discrimination and oppression of lesbians and gays. NCOLGI further believes that use of these therapies violates the professional Code of Ethics. . . . All social workers have an ethical obligation to work actively against oppression and homophobia in all of its forms, including the oppression and homophobia so explicit in the so-called reparative therapies.[12]
February 1992

Although some individuals, including parents of children and adolescents who are believed to be lesbian or gay, clearly request "reparative" therapy aimed at changing sexual orientation, these and other professional associations caution against such acts, warning that such persons are misguided and such attempts can be harmful.[2,4,12]

Mental Health Referrals

When making a psychiatric referral, providers should ensure that mental health practitioners are able to provide appropriate, nonjudgmental counseling and support. When youth are questioning or confused about sexual identity, vulnerability is increased, and support is particularly important. The need for supportive counseling is underscored by the American Academy of Pediatrics policy statement about homosexuality:

> Any youth struggling with sexual orientation issues should be offered appropriate referrals to providers and programs that can affirm the adolescent's intrinsic worth regardless of sexual orientation. Providers who are unable to be objective because of religious or other personal convictions should refer patients to those who can.[2]

Providers should assess the agency's or individual practitioner's attitudes, experience, and willingness to work with lesbian and gay clients. (*See* referral checklist, Fig. 10.2, to assist in identification of appropriate referral sources for lesbian, gay, and bisexual youth.)

References

1. American Academy of Child and Adolescent Psychiatry: Level of care placement criteria for psychiatric illness. Washington, DC, American Academy of Child and Adolescent Psychiatry, 1996.
2. American Academy of Pediatrics: Homosexuality and adolescence. Pediatrics 92:631, 1993.
3. American Psychiatric Association: Diagnostic and Statistical Manual of Mental Disorders, 4th ed. Washington, DC, American Psychiatric Association, 1994.
4. American Psychiatric Association: Gay and lesbian issues. Fact Sheet. Washington, DC, American Psychiatric Association, 1994.
5. American Psychological Association: Discrimination against homosexuals. American Psychological Association Policy Statements on Lesbian and Gay Issues. Washington, DC, American Psychological Association, 1991.
5a. American Psychological Association: Resolution on appropriate therapeutic responses to sexual orientation. Washington, DC, American Psychological Association, 1997.
6. Boxer A, Haas J: Protocol for mental health care of lesbian and gay adolescents. Conference on the Primary Care Needs of Lesbian and Gay Adolescents, Health Resources and Services Administration, Washington, DC, December 5–6, 1994.
7. Bradford JB, Ryan CC: The national lesbian health care survey.[Unpublished data, 1987.]
8. Garnets L, Herek GM, Levy B: Violence and victimization of lesbians and gay men: Mental health consequences. In Herek G, Berrill K (eds.): Hate crimes: Confronting violence against lesbians and gay men. Newbury Park, CA, Sage Publications, 1992.
9. Hamilton JA. Emotional consequences of victimization and discrimination in "special populations" of women. Psychiatr Clin North Am 12:35, 1989.
10. Herdt G, Boxer A. Children of Horizons: How Lesbian and Gay Teens are Leading a New Way Out of the Closet, 2nd ed. Boston, Beacon Press, 1996.
11. National Association of Social Workers: Lesbian and gay issues. Washington, DC, NASW Delegate Assembly, 1993.
12. National Association of Social Workers, National Committee on Lesbian and Gay Issues: Position statement regarding "reparative" or "conversion" therapies for lesbians and gay men. Washington, DC, National Association of Social Workers, 1992.
13. Remafedi G, Farrow JA, Deisher RW: Risk factors for attempted suicide in gay and bisexual youth. Pediatrics 87:869, 1991.
14. Sales E, Baum M, Shore B: Victim readjustment following assault. J Soc Issues 40:117, 1984.

Part 3

HIV/AIDS

Adolescents face unique challenges in coming of age during the 1990s. At a time when exploration and experimentation are the developmental norms, they must learn to protect themselves from a life-threatening sexually transmitted disease, often without appropriate educational materials or guidance. This is particularly true for lesbian and gay adolescents, who rarely receive health education and counseling in a way that is relevant to them.

Increasing concern about adolescents' risks for HIV has led to the development of a special report for President Clinton on *Youth and HIV/AIDS*,[30] which recommends that all adults who work with teens provide HIV prevention information, and to recommendations from the American Medical Association[16] and the American Academy of Pediatrics[2] urging that providers include HIV education as part of routine care.

Part 3 provides an overview of HIV infection in adolescents, including risk behaviors and prevention; protocols for assessment, treatment, and psychosocial care; and guidance on offering counseling and testing for adolescents, including a protocol for providing HIV counseling and testing for adolescents in primary care settings.

CHAPTER 12

Overview: HIV Infection in Adolescents, Including Lesbians and Gay Males

If you go for HIV testing, people assume you're gay. We have so little access to information on how or where to get tested. Most information about HIV isn't written for us. We're afraid to talk to our family doctor—he may tell our parents. So where can you go for help if you're young and gay?

—Gay Youth

Adolescents are at high risk for HIV infection (Table 12.1). Worldwide, 1 of every 2 people with HIV became infected during adolescence or early adulthood—during ages 15–24.[21] By 1988, AIDS had become the sixth leading cause of death in this age group in the United States.[29] However, the long incubation period from infection to onset of disease helps to disguise the level of risk. For example, although a relatively small number of youth (2,574, ages 13–19, as of June 1996) were diagnosed with AIDS during adolescence, nearly 8 times as many young adults, ages 20–24, were diagnosed during the same period; the majority were infected during their teens.

Among adolescents with HIV, minorities, women, and gay and bisexual males are disproportionately affected. Within the general population, African Americans account for 14% of 13–19 year-olds; however, they comprise 33% of male and 65% of female adolescents with AIDS. Similarly, Hispanics account for 8% of the nation's teens, while representing 20% of male and 16% of female adolescents with AIDS.[6] Adolescent females account for a much larger proportion of AIDS cases than adult females (34% vs. 14%), and male-to-male sexual contact accounts for more than one-third of all adolescent AIDS cases and nearly two-thirds of cases among 20–24 year-olds. Beginning at age 20, men who have sex with other men represent the largest transmission category, highlighting the continued high risk of young gay and bisexual males for HIV infection and the need for consistently reinforcing prevention strategies during routine health visits.

HIV Seroprevalence in Adolescents

As with adults, prevalence among adolescents has increased significantly during the past decade. Among 20-year-olds attending a Baltimore STD clinic, for, example, HIV seroprevalence increased from 1.8 per 1000 in 1979–1983 to 21 per 1000 during 1987– 1989.[32] During the 1980s, the median age of persons infected with HIV was over 30. Between 1987 and 1991 the age dropped to 25 years old, and 1 of 4 newly infected persons was 22 or younger.[35]

Although HIV prevalence information is limited for adolescents, available data underscore the need for prevention and early intervention, including counseling and testing. Among Job Corps applicants tested from October 1987 through February 1990, 3.6 per 1000 were found to be HIV positive; prevalence ranged from 5.3 per 1000 in African Americans, to 2.6 per 1000 in Hispanics, to 1.2 per 1000 in whites.[11]

TABLE 12.1.   Reported AIDS Cases in Adolescents and Young Adults
(Through June 1996)

Exposure Category	13–19 (n = 2,574)		20–24 (n = 19,997)	
	Males (%)	Females (%)	Males (%)	Females (%)
Men who have sex with men	33	—	63	—
Injecting drug use	7	15	13	30
Men who have sex with men and inject drugs	5	—	11	—
Hemophilia	41	1	4	0
Heterosexual contact	3	55	4	52
No identified risk	7	22	6	15

From Centers for Disease Control and Prevention: HIV/AIDS Surveillance Report. Washington, DC, U.S. Department of Health and Human Services, Mid-year ed. 7, June 1995.

Findings show that prevalence increased with age. Among adolescents treated at a hospital serving children and youth in Washington, D.C., 3.7 per 1000 were found to be HIV-infected, with highest rates in females (4.7 per 1000) and older adolescents, aged 18–19 (5.6 per 1000).[13] Prevalence rates among adolescents seeking treatment at an STD clinic were 22 per 1000 for youth aged 15–19 and 36 per 1000 for 20–24 year-olds.[32]

A smaller study of homeless and runaway youth, who are at high risk for HIV infection, showed an HIV prevalence rate of 6% for adolescents, aged 16–21 years, and 16% for older adolescents, aged 18–21 years.[38]

Studies of young gay men consistently show high levels of infection. In a sentinel study of STD clinics around the country, on average, 30% of young gay males were infected with HIV.[39] Data from the national Multi-center AIDS Cohort Study (MACS), used to project overall risk of infection, estimate that a 20-year-old male who has sex with men has a 1 in 5 chance of becoming infected before age 25.[11] In studies of young gay men in San Francisco and New York,[14,27] 9% were already infected, with highest rates (21%) among African-Americans. According to the recent report to President Clinton on adolescent AIDS, the rate of infection in young men who have sex with other men may be seven times greater than for the general population.[30] And although older gay men in urban areas have reduced many high-risk behaviors, a second wave of HIV infection is affecting young gay males.[11,30]

Seroprevalence information about lesbians is limited. One survey of lesbian and bisexual women in California found a prevalence rate of 1.2% (compared with 0.2% for childbearing women and 0.4% for women in population-based surveys).[28] Although a small number of lesbians are reported to have AIDS, they were infected through sex with men or needle sharing. Instances of female-to-female transmission are extremely rare, although several cases have been reported.[10,25] However, HIV risk behaviors for lesbians and other women who have sex with women are obscured since they are reported under other exposure categories (e.g., injection drug use, heterosexual contact, no identified risk). As a result, many lesbians, including lesbian adolescents, do not perceive that they are at risk for HIV and do not use precautions (e.g., condoms and barrier protection) during sex with males or females, despite the fact that lesbian and bisexual females who have intercourse with gay and bisexual males may be at increased risk for infection.

TABLE 12.2.   Risk Factors for HIV Infection in Adolescents

Unprotected anal, vaginal, and oral intercourse	Piercing or tattooing
Needle sharing	Alcohol and drug use before/during sexual
Injecting heroin, cocaine or amphetamines	intercourse
Injecting anabolic steroids or hormones	Sexual abuse victimization
Use of crack cocaine or other highly addictive substances	Living in communities with high rates of HIV

Risk Factors for HIV Infection in Adolescents (Table 12.2)

Sexual Intercourse. Sexual intercourse is the major route of HIV transmission for adolescents and young adults. Young gay males represent the highest exposure category in these age groups, although young females are at increasing risk, accounting for 14% of adolescent AIDS cases in 1987 and 43% in 1994.[30] Studies of condom use show a range of behaviors among sexually active youth. In a national survey, 3 out of 5 adolescent males (ages 17–19) reported using condoms during their last intercourse. However, use was significantly lower among higher risk males—those with five or more partners or who also used injection drugs.[8]

Although adolescents are also at risk for infection through oral intercourse, studies of condom use show less frequent compliance during oral sex.

Blood Products and Transfusions. Among adolescent males, hemophilia has represented the largest single exposure category, although cases of AIDS are steadily decreasing since blood products have been treated and screened, dropping from 43% of cases in June 1994 to 35% in June 1995.[6] Among sexually active adolescents with hemophilia, HIV prevention information appears more widespread than condom use. According to one study, adolescents with hemophilia had accurate information about prevention, but only 1 in 9 consistently used condoms.[31]

Needle-Sharing and Crack Use. Needle-sharing and use of crack cocaine are both closely linked with HIV transmission. Among all adolescents with AIDS, injecting drug use (IDU) was the only risk factor for 1 out of 10 adolescents. Rates of IDU-related transmission are higher among females than males in both adolescent and young adult age groups (*see* Table 12.1). Within the general adolescent population, injection use of heroin, cocaine, or amphetamines is low (1% in adolescents, aged 12–19), although rates vary according to group and geographic area. Among New York City teens with AIDS, for example, 16% of males and 30% of females reported injection drug use, and among street youth in the western states, 25–40% had used injection drugs.[8,17] Crack, a highly addictive smokable form of cocaine that can impair judgement and increase sexual arousal, is associated with exchange of sex for money and drugs. In the late 1980s, 40% of New York City teens treated in an adolescent AIDS clinic reported heavy crack use and denied having injected drugs.[20] Of these, over 80% engaged in "survival sex"—sex for food, shelter, or drugs.

Steroid and Hormone Injection. Adolescents are also at risk for HIV infection through needle-sharing related to anabolic steroid use and street injection of hormones (usually estrogen to induce development of female secondary sex characteristics). In a study of steroid use among adolescents involved in strength training, researchers found a significant association between anabolic steroids and multiple drug use, including cocaine, amphetamines, heroin, alcohol, and tobacco.[15] Strength training was also found to be associated with anabolic steroid use. Transgendered persons, particularly males fearful of rejection and discrimination from health care workers, buy hormones on the street to self-inject, thus exposing themselves to HIV through needle-sharing.[36]

Although risk has not been directly established, body piercing and tattooing with unsterilized needles may also increase risk of infection.

Alcohol and Drug Use. Research has shown a strong correlation between alcohol and drug use and unprotected sex: use of alcohol and drugs impairs judgement and increases risk for HIV.[9,26] Adolescents who use alcohol and smoke marijuana before engaging in sexual activity are much less likely to use condoms (2.8 times and 1.9 times, respectively).

Sexual Abuse. Victims of childhood sexual abuse are at higher risk for HIV infection. They also begin having sex at an earlier age and have more sexual partners.[5,22] In a study of childhood sexual abuse and risk for HIV, men who had been sexually abused as children were twice as likely as nonabused males to be infected with HIV.[40] Both males and females abused as children showed a range of high-risk behaviors, including prostitution, anonymous and multiple partners, and alcohol and drug abuse. These findings are similar to results of a study of gay and bisexual men attending STD clinics,[3] and they are corroborated by a comprehensive assessment of adolescents with AIDS, which showed an association between childhood sexual abuse in males and findings of child sexual abuse in 1 out of 3 females.[20]

Perinatal Infection. Increasingly, as more effective treatment is developed, children who were infected perinatally will reach puberty, and some may not be diagnosed until adolescence. Several cases of congenitally infected adolescents have already been described.[18] Providers are likely to see more cases in coming years. In addition to ongoing medical care, these youth need support in learning to cope with HIV disease and meeting their developmental needs, including emerging sexuality.

Identity ≠ Always Behavior

Misperceptions about sexuality and sexual identity lead to false assumptions about behavior. Not all adolescents who engage in same-sex behavior later identify as lesbian or gay, and vice versa. In four surveys of young males, the prevalence of same-sex activity to orgasm ranged from 17–37%;[33] however, the percentage who later self-identify as gay is much lower. Moreover, many adolescents who later identify as lesbian or gay may self-label as bisexual when they are younger. In a survey of lesbian and gay youth, ages 14–21, for example, more than half had previously identified as bisexual.[34]

The discrepancy between behavior and identity has important implications for prevention and care, and underscores the need for broad-based education for all teens. Of adolescents who tested positive for HIV infection at an adolescent AIDS clinic, 9 out of 10 males reported same-sex intercourse, but only half (54%) identified as gay (23% identified as bisexual and the rest, heterosexual).[19] Among adolescents receiving treatment for HIV/AIDS, 12% who initially reported "no identified risk" had clinical evidence of same-sex activity (e.g., perianal warts or herpes).[20]

In a study of lesbian and gay adolescents, heterosexual activity was common: 4 out of 5 young lesbians had been sexually active with male partners and had initiated sex with males at an earlier age than with females, and more than half of gay male adolescents (56%) reported a history of heterosexual intercourse.[34] Among young women aged 13–21, 26% had engaged in anal intercourse and three-quarters were sexually active;[23] among lesbian youth, 15% reported having anal sex.[34] Providers can assess risk for HIV and other STDs most effectively by asking the same questions of all adolescents (*see* Interview, Table 10.2 and Tables 13.4 and 13.5 in the next chapter)

TABLE 12.3. Lesbian and Gay Adolescents: Factors that Increase Vulnerability for HIV

Stress from coping with stigma associated with homosexuality
Need for secrecy to protect emerging lesbian/gay identity
Lack of appropriate outlets for socialization and exploration of sexual identity (secrecy and fear of discovery promote high-risk, anonymous behaviors)
Tendency, particularly among young gay males, to have older partners who have greater likelihood of exposure to HIV infection
Reaction to pervasiveness of AIDS within the lesbian/gay community: denial or perception that infection is inevitable, so prevention is futile.
Lack of awareness and limited knowledge among providers about sexuality (identity and behavior)
Lack of clear prevention messages that include lesbian and gay adolescents

and by not making assumptions about an adolescent's behavior or identity on the basis of appearances or other indirect means.

Risks and Vulnerabilities for Lesbian and Gay Adolescents (Table 12.3)

In addition to risks faced by all adolescents who are entering the most sexually active period of their lives, lesbian and gay adolescents experience additional vulnerabilities as a result of their stigmatized status and invisibility. Coming out—the process of self-identifying as lesbian or gay—is inherently stressful; without access to a supportive environment, the stress of managing a stigmatized identity may foster negative coping behaviors that increase risk for HIV infection. Sustained stress may result in immunosuppression, depression, and low-self esteem, which further affect the immune system.[12,24] The need for secrecy to avoid rejection, ridicule, and anti-gay violence encourages lesbians and gay youth to hide, which increases social isolation. Lack of appropriate outlets for socialization encourages youth to seek out gay peers and adults in high-risk environments in which risk behaviors are reinforced and they are more apt to be exploited. Many gay males learn about being gay from older males who are more likely to be exposed to HIV infection. In one study, for example, the average age of partners of gay male adolescents with HIV was nearly four years older.[19] Moreover, the pervasiveness of AIDS within the gay community has resulted in feelings of futility among many young gay males; they may believe that HIV infection is inevitable and thus that prevention is useless.

Extremely high prevalence rates within the gay community increase the urgency for active education and prevention efforts with lesbian and gay youth who may initiate sexual activity with older partners. HIV prevalence estimates among men who have sex with men range from 28% in Denver, to 31% in Miami, to 27% in Dallas and Houston, to 30% in New York, and 41% in San Francisco.[11] Unprotected anal sex and multiple partners are the strongest predictors of HIV infection in adult gay men. Studies of lesbian and gay adolescents show that some youth consistently fail to use condoms during intercourse and continue to engage in these and other high-risk behaviors. In addition to providing anticipatory guidance about HIV/AIDS for all adolescents and developing a risk-reduction plan for youth who are sexually active, providers should recommend voluntary HIV testing with informed consent and provide routine counseling for all sexually active adolescents.

References

1. Alan Guttmacher Institute: Teenage Pregnancy: The Problem That Hasn't Gone Away. New York, Alan Guttmacher Institute, 1981.

2. American Academy of Pediatrics: Adolescents and human immunodeficiency virus infection: The role of the pediatrician in prevention and intervention. Pediatrics 92:626, 1993.

3. Bartholow BN, Doll LS, Joy D, et al: Emotional, behavioral and HIV risks associated with sexual abuse among adult homosexual and bisexual men. Child Abuse Negl 18:747, 1994.

4. Bell TA, Hein K: Adolescents and sexually transmitted diseases. In Holmes K, Mardh P, Sparling P, Wiesner P (eds): Sexually Transmitted Diseases. New York, McGraw Hill, 1984.

5. Cassesse J: The invisible bridge: Child sexual abuse and the risk of HIV infection in adulthood. SIECUS Report 21:1, 1993.

6. Centers for Disease Control and Prevention: HIV/AIDS Surveillance Report. U.S. Department of Health and Human Services, Mid-year edition 7, June 1995.

7. Centers for Disease Control and Prevention: HIV/AIDS Surveillance Report. U.S. Department of Health and Human Services 8:1, 1996.

8. Centers for Disease Control: Youth risk behavior surveillance—US 1993. MMWR 44:1, 1995.

9. Chitwood DD, Comerford M: Drugs, sex and AIDS risk. Am Behav Sci 33:465, 1990.

10. Chu SY, Buehler JW, Fleming PL, Berkelman RL: Epidemiology of reported cases of AIDS in lesbians, United States 1980–89. Am J Public Health 80:1380, 1990.

11. Coates TJ, Faigle M, Stall RD: Does HIV Prevention Work for Men Who Have Sex With Men? Report for the Office of Technology Assessment. San Francisco, University of California, Center for AIDS Prevention Studies, February 1995.

12. Coates TJ, Temoshok L, Mandel J: Psychosocial research is essential to understanding and treating AIDS. Am Psychol 39:1309, 1984.

13. D'Angelo LJ, Getson PR, Luban NLC, Gayle HD: Human immunodeficiency virus infection in urban adolescents: Can we predict who is at risk? Pediatrics 88:982, 1991.

14. Dean L, Meyer I: HIV prevalence and sexual behavior in a cohort of New York City gay men (aged 18–24). J Acquir Immune Defic Syndr 8:208, 1995.

15. DuRant RH, Escobedo LG, Heath GW: Anabolic-steroid use, strength training and multiple drug use among adolescents in the United States. Pediatrics 96:23, 1995.

16. Elster AB, Kuznets NJ: AMA Guidelines for Adolescent Preventive Services (GAPS): Recommendations and Rationale. Baltimore, Williams & Wilkins, 1994.

17. Fullilove MT, Fullilove RE: Intersecting epidemics: Black teen crack use and sexually transmitted disease. J Am Med Wom Assoc 44:146–153, 1989.

18. Futterman D, Hein K: Management of adolescents with HIV infection for pediatric AIDS. In Pizzo P, Wilfret C (eds): The Challenge of HIV Infection in Infants, Children and Adolescents. Baltimore, Williams & Wilkins, 1994.

19. Futterman D, Hein K, Kipke M, et al: HIV+ adolescents: HIV testing experiences and changes in risk-related sexual and drug use behavior. Presented at the Sixth International Conference on AIDS, San Francisco, CA, June 1990.

20. Futterman D, Hein K, Reuben N, Dell R, Shaffer N: Human immunodeficiency virus-infected adolescents: The first 50 patients in a New York City program. Pediatrics 91:730, 1993.

21. Goldsmith MF: Medical news and perspectives. JAMA 270:16, 1993.

22. Harrison PA, Hoffman NA, Edwall GE: Differential drug use patterns among sexually abused adolescent girls in treatment for chemical dependency. Int J Addict 24:499, 1989.

23. Jaffe L, Seehaus M, Wagner C, et al: Anal intercourse and knowledge of AIDS among minority-group female adolescents. J Pediatr 9:136, 1988.

24. Kaplan GA: Psychosocial aspects of chronic illness: Direct and indirect associations with ischemic heart disease mortality. In Kaplan RM, Criqui MH (eds): Behavioral Epidemiology and Disease Prevention. New York, Plenum, 1985.

25. Kennedy MB, Scarlett MI, Duerr AC, Chu SY: Assessing HIV risk among women who have sex with women: Scientific and communication issues. J Am Med Wom Assoc 50:103, 1995.

26. Leigh BC, Stall R: Substance use and risky sexual behavior for exposure to HIV. Am Psychol 13:359, 1993.

27. Lemp GF, Hirozawa AM, Givertz D, et al: Seroprevalence of HIV and risk behaviors among young gay and bisexual men: The San Francisco/Berkeley Young Men's Survey. JAMA 272:449, 1994.

28. Lemp GF, Jones M, Kellogg TA, et al: HIV seroprevalence and risk behaviors among lesbians and bisexual women in San Francisco and Berkeley, California. Am J Public Health 85:1549, 1995.

29. Novello AC: Report of the Secretary's Work Group on Pediatric HIV Infection and Disease. Washington, DC, U.S. Department of Health and Human Services, 1988.

30. Office of National AIDS Policy: Youth & AIDS: An American Agenda. Report to the President. Washington, DC, Office of National AIDS Policy, 1996.

31. Overby KJ, Lo B, Litt IF: Knowledge and concerns about acquired immune deficiency syndrome and their relationship to behavior among adolescents with hemophilia. Pediatrics 83:204, 1989.

32. Quin TC: Evolution of HIV epidemic among patients attending STD clinics. J Infect Dis 165:541, 1992.
33. Remafedi G: Preventing the sexual transmission of AIDS. J Adolesc Health Care 9:139, 1988.
34. Rosario M, Meyer-Bahlburg H, Hunter J, et al: The psychosexual development of urban lesbian, gay and bisexual youths: Sexual orientation, identity, activity and practices. Paper presented at the 2nd International Conference on the Biopsychosocial Aspects of HIV Infection, Brighton, UK, July 1994.
35. Rosenberg PS, Biggar RJ, Goedert JJ: Declining age at HIV infection in the United States. N Engl J Med 330:789, 1994.
36. Sbordone AJ: Transgenderism: Social and psychological issues in the treatment of HIV/AIDS, a case study. Paper presented at the Sixteenth National Lesbian and Gay Health Conference and AIDS Forum, New York, June 1994.
37. St. Louis ME, Conway GA, Hayman CR, et al: Human immunodeficiency virus infections in disadvantaged adolescents: Findings from the US Job Corps. JAMA 266:2387, 1991.
38. Stricof RL, Kennedy JT, Natell TO, et al: HIV seroprevalence in a facility for runaway and homeless adolescents. Am J Public Health 81:50, 1988.
39. Wendall DA, et al: Youth at risk: Sex, drugs and human immunodeficiency virus. American Journal of Diseases of Children 146:76, 1992.
40. Zierler S, Feingold L, Laufer D, et al: Adult survivors of childhood sexual abuse and subsequent risk of HIV infection. Am J Public Health 81:572, 1991.

CHAPTER 13

HIV Counseling, Testing, and Prevention

Although adolescents are at increasing risk for HIV infection, relatively few have access to HIV counseling and testing. Until recently, publicly funded programs have not targeted adolescents, and many providers are not comfortable offering HIV testing to youth, fearing that they will not be able to handle positive results. Existing counseling and testing programs are not generally accessible to young people, who often do not know where to go for testing and may not be able to pay for such services. This is beginning to change as the impact of the AIDS epidemic on the nation's youth finally is being acknowledged.

The report to President Clinton on adolescent AIDS calls for making counseling and testing programs accessible to adolescents, including developing CDC guidelines addressing the special needs of youth in counseling and testing services (CTS).[15] Moreover, a policy statement from the AIDS Policy Center for Children, Youth and Families calls for all health care programs to review existing policies and to ensure that providers are trained in the developmental needs of youth.[1] Until these services are more widespread, however, adolescents who are sexually active and who use injection drugs remain unidentified and unserved. Providing routine counseling about HIV and offering voluntary testing are critical elements of early intervention, risk assessment, and client education. Guidelines are available to assist providers in incorporating HIV testing into routine adolescent primary care.[12] In addition, specific guidelines are included in this chapter, and a comprehensive protocol is provided in Appendix E.

Goals and Principles of HIV Counseling and Testing (Table 13.1)

Like other underserved populations, many adolescents generally are diagnosed late in the course of illness when intervention with emerging treatment strategies may be less effective.[19] Relatively few currently receive care for HIV disease, and most do not know they are infected. For example, nearly half of adolescents seen at an adolescent AIDS clinic showed significant immune dysfunction at the time of their initial visit.[6] With few options for case finding, including limited availability of counseling and testing services, adolescents are medically disadvantaged, and their HIV prevention and care needs are neglected and often ignored.

The development of new anti-viral drugs for treating HIV infection offers promising treatment possibilities through combination therapy and use of protease inhibitors, a new class of drugs that significantly reduce the amount of HIV in the body and that have been shown to prolong life and decrease AIDS-related disorders. To be most effective, however, providers must be able to monitor levels of HIV (viral load) to determine disease progression and make decisions about when to intervene. Without knowledge of HIV status and access to HIV-related care, these options are not possible.

The primary goal of offering HIV counseling and testing to adolescents is to identify HIV-positive youth, to provide ongoing medical care and support services,

TABLE 13.1.   Benefits of HIV Counseling and Testing for Adolescents

Identify HIV+ adolescents and provide medical and support services
Relieve anxiety for HIV-negative adolescents
Discuss sexual orientation, behaviors, and practices
Provide risk assessment and identify high-risk behaviors
Provide HIV education, risk reduction information, and skills training
Provide appropriate referrals for non–HIV-related care and support services, if
    HIV negative (e.g., alcohol and drug treatment, counseling)

and to relieve anxiety for youth who are HIV-negative. Counseling and testing also offer other benefits for risk reduction, prevention, and ancillary care. During pre- and post-test counseling, providers have an opportunity to talk about sexual behaviors and orientation, to identify high-risk behaviors and practices that may not have been acknowledged or discussed previously, to develop an individualized risk-reduction plan, and to refer adolescents for other health problems such as alcohol and drug treatment and mental health services.

Lack of generalized training for providers about HIV counseling and testing and poor integration of CTS services into primary care (most counseling and testing services have been offered either at separate sites or provided in conjunction with STD clinics) have contributed to the perception among many providers that counseling and testing require specialized skills and abilities and are difficult to include as a part of routine patient care. Although an understanding of the principles and goals of counseling and testing is important, providers can readily incorporate HIV counseling and testing into routine assessment and care by following the guidelines included in Appendix E and by familiarizing themselves with related state laws.

Studies have shown that health care providers play an important role in helping teens to identify risk behaviors and to make decisions about HIV testing. A survey of Boston-area high school students found that most adolescents want physicians to ask personal questions about HIV-related risk behaviors and prefer that providers initiate this discussion.[16] After receiving routine counseling with the option of HIV testing from primary care providers, a significant proportion of high-risk adolescent girls chose to be tested.[8] Provider initiation is essential because many high-risk youth may not acknowledge risk behaviors. For example, more than three-quarters of adolescents tested in Houston public health programs over a 2-year period denied having any risk behaviors, including nearly half (49%) of all youth who tested positive for HIV.[10]

Principles of HIV Counseling and Testing (Table 13.2)

HIV counseling and testing should be voluntary and should include specific informed consent. Clinicians have found that most adolescents are capable of understanding the risks and benefits of medical treatment and thus can give informed consent.[14] Moreover, a comprehensive analysis of research on adolescent decision-making shows that adolescents, particularly those aged 14 years and over, have the capacity to make their own health care decisions.[7] Because the decision to take an HIV test is anxiety-provoking and has a significant impact on the lives of youth who are found to be positive, providers should help to identify a supportive adult who can be involved in the testing process. The adult may be a parent, teacher, counselor, or older friend.

Providers should carefully explain the benefits of HIV testing and potential impact of disclosure, including discrimination, on persons who are known to be HIV-

TABLE 13.2.   Principles of HIV Counseling and Testing with Adolescents

HIV counseling and testing should be voluntary and should include specific informed consent.

All sexually active adolescents should be offered HIV testing; however, testing should not be coercive. Providers should carefully explain the benefits of HIV testing, discuss confidentiality, potential discrimination, and disclosure requirements (if any), based on state law.

Providers should help the youth to identify a supportive adult to be involved in the testing process and to provide ongoing assistance and support.

Information on HIV testing, prevention, and follow-up care should be presented in clear, culturally, linguistically, and developmentally appropriate language.

Adolescents should be informed clearly that they continue to receive ongoing care, whether or not they choose to be tested. Some adolescents may need several sessions to talk about their concerns before making a decision about testing.

Special care should be taken to protect confidentiality in residential programs, institutional settings, detention facilities, and foster care.

HIV counseling and testing should be made available and accessible to adolescents. This includes offering CTS during evening hours, providing CTS in settings in which adolescents routinely receive care, and offering anonymous as well as confidential testing (with strong linkages to follow-up care if testing is anonymous).

Providers who recommend HIV testing should assist and follow-up actively after making the referral (if counseling and testing are not on-site).

Providers should develop a practical, achievable risk-reduction plan with adolescents who are HIV-negative; although risk reduction is also a goal for HIV-positive youth, the primary goal of post-test counseling is emotional stabilization, medical referral, and psychosocial follow-up.

All pregnant adolescents with HIV should receive information about the benefits and potential risks of anti-retroviral use during pregnancy to reduce perinatal transmission of HIV, based on HRSA implementation guidelines.[47] This information should include age-appropriate discussion, inclusion of family members in decision-making, and adequate time to discuss concerns.

---

infected. Confidentiality should be clearly delineated; in some states, test results may be disclosed to others upon request. Providers should ensure that adolescents are not coerced and do not perceive that their health care will be jeopardized if they refuse to be tested. If testing does not occur on site, providers should make the referral and follow-up personally to ensure that results are received and that needs are addressed. All settings where youth are referred for care, including CTS sites, should be assessed for sensitivity to adolescent needs, policies related to HIV testing, capacity to provide comprehensive care, and linkages to care in other settings. Agencies that serve adolescents also should ensure that primary care and CTS services are accessible. This may include providing services at times that do not conflict with school or work, ensuring that services are located near public transportation, and addressing financial barriers.

Legal Issues

Adolescents aged 18 years or older are considered adults legally in almost all states and can thus consent to treatment. Those under 18 years of age are considered to be minors, and although parental consent generally is required for health care, all states have laws that allow minors to consent to diagnosis and treatment of STDs.[5] However, not all states have classified HIV as an STD or a venereal disease (classifications that permit adolescents to consent to treatment under these statutes). Most states have also enacted laws enabling minors to consent to treatment for other health concerns, including mental health, alcohol and drug problems, rape, sexual assault, and pregnancy.

By the mid-1980s, states had enacted a broad range of HIV-related laws, the largest portion of which dealt with HIV testing. Approximately 32 states allow minors to consent to HIV testing and treatment.[2] In other states, minors may be able to consent under laws that cover specific services, such as those for STDs, contagious or communicable diseases, pregnancy, or family planning, or under laws that authorize minors' consent on the basis of their status.[5]

In addition to consent to testing laws and existing confidentiality laws that cover HIV, some states, including Delaware, Florida, and Iowa, have passed legislation that restricts adolescent testing or treatment information from disclosure.[2] In particular, Delaware and Florida's laws prohibit health care providers from indirectly divulging confidential information through such practices as sending a bill for services to a minor's home or to a person other than the minor.[2] Laws in three states allow disclosure of HIV testing and treatment to a minor's parent or legal guardian. Colorado allows disclosure for unemancipated minors or those under age 16; Michigan allows disclosure when the minor's parent or legal guardian requests written disclosure; and Iowa requires minors to be informed before testing that HIV-positive results will be disclosed to their parents or legal guardians.

Providing HIV Counseling and Testing for Adolescents

Recent treatment advances with combination therapy and protease inhibitors call for proactive case finding and outreach efforts to identify and initiate treatment for HIV-positive adolescents. However, access to care requires wider access to age-appropriate counseling and testing services, and greater commitment among providers to counsel and routinely offer HIV testing with informed consent to all sexually active adolescents.

Providers should counsel all sexually active adolescents about the need for HIV testing and offer voluntary testing with informed consent. Providers should help youth determine appropriate timing for the test. Some teens may choose to be tested when the option is offered; others may need more time to talk about it or may choose to defer testing to a less stressful time (e.g., after exams). This section includes an outline for providing HIV counseling and testing in primary care settings. (*See* Appendix E for complete guidelines.)

Pre-Test Counseling (*see* Table 13.8)

When discussing the need for HIV testing, providers should explain the increasing prevalence of HIV infection in adolescents, especially the high prevalence among young gay males. They should help youth personalize risk and discuss how specific sexual or drug-using behaviors have put them at risk for HIV infection. Testing should never be coercive. Adolescents should be informed clearly that they will continue to receive ongoing care, whether or not they choose to be tested. Information should be presented in clear, culturally, linguistically, and developmentally appropriate language. Providers can assess an adolescent's developmental level by considering how youth respond to the following during the counseling session: (a) thought process (concrete vs. abstract), (b) future orientation, (c) ability to plan, (d) capacity to weigh options, (e) ability to assess risk realistically, and (f) ability to assess skills for implementing behavioral change.[12]

If an adolescent is considering the test, providers should help identify a supportive adult to be involved in the testing process and to provide ongoing assistance and support; this adult should be someone on whom the youth can rely and with whom he or she has a trusting relationship (e.g., parent, teacher, counselor).

RISK ASSESSMENT AND HIV EDUCATION (Tables 13.3–13.5)

If an adolescent has not been seen before, providers should conduct a risk assessment and review previous test history. The assessment includes determining risk for transmission through sexual behavior, needle sharing, blood products, and perinatal transmission. It also includes a sexual and substance use history, including use of drugs and alcohol during sexual intercourse (*see* Appendix E).

Whether test results are positive or negative, HIV counseling offers an opportunity for identifying risk behaviors, fostering communication and interaction skills, and developing strategies for minimizing risk. Providers should determine an adolescent's knowledge of HIV transmission and AIDS; many youth have misconceptions about how HIV is transmitted (*see* Table 13.3). Ask the adolescent to explain what he or she knows, and fill in the gaps. Discuss the risks of various behaviors: unprotected anal, vaginal, and oral sex; use of alcohol and drugs during sex; and needle sharing. If an adolescent is not sexually active, counseling provides an opportunity to talk about sexual readiness, delaying intercourse, and ways to increase intimacy other than risky sexual behaviors.

Even if an adolescent does not acknowledge engaging in specific behaviors, providers should review all risk behaviors, carefully distinguishing between low-risk and high-risk activities. Some adolescents, particularly those who may be lesbian or gay, are reluctant to ask questions about safer sex or condom use, fearing negative or judgmental reactions. Providers should demonstrate condom use, preferably with an anatomic model, and explain use of the female condom, as well as dental dams for oral-anal and oral-vaginal sex. Asking questions about the difficulties teens routinely experience when using condoms may help to identify specific barriers (e.g., if condoms break, providers can discuss proper use and recommend nonoxynol 9 for lubrication).

Providers should help youth to strategize ways to reduce risk, with the interim goal of reducing harm or minimization of risk for HIV infection. For example, many teens are unaware that alcohol and drug use before and during sex can affect judgment and increase risk for HIV. Experimentation with alcohol and marijuana is common among adolescents. Expecting them to abstain entirely is unrealistic for most; however, getting them to agree not to use alcohol or drugs during or immediately before sex is a more practical and achievable goal. Likewise, youth who inject drugs may not be

---

TABLE 13.3. Basic Concepts for Explaining HIV to Adolescents

The HIV antibody test is a test for HIV infection, not AIDS.
An antibody is like a "footprint" indicating that someone has been exposed to HIV.

People may carry the virus in their bodies for many years before developing HIV-related symptoms or AIDS.

HIV affects the ability of the immune system to function properly.

New drugs are intended to prevent the virus from reproducing in the body to keep the immune system working for as long as possible.

Continuing to practice unsafe sex or needle sharing can cause reinfection, which may make HIV disease worse and cause symptoms to appear sooner.

Practicing safer sex and not sharing needles are essential to protect one's health and one's partner's health.

Partners also should be tested for HIV infection.

TABLE 13.4.   Elements of a Sexual Risk History

1. How old were you when you first had sexual intercourse (oral, vaginal, or anal)? How old was your partner?
2. Do you consider yourself heterosexual, gay or lesbian, or bisexual? Or are you unsure?
3. Do you have sex with men, women, or both?
4. Tell me about your sexual experiences: how often have you had oral, vaginal, or anal sex? How many partners have you had? Did you give or receive oral, vaginal, or anal sex (insertive or receptive)? What percentage of the time did you use condoms? Tell me about your sexual experiences during the past month.
5. Tell me about the number of partners you have had. How old were they? Did any have risk factors for HIV infection? (Did they use injection drugs? Did they have multiple partners? Were they gay or bisexual?)
6. Have you ever had an STD? (Provider should describe symptoms of common STDs.) Tell me what kinds you may have had or what the symptoms may have been. Did you receive treatment? What kind?
7. What kinds of birth control have you used? Have you ever tried to prevent STDs? If so, how?
8. Have you ever been pregnant, had a baby, had an abortion or miscarriage?
9. Have you ever used drugs or alcohol before or during sex?
10. Have you ever had sex in exchange for food, money, drugs, or a place to live or sleep?
11. Has anyone ever forced you to have sex or do something sexually that you did not want to do?
12. Do you have any questions or concerns about your current sexual experiences?
13. What do you know about "safer sex"? Are you doing anything to protect yourself and your partners from being infected with HIV? How do you feel about changing your sexual behavior to prevent HIV infection or reinfection? What sexual behavior will you miss? How does your partner feel about safer sex? Does your partner know that you have HIV? Do you need help telling your partner?
14. Do you think condoms can prevent HIV and STDs? If you do, what makes it hard to use condoms? Did you use a condom the last time you had intercourse? Why or why not? What would make it easier for you to use condoms?

From Kunins H, Hein K, Futterman D, et al: Guide to adolescent HIV/AIDS program development. J Adolesc Health 14:1S, 1993, with permission.

ready to enter a treatment program. While continuing to offer substance abuse treatment, providers can help minimize risk by showing teens who use injection drugs how to clean equipment, encouraging them to teach their needle-sharing friends and strongly recommending not sharing needles. In addition, providers should caution adolescents to avoid sharing ear-piercing and tattooing equipment.

Risk education should culminate with the development of an individualized risk-reduction plan. As with other tasks that require negotiation and communication skills, providers may assist adolescents by asking concrete questions, planning specific responses, and conducting role plays to enhance self-efficacy and increase confidence.

CONFIDENTIALITY AND DISCLOSURE

Providers should explain the benefits of HIV testing (e.g., risk reduction, early intervention), and discuss confidentiality of test results, including disclosure requirements (if any) based on state law, as well as potential negative reactions of others when positive results are disclosed (discrimination and stigma). Adolescents should understand the difference between anonymous and confidential testing.* Although confi-

---

*Providers should be aware that some adolescents may ask for anonymous testing because they falsely assume that being "anonymous" will prevent others from learning their HIV status. Their motivation for seeking anonymous testing is based on concrete thinking, and not on an accurate understanding of the actual difference between anonymous and confidential testing. If they are HIV+, their care will be confidential, not anonymous.

TABLE 13.5.   Elements of a Drug Use History

1. Do you, any of your friends, or your sexual partners ever use any of these drugs: alcohol, marijuana, crack, cocaine, heroin, amphetamines, hallucinogens (LSD, PCP), barbiturates, sedatives, or steroids? Do you take any of them at the same time? Which ones?

2. For each drug you use, tell me about how old you were when you started using it, how often you have used it during the past month, how often you use it each day, and the ways you use it (pills, snorting, sniffing, injection).

3. Where do you use drugs? Alone, with friends, lovers, at parties? Where do you buy drugs (friends, the street, crack houses, shooting galleries)?

4. If you have injected drugs, tell me about your needle use. How often do you share needles and with whom; how do you clean them; how often do you use works in a shooting gallery?

5. If you smoke crack, tell me about your crack use. How often do you use crack? What percentage of the time do you use in crack houses? How often do you have sex in crack houses, and what types of sex do you have?

6. Have you ever exchanged sex for drugs?

7. How do you get money to buy drugs?

8. Have you ever had medical problems because of drug use (visited a doctor or hospital), overdosed, or tried to hurt or kill yourself because of drugs?

9. Have you ever been in trouble with the law or had problems with your family, school, or work because of drugs?

10. Do you think you are addicted or have a problem with drugs, including alcohol?

11. Have you ever tried to get off drugs or tried to stop drinking? How have you tried? What kinds of treatment programs have you tried?

From Kunins H, Hein K, Futterman D, et al: Guide to adolescent HIV/AIDS program development. J Adolesc Health 14:1S, 1993, with permission.

dential testing is preferred because linkages to care are ensured more effectively, anonymous testing may be more appropriate for some youth, particularly when concerns about disclosure are paramount. If anonymous testing is warranted, providers should make arrangements for the test, which include addressing transportation needs, and follow-up after testing to ensure that results have been received and that care and support needs are addressed.

HIV ANTIBODY TEST

Providers should (1) explain the long latency period between infection and symptoms and explain how HIV affects the immune system; (2) describe how the antibody test works and what it may indicate if a person is negative or positive; and (3) explain the "window period" and why retesting is necessary within 6 months if someone has recently been exposed to HIV.

Use of the terms "positive" and "negative" to indicate test results may be confusing for teens because they understand the opposite meanings in everyday use; i.e., positive connotes good and negative means bad. Adolescents must understand clearly that a positive result means they have been exposed to HIV and have been infected. Not everyone who tests positive to the antibody test has or develops AIDS. People may carry the virus in their bodies for many years before developing HIV-related symptoms or AIDS. Describing how HIV works on the immune system helps adolescents to understand why early intervention is important and helps to underscore the need for avoiding reinfection. Providers should raise the issue of partner notification during the pretest session. Adolescents generally are uncomfortable talking about partner notification; nevertheless, this issue should be addressed routinely during follow-up sessions, with providers offering to help if an adolescent feels he or she is unable to do so. Providers might explain the need for notifying partners by saying: "If you test positive for HIV, it is important to let your sexual or needle-sharing partners know so that they can find out if they are infected, get counseling and care, and protect themselves and others from infection. They can decide whether or not to get tested."[12]

NEW HIV TESTING OPTIONS

Providers should be aware of new testing developments that expand options for HIV testing (Table 13.6). The developments include same-day testing (rapid assay), non–serum-based testing (urine and oral fluids), and home collection kits. Although providers may prefer drawing blood on site and following routine testing procedures, they may encounter youth who have used a home collection kit and require appropriate counseling and followup, or they may choose new testing options to maximize flexibility in various settings, such as outreach programs or situations in which immediate results are needed.

TABLE 13.6. Expanded HIV Testing Options

Type of Test	Sensitivity*	Specificity†	Results	Procedure
Home collection system • Confide • Home Access	100% 100%	99.95% 100%	7 days 3–7 days	Test kit includes pretest counseling and blood collection items; user pricks finger, drops blood sample on enclosed test card and mails to the lab in a preaddressed envelope. No identifying information is required; results are obtained by calling the counseling center and giving the test identification number supplied with the kit. Positive results are retested twice, with a confirmatory Western blot. Counseling is provided by phone with local referral information.
Oral fluid test • OraSure	99.5%	99.5%	3 days	Oral fluids are collected on a cotton pad placed in the mouth for 2–5 minutes (test available only through a physician). Specimen is sent to the lab; positive results are retested and confirmed with an oral Western blot test. Results are given by provider.
Rapid serum test • Single-use	99.9%	99.6%	10 minutes	Blood is drawn and mixed with reagent in a test tube; within 10 minutes, a potentially positive result changes color. Test can be used to confirm HIV-negative status, but positive results require follow-up with a standard HIV test to confirm HIV infection. Results are given by provider.
Urine test • Sentinel	98.7%	99.1%	2.5 hours	Urine specimen is mixed with reagent; a potentially positive result changes color. Test can be used to confirm HIV-negative status, but positive results require follow-up with a standard HIV test to confirm HIV infection. Results are given by provider.

* Ability to accurately identify HIV-infected persons.
† Ability to screen out uninfected persons.
Adapted from Massachusetts Medical Society: Novel approaches to HIV antibody testing. AIDS Clinical Care 9:1, 1997.

With the exception of the home collection system, through which testing is controlled by the individual, other testing options must be administered in the presence of a health care provider. However, the shorter turn-around time for results and the ability to avoid drawing blood (e.g., oral fluids and urine tests) increase their utility and appeal. In addition, most tests have acceptable and, in some cases, excellent sensitivity (ability to accurately identify HIV-infected persons) and specificity (ability to screen out uninfected persons).[1a] With adolescents who are extremely anxious, the ability to reduce waiting time and confirm negative results makes these tests the preferred option.

ADVANTAGES AND DISADVANTAGES OF HIV TESTING

Providers should help adolescents explore the benefits and potential drawbacks of learning their HIV status (Table 13.7). They might introduce the topic by asking: "What do you think are the benefits of knowing your HIV-positive status?" In addition to responses the youth may give, the benefits include (1) providing an opportunity for early intervention and enhancing quality of life; (2) avoiding reinfection or other STDs; (3) enabling youth to develop positive self-care and coping skills and to adjust to living with HIV before receiving an AIDS diagnosis; (4) providing important information for family planning decisions; and (5) protecting others from infection.

A similar question should be asked about disadvantages: "What are some of the drawbacks of knowing you are HIV-positive?" The drawbacks include (1) negative reactions from family and friends; (2) discrimination and stigma if others find out; (3) intense emotional distress and feelings of wanting to harm oneself or others; (4) difficulty getting or paying for care; and (5) fears about dying.

The goals of this discussion are to help adolescents understand the significance of being tested and the potential implications if they are infected and to help providers learn more about each adolescent's ability to handle the results.

COPING SKILLS—MANAGING RESULTS

Understanding more about how adolescents cope with other major life events may provide key information about how they may respond to positive HIV results and what kinds of support may be needed. Providers might ask: "Have you ever had to deal with difficult situations or really upsetting news in the past? How did you (might you) handle something like that?" Responses that youth provide should be applied to

TABLE 13.7.   Advantages and Disadvantages of Anonymous vs. Confidential HIV Testing

Type of Testing	Advantages	Disadvantages
Anonymous testing	Blood samples are labeled with an identifying number; the person's name is not used. No one but the test recipient gets the results, so negative reactions are avoided.	Anonymous testing makes it more difficult to provide followup care because providers do not know a person's test result. Services for HIV+ adolescents are limited and are more difficult to assess without the support of a knowledgeable provider.
Confidential testing	Testing can be provided by the primary care provider so that followup care, support, and advocacy can be delivered. Adolescents can receive care from a provider with whom they have an ongoing relationship.	In states with disclosure laws, results may be shared with parents or other agencies. Even under the best of circumstances, confidential information may sometimes be disclosed inadvertently or accidentally.

TABLE 13.8.   Protocol for HIV Pre-Test Counseling with Adolescents

Provide HIV counseling for all adolescents.
Offer HIV testing to all sexually active adolescents with informed consent.
Testing should not be coercive.
  • Clearly inform youth they they will continue to receive ongoing care, whether or not they choose to be tested.
  • Help youth to identify a supportive adult to be involved in the testing process and to provide ongoing assistance and support; identify support system.
  • Review previous test history, if any.

Risk assessment
1. Discuss risk in the context of an adolescent's sexual, drug-use, or other risk behaviors.
2. For new clients, conduct risk assessment.
    a. Sexual behavior and condom use
    b. Alcohol, drug, and needle use
    c. Blood products
    d. Perinatal transmission

HIV/AIDS knowledge
1. Discuss adolescent's knowledge of HIV transmission and course of disease
    a. Routes of transmission
    b. Difference between HIV and AIDS
    c. Latency period and effect on immune system

Risk reduction education
1. Provide risk reduction education.
    a. Discuss readiness for sexual activity (if not yet sexually active).
      – Recommend delaying sex.
      – Discuss ways to increase intimacy without having sex.
2. Discuss safer sex and demonstrate protection methods.
    a. Condoms
    b. Dental dams
    c. Female condoms
3. Discuss strategies for partner negotiation.
    a. Role play and talk about appropriate responses
4. Discuss safer needle use.
    a. Harm reduction (talk about cleaning injection equipment)
    b. Needle exchange programs
    c. Avoid sharing tattoo and ear-piercing equipment
5. Discuss use of alcohol and drugs during sex.
    a. Develop strategies to minimize risk.

Testing issues
1. Explain differences between anonymous and confidential testing.
2. Explain meaning of test results.
    a. Antibody response following infection
    b. Negative, positive, indeterminate
3. Explain the pros and cons of HIV testing.
4. Discuss confidentiality, potential discrimination and stigma, and disclosure requirements (if any), based on state law.
5. Obtain consent.
6. Draw blood.
7. Answer questions and discuss coping strategies until results are available.
8. Schedule appointment for test results (in person).

Follow-up and referral

Adapted from Chabon B, Futterman D, Jones C: Adolescent HIV Counseling and Testing Protocol, Adolescent AIDS Program, Montefiore Medical Center, 1995.

how they may deal with waiting for/coping with their test results. Providers should help teens to anticipate their results and imagine what their responses may be by asking: "If you decide to get tested, what do you think your results might be?"

Using a role play to explore feelings about being positive (or negative) helps an adolescent get in touch with his or her feelings and helps providers determine the youth's capacity to handle test results and the level of support he or she may require initially. Providers may introduce the role play by saying:

> I'd like you to pretend that you have decided to take the HIV test. Let's pretend that it is 2 weeks from today, and you have come back to get your test results. Can you imagine what that would feel like? Close your eyes if it makes it easier to imagine.

> You are going to get your test results today. You have come to see me, and I ask you to sit down. I tell you that your results are positive. How would you feel? What would you say or do?[12]

Continue to role play for a few minutes while the youth describes his or her reactions. Role play giving a negative test result, and use the session to talk about the "window period" and the need for possible retesting if the youth has recently been exposed to HIV. This is a good opportunity to reinforce the need for avoiding risky behavior in the future.

Using this information, providers need to let the adolescent know how long he or she will have to wait to get results, to talk about how he or she expects to cope during that time, and to identify sources of support if they require it. The provider might ask:

> How do you think you are going to feel while you are waiting for your test results?

> Can you talk about being tested with anyone? If so, with whom, and what would you tell him or her?

> What can you do if you feel really upset or nervous?[12]

If an adolescent has no additional support, the provider should identify an interim referral and provide contact information during the waiting period (in some cases, the waiting period for routine HIV testing may take 2 weeks or longer).

CONSENT FOR HIV TESTING

The provider and adolescent should determine whether the adolescent is ready for testing. Some youth may lack adequate support or appear emotionally unready. If so, testing should be delayed until he or she is ready. If the adolescent decides to be tested, he or she should read and sign an appropriate consent form that meets legal and institutional standards.

The provider should answer any additional questions, reinforce plans for coping during the waiting period, provide contact numbers, and encourage the youth to call with questions or concerns in the interim. Schedule a followup appointment to provide test results, which are not given over the phone, and let the youth know that he or she will be contacted if he or she fails to return for results.

Post-Test Counseling (Table 13.9)

The components of post-test counseling for adolescents are similar, whether results are negative, positive, or indeterminate. When informing adolescents of test results, providers should be straightforward, give results at the beginning of the session, and allow adequate time for the youth to respond. The session should include risk reduc-

TABLE 13.9.   Protocol for HIV Post-Test Counseling with Adolescents

Post-Test Counseling for HIV+ Adolescents
- Provide results and answer questions.
- Allow youth time to respond.
- Encourage expression of feelings; anticipate traumatic reaction (may include denial, panic, crying, anger, fear, self-blame, relief).
- After youth has adequately expressed feelings, reflect back their response.
  - Explore fears (fear of dying is common).
- Assess potential for suicide and need for immediate mental health intervention.
- Explain meaning of positive test results.
  - Exposure/infection with HIV
  - Describe difference between HIV and AIDS.
- Explain that people with HIV can live active productive lives for many years.
  - Remind youth of treatment options.
- Discuss support system.
  - Explore who they can tell about their HIV positive status.
    - Caution about inappropriate disclosure (e.g., potential discrimination).
    - Provide information about what to do if they experience discrimination.
    - Offer to assist with disclosure, if necessary (e.g., meeting with parents).
- Assess immediate needs (e.g., housing, safety) and develop plans to address them.
- Review routes of transmission and prevention (blood, semen, tissue, organs, razors, toothbrushes, breastfeeding, needle-sharing).
- Reinforce risk reduction strategies.
  - Practice safer sex and condom use.
  - Avoid sharing needles or works.
  - Clean needles before use.
  - Seek drug treatment referral, if appropriate
  - Partner negotiation/disclosure
- Discuss strategies for partner notification.
- If adolescent is pregnant, provide information on the benefits and potential risks of antiretroviral use during pregnancy to reduce perinatal transmission of HIV. Provide additional counseling to the adolescent and family/support system to assist in decision-making; include adequate time to discuss concerns.
- Establish support plan for next 48 hours and longer term (next week).
- Make followup appointment for medical care and provide contact information.
  - 24-hour crisis hotline
  - Emergency mental health care
- Ensure emotional stability before session ends.

Post-Test Counseling for HIV-Negative Adolescents
- Provide results and answer questions.
- Allow youth time to respond.
- Encourage expression of feelings.
- Explain meaning of negative test results.
  - No evidence of exposure/infection with HIV
  - Not necessarily free of HIV ("window" period)
  - Need to be retested if engaged in risky behavior within past 6 months
- Review and reinforce risk reduction strategies.
  - Practice safer sex and condom use.
  - Avoid sharing needles or works.
  - Clean needles before use.
  - Seek drug treatment referral, if appropriate.
  - Partner negotiation/disclosure
- Address additional questions.
- Assess need for additional referrals and make appointments (e.g., health and social services, mental health services, etc.).
  - Provide health education literature.

Adapted from Chabon B, Futterman D, Jones C: Adolescent HIV Counseling and Testing Protocol, Adolescent AIDS Program, Montefiore Medical Center, 1995.

tion counseling, reinforce negotiation skills, and identify additional referral needs. Before the session ends, providers should make required appointments for followup services with other agencies. Predictably, counseling HIV-positive adolescents requires additional time to express and acknowledge feelings, identify immediate needs, assess for suicide potential, and develop a plan for coping and mobilizing support.

POST-TEST COUNSELING FOR HIV+ ADOLESCENTS

Provide Results. Providers should give results directly without engaging in casual conversation and wait for the youth to respond. A forthright approach is best: "Your test results show that you are HIV-positive, which means that you have HIV infection."

Encourage and Validate Response. An immediate response to others' distress is to try to comfort them. However, providers should allow the adolescent time to react; this may require sitting in silence while the youth absorbs the information. If the adolescent does not react directly, giving him or her permission to express feelings is often helpful: "You must be having a lot of feelings right now. It might be helpful to sort them out. Which one feels most intense?"

Common reactions include denial, panic, crying, anger, fear, guilt and self-blame, and even relief. After the adolescent has expressed immediate reactions, acknowledge his or her feelings and help interpret test results. A common though often unexpressed concern is fear of dying. Understanding that HIV infection is a chronic infection, not a "death sentence," may help motivate development of appropriate self-care and health utilization skills. For example, a provider might say:

> HIV infection is a chronic illness that requires medical care and support. Many people with HIV live active, productive lives for many years. HIV is not a death sentence. New treatments can help your body fight HIV and resist infections. Over time, HIV slowly weakens the body's ability to fight infection. That is why it is really important to get a lot of support and learn how to take care of yourself. You need to learn how to reduce stress, prevent reinfection with HIV, and get proper medical care. We need to take this one step at a time.

Establish Counseling Goals. In addition to helping youth to label and express their feelings about being HIV-positive, goals of post-test counseling with HIV+ adolescents include (1) ensuring that adolescents understand that HIV infection is a treatable, chronic illness; (2) helping identify and mobilize the adolescent's support system; (3) reinforcing risk-reduction messages and skills, including the need for partner notification; (4) assessing immediate mental health needs and suicide potential; and (5) developing short- and long-term plans for continued care and follow-up.

Identify Support System. Adolescents need help to identify and mobilize their support system. This includes (1) identifying persons in their lives who provide ongoing emotional and financial support; (2) discussing potential reactions to their HIV status, including discrimination and rejection; (3) determining persons with whom they can safely share their HIV test results; and (4) developing a plan for informing appropriate persons. If a supportive adult has participated in the post-test session, he or she can assist with notifying key persons in the youth's support system.

Inform Key Persons. Many youth express concerns about confidentiality and feel overwhelmed by the prospect of having to inform their parents and notify partners. Providers can offer to help by scheduling a meeting with the adolescent and his or her family, and by assisting with partner notification through role play or a face-to-face meeting.

Reinforce Risk Reduction Behaviors. As with pre-test counseling, providers should reinforce the need for risk reduction and review strategies, such as using condoms and dental dams; cleaning and not sharing needles; avoiding alcohol and drugs before or during sex; and negotiating risk reduction with partners to avoid risky behaviors.

Develop Response Plan. In addition to addressing needs for immediate support, providers should help the adolescent develop an immediate and long-term plan for managing emotional and health-related needs. This includes coping with test results, managing fears and feelings, and asking for help when they need it. Providers may prompt discussion by asking several basic questions:

What do you think you need to do next?

What will you do when you leave here today?

Let's talk about some other options.

Is ____ someone you might be able to talk with?

What can you do if you are alone and feel scared or overwhelmed?[12]

Referral and Follow-up. After scheduling a followup medical appointment, providers should give the youth a list of contact persons, including phone numbers for a 24-hour crisis line and emergency mental health services. Providers should develop a specific plan for addressing traumatic reactions following receipt of test results: the adolescent should be encouraged to call the provider with specific concerns before the next appointment; if the youth feels suicidal or extremely anxious, he or she should immediately call the crisis hotline or emergency mental health services.

Before the session ends, providers should assess the adolescent's level of emotional stability. If additional emotional support is needed, the provider should make an immediate referral for mental health services.

POST-TEST COUNSELING FOR HIV-NEGATIVE ADOLESCENTS

Providers should follow the protocol for post-test counseling with HIV-negative adolescents (*see* previous pages and Appendix H). The goals of counseling with HIV-negative youth include (1) determining whether a followup test is needed (youth who have engaged in risky behavior within the past 6 months should be retested within 6 months); (2) reinforcing risk-reduction messages and skills; and (3) developing an individualized risk-reduction plan that will be reassessed during subsequent primary care visits. A negative test result provides an important opportunity for reinforcing low-risk behaviors. However, adolescents who have engaged in high-risk acts within the past 6 months are not necessarily HIV-negative. Providers should carefully explain the "window" period during which antibodies routinely develop and should reschedule a follow-up test within the next 6 months.

Prevention (Tables 13.10 and 13.11)

A common argument against educating adolescents about sex is that providing information encourages them to become sexually active. In fact, the opposite is true. A comprehensive review of 23 school-based programs designed to reduce risky sexual behaviors found that teens who received AIDS education were actually less likely to engage in sex and more likely to practice safer sex than peers who did not.[11]

Without an effective vaccine, prevention remains the most important strategy for reducing the spread of HIV infection. Promoting risk reduction with adolescents is

TABLE 13.10.   Developmental Characteristics that Increase Adolescents' Risk
for HIV Infection

Perceptions of invulnerability	Concrete rather than abstract thinking
Present time orientation and impulsivity	Reliance on peer approval
Denial of danger	Fatalistic attitudes among many high-risk teens

particularly challenging because developmental characteristics foster concrete, short-term thinking, encourage experimentation and risk-taking, and increase reliance on peers. Behavioral interventions have been successful in reducing short-term risk, although long-term changes are much more difficult to maintain.[22] For example, a study of responses to an HIV-prevention program for gay and bisexual males showed significant reduction in the number of unprotected, same-sex anal and oral sex activities.[21] Youth maintained reduced risk through a 12-month follow-up, although frequency increased over a 2-year period.[20] Abstinence was significantly more likely among younger adolescents and those who had not been sexually active prior to the intervention; even with prevention intervention, however, gay and bisexual adolescents who engaged in commercial sex increased their sexual risk behaviors. In another study evaluating a similar intervention among mid-western gay and bisexual youth, 60% showed a decrease in unprotected anal sex during follow-up, including more consistent use of condoms.[17] Findings underscore the need for early intervention (before age 13), for anticipating relapse and for consistent reinforcement of prevention messages by providers.

Predictors of unsafe sex for gay and bisexual youth have been identified; these include high levels of anxiety and depression, frequent alcohol use,[20] substance abuse,[18] lack of communication with partners about risk reduction, having a steady partner, and having frequent intercourse.[18] Among the limited, nonrepresentative studies of gay male adolescents, three risk patterns have been identified: (1) young gay males are more likely than older gay men to engage in risky sexual behavior; (2) reported substance use is high and linked to risky sexual behavior; and (3) some young gay males barter sex, use condoms infrequently, and have multiple male partners, generally older adult males.[20] Although similar data are not available for lesbian adolescents, reported frequency of heterosexual activity, sex with gay male peers, and inconsistent condom use puts them at high risk for HIV infection. These data emphasize the need to provide support for lesbian and gay adolescents to build self-esteem and enhance self-care behaviors, particularly when youth are struggling with issues related to coming out.

PROMOTING RISK REDUCTION AND PREVENTION

Knowledge of the basic principles and goals for risk reduction can help providers respond most effectively to adolescents' behavioral learning needs (Table 13.12). Even highly motivated adults have difficulty maintaining healthy behaviors consistently.

TABLE 13.11.   Factors that Promote Successful Risk Reduction for Adolescents

Capacity to personalize risk and belief that one's actions can make a difference
Knowledge and opportunity to practice risk-reduction skills
Perception that peer group supports risk-reduction behaviors
Opportunity to experience repeated messages to reinforce health-promoting behaviors

TABLE 13.12.　Principles for Promoting Positive Behavioral Change in Adolescents

Help adolescents to personalize their risk and believe that their actions can make a difference.
Develop individualized risk reduction goals based on each adolescent's needs: Help to identify a range of options for behavioral change.
Clarify the difference between high- and low-risk behaviors; demonstrate condom use.
Set *realistic* behavioral goals that focus on minimizing risk rather than eliminating it entirely.
Build communication, decision-making, and assertiveness skills, through role playing and interactive exercises, to enable adolescents to resist negative peer pressure and to negotiate safer sex and safer drug use.
Encourage youth to delay sexual activity and to protect themselves if they become sexually active.
Identify and discuss values and beliefs (family, adolescent, and peers).
Address cultural attitudes about sexuality and condom use.
Include sexual orientation and behavior in discussions with all adolescents.
Consistently repeat risk-reduction messages and reinforce health-promoting behaviors.

Expecting adolescents to comply with difficult, awkward, or embarrassing behavioral changes without implementation skills sets them up to fail. Teaching adolescents how to reduce risk for HIV before they initiate sex or drug use is much more effective than trying to change established behaviors. Because adolescents are developmentally inclined toward risk-taking and sensation-seeking and because peer pressure is often extreme, providers should encourage youth to delay sexual activity and, at the same time, teach them how to protect themselves. "Don't drink, but if you do, don't drive" is a comparable prevention paradigm.

Providers must also recognize that change is incremental and that behaviors are best modified by setting realistic goals. This requires a thorough risk assessment and development of an individualized risk-reduction plan. Lesbian and gay adolescents may feel overwhelmed by the severity of the AIDS epidemic within the gay community. Providers can help them understand that change is possible by discussing the remarkable changes that have occurred in gay male sexual behavior during the 1980s, described as the most profound behavioral change ever occurring in public health.[4] In order to develop and sustain health-promoting behavior, adolescents must believe that they have the ability to practice and/or change their behaviors. This includes demonstrating condom use and engaging in role playing and interactive exercises to help build communication, decision-making, and assertiveness skills.

Unlike other life-threatening diseases that develop over a period of years, resulting from poor diet, smoking, or a sedentary lifestyle, HIV can be contracted through a single episode of risky behavior. Thus, HIV prevention and risk assessment are no longer optional elements of care, but must be included as a routine part of primary care for all adolescents.

References

1. AIDS Policy Center for Children, Youth and Families: Position statement on youth and HIV testing. Washington, DC, March 1996.
1a. Brodie S, Sax P: Novel Approaches to HIV Antibody Testing. AIDS Clinical Care. Massachusetts Medical Society 9:1–8, 1997.
2. Bowleg L: Changing Faces, Changing Directions: State Responses to the Demographic Shifts in the HIV/AIDS Epidemic. Washington, DC, Intergovernmental Health Policy Project, 1995.
3. Chabon B, Futterman D, Jones C: Adolescent HIV Counseling and Testing Protocol, Adolescent AIDS Program, Montefiore Medical Center, 1995.
4. Ekstrand ML, Coates TJ: Maintenance of safer sexual behaviors and predictors of risky sex: The San Francisco Men's Health Study. Am J Public Health 80:973, 1990.
5. English A: Expanding access to HIV services for adolescents: Legal and ethical issues. In Clemente RJ (ed): Adolescents and AIDS: A Generation in Jeopardy. Newbury Park, CA, Sage, 1992.

6. Futterman D, Hein K, Reuben N, et al: Human immunodeficiency virus-infected adolescents: The first 50 patients in a New York City program. Pediatrics 91:730, 1993.
7. Gittler J, Quigley-Rick M, Saks MJ: Adolescent Health Care Decision Making: The Law and Public Policy. New York, Carnegie Council on Adolescent Development. Report for the US Congress Office of Technology Assessment, June 1990.
8. Goodman E, Tipton AC, Hecht L, Chesney MA: Perseverance pays off: Health care providers' impact on HIV testing decisions by female adolescents. Pediatrics 94:878, 1994.
9. Health Resources and Services Administration: ZDV therapy for reducing perinatal HIV: Implementation in HRSA-funded programs. Program Advisory. US Department of Health and Human Services, December 1995.
10. Ilegbodu AE, Frank ML, Poindexter AN, Johnson D: Characteristics of teens tested for HIV in a metropolitan area. J Adolesc Health 15:479, 1994.
11. Kirby D, Short L, Collins J, et al: School-based programs to reduce sexual risk behaviors: A review of effectiveness. Public Health Rep 109:339, 1994.
12. Kunins H, Hein K, Futterman D, et al: Guide to adolescent HIV/AIDS program development. J Adolesc Health. 14:1S, 1993.
13. Massachusetts Medical Society: Novel approaches to HIV antibody testing. AIDS Clin Care 9:1, 1997.
14. Morrissey JM, Hofmann AD, Thrope JC: Consent and Confidentiality in the Health Care of Children and Adolescents: A Legal Guide. New York, Free Press, 1986.
15. Office of National AIDS Policy: Youth & AIDS: An American Agenda. Report to the President. Washington, DC, 1996.
16. Rawitscher LA, Saitz R, Friedman LS: Adolescent's preferences regarding human immunodeficiency virus (HIV)-related physician counseling and testing. Pediatrics 96:52, 1995.
17. Remafedi G: Cognitive and behavioral adaptations to HIV/AIDS among gay and bisexual adolescents. J Adolesc Health 15:142, 1994.
18. Remafedi G: Predictors of unprotected intercourse among gay and bisexual youth: Knowledge, beliefs and behavior. Pediatrics 94:163, 1994.
19. Rodgers AS, Futterman D, Levin L, D'Angelo L: A profile of human immunodeficiency virus–infected adolescents receiving health care services at selected sites in the United States. J Adolesc Health Care 19:401, 1996.
20. Rotheram-Borus MJ, Hunter J, Rosario M: Coming out as lesbian or gay in the era of AIDS. In Herek G, Greene B (eds): AIDS Identity and Community: The HIV Epidemic and Lesbians and Gay Men. Thousand Oaks, CA, Sage, 1995.
21. Rotheram-Borus MJ, Reid H, Rosario M: Factors mediating changes in sexual HIV risk behaviors among gay and bisexual male adolescents. Am J Public Health 84:1938, 1994.
22. Stryker J, Coates TJ, DeCarlo P, et al: Prevention of HIV infection: Looking back, looking ahead. JAMA 273:1143, 1995.

CHAPTER 14

Clinical Care

Although treatment advances greatly increase quality of life and offer hope for HIV-infected persons and their families, relatively few HIV-infected adolescents are currently receiving care. A recent survey of federally-funded adolescent AIDS treatment programs found less than 1,000 adolescents who were receiving care for HIV disease;[16] of these, most were identified late in the course of disease when treatment may be less effective. Of adolescents seen in a New York City program, for example, the median CD4 count was 500/ml when they entered care.[6] Because most HIV-infected youth are in relatively early stages of HIV disease (having been infected during adolescence), early intervention is clinically viable and increasingly is expected to become the standard of care.[11]

Primary Care for HIV+ Adolescents

A key task in working with adolescents with HIV is helping them adjust to their HIV status. Access to support and psychosocial care is a critical component of clinical care, particularly because early intervention and optimal treatment require aggressive drug therapy on a relatively inflexible schedule.

Overall goals for primary care include (1) determining the stage of HIV disease and health status; (2) providing ongoing health maintenance for HIV and primary care needs; (3) monitoring immune function and viral load; (4) providing access to state-of-the-art treatment; (5) providing education on HIV and risk reduction; (6) identifying and addressing psychosocial concerns; and (7) providing access to appropriate clinical trials (Table 14.1).

Like adults with HIV, adolescents have a range of psychosocial and support needs that change with the stage and course of illness. These include a need for emotional support, empowerment to promote quality of life and to enhance treatment adherence, counseling and management of psychological and adjustment problems related to HIV status, assistance in dealing with discrimination and isolation, and help in meeting basic life needs such as transportation, access to food, and shelter. In addition, adolescents must deal with developmental stressors and multiple barriers to care, including lack of financial resources, lack of experience negotiating complex systems, and lack of sensitivity to their developmental and care needs.

Psychosocial care is an intrinsic part of primary care for all persons with HIV/AIDS; for adolescents, psychosocial needs are paramount. Without appropriate support, adolescents have enormous difficulty accessing care and adhering to treatment. Goals of psychosocial care for adolescents with HIV include (1) identifying and addressing crises (e.g., suicidal behavior, homelessness); (2) providing access to benefits, entitlements, and services; (3) promoting adherence to medical regimens; (4) assessing and expanding social support (if needed); (5) supporting development of self-care and life-enhancing practices; (6) identifying and treating chronic problems (e.g., depression, drug, and alcohol addiction); (7) promoting skills to live independently and to make the transition to adulthood, which include establishing life, education, and career goals; (8) reinforcing and sustaining safer sex behaviors; and (9) promoting harm reduction, encouraging drug treatment, and supporting recovery to prevent relapse (Table 14.2).

TABLE 14.1. Goals: Primary Care for HIV+ Youth

Determine staging of HIV illness and health status. Provide health care maintenance: HIV and primary care. Identify and treat concurrent medical problems. Provide ongoing monitoring: immunologic/virologic.	Provide state-of-the art treatment/therapies: antiretrovirals and opportunistic infection prophylaxis, complementary therapies. Provide education on HIV disease. Maximize health and nutritional status. Identify and address psychosocial concerns. Establish linkages with appropriate clinical trials

Clinical Care (Table 14.3)

Although the natural history of HIV infection in adolescence has not been fully defined, most adolescents are infected after their immune system has developed; the course of disease parallels that of adults, although there might be subtle differences in the adolescent immune system. In particular, clinicians have noted that adolescents who were infected through sexual contact or injection drug use have a clinical course more like that of adults than of children,[5] and long-term survivors of perinatal infection may have a unique clinical course that differs from that of other adolescents.[9] NIH has funded a prospective study, Adolescent Medicine HIV/AIDS Research Network (AMHARN), to identify clinical issues unique to adolescents, including course and spectrum of disease, puberty, and developmental and psychosocial interactions,[7] which will inform future treatment guidelines.

Assessment

MEDICAL HISTORY

Initial evaluation of an adolescent with HIV infection includes a medical, sexual, and substance use history, psychosocial assessment, physical examination, and laboratory evaluation. These may be divided over 1–3 visits so as not to appear overwhelming. An initial medical history should assess for prior illness that may be HIV-related, especially evidence of seroconversion (e.g., fever, malaise, lymphadenopathy, and involvement of organ systems). This history helps identify when infection may have occurred to assist in staging HIV infection. When congenital infection is suspected, providers should obtain information on parents' risk behaviors, including injection drug use.

A comprehensive history records sexual behavior and drug use; prior illnesses, including STDs, recurrent pneumonia, or tuberculosis, which may be reactivated in adolescents with HIV; hospitalizations; use of condoms and contraception; menstrual

TABLE 14.2. Goals: Psychosocial Care for HIV+ Youth

Identify needs and stabilize, if necessary (e.g., crisis intervention to manage suicidal behavior, homelessness, etc.). Provide access to benefits, entitlement, available services. Promote adherence to medical regimens. Develop trusting relationships Identify and expand social support, if needed.	Support health promotion, self-respect, self-care, and life-enhancing practices. Identify and treat chronic problems (e.g., depression, post-traumatic stress disorder, drug and alcohol addiction) Promote self-confidence and skills to live independently—transition to adulthood. Reinforce and sustain safer sex behaviors Promote harm reduction; encourage drug treatment, and support recovery to prevent relapse

TABLE 14.3. Protocol for HIV-Related Care

1. Medical and psychosocial history	6. Medications/treatment
2. Review of systems	7. Access to clinical research
3. Physical examination	8. Entitlements/case management
4. Laboratory assessment	9. Patient education and empowerment
5. Immunizations	10. Referral to support services

***

Medical history
- Allergies (particularly medication related)
- Childhood and family illnesses
- Hospitalization and medication history
- Sexual history: sexuality, sexually transmitted/gynecologic diseases
- Tuberculosis/pneumonia and other infections
- Substance use

Psychosocial history
- Psychosocial status and needs (comprehensive history)
- Coping behaviors and skills
- Access to counseling and support
- Disclosure: family, partners, friends
- Living will
- Child custody/permanency planning

Review of systems
- Sense of well-being/illness
- Symptoms of seroconversion illness
- Appetite, weight loss or gain, nausea, vomiting, diarrhea
- Lymphadenopathy: presence or regression, tenderness
- Oral health: dentition, gum disease, thrush, herpes, lesions
- Sino-pulmonary: cough, shortness of breath, wheezing, sinusitis
- Anogenital complaints
- Skin or hair changes
- Mental status or neurologic changes
- Visual changes
- Unusual bleeding

Physical examination
- General: appearance, weight, fever
- Skin: HIV-related lesions appear throughout course of HIV, dermatological problems common among adolescents
- HEENT: visual fields and thorough retinal examination (consider referral for ophthalmologic examination when CD4 < 100/mm^3), oral examination: dentition, gums, thrush, herpes
- Lymph nodes: note presence and regression
- Breast: masses, discharge, enlargement 2' hormones
- Lungs and cardiac function
- Abdominal: hepatosplenomegaly

Physical examination *(cont.)*
- Gynecologic: speculum and bimanual examination incorporated into full examination, not referred out
- Genital: inspection for lesions
- Anal: inspection for all youth (including lesbians and males denying male-male sex)
- Neurologic/mental status: may be difficult to sort out HIV issues from substance use in active users; assess developmental/cognitive level

Laboratory assessment *(at entry and suggested minimal interval; as clinically indicated and needed to monitor medications)*
- Repeat HIV Ab for confirmation
- CD4 and viral load count every 3 months and with medication changes
- Complete blood count every 3–12 months
- Chemistry and enzyme panel every 12 months
- Urinalysis every 12 months
- Toxoplasmosis titer every 2–3 years in unexposed patients when CD4 < 200/mm3
- Tuberculosis: PPD with anergy every 12 months unless anergic for 2 years (chest x-ray if anergic)
- Syphilis serology every 6–12 months
- Gonorrhea (genital, oral, anal) every 6–12 months
- Chlamydia (genital) every 6–12 months
- Cervical cytology (Papanicolaou) every 6–12 months (colposcopy when indicated)
- Vaginal wet preparation every 6–12 months

Immunizations
- Influenza—yearly
- Pneumococcal—baseline
- Measles, mumps, and rubella—baseline
- Tetanus—every 10 years
- Hepatitis B—3-in-series (pre- and post-vaccine titers)

Medications/treatment *(consult most recent guidelines)*
- Dosing by Tanner stage not age
- Impact of puberty and gender inadequately defined
- Antiretrovirals: indications for initiation, combinations
- Opportunistic infection prophylaxis: primary and secondary
- Birth control, pre- and perinatal medications
- Adherence issues
- Complementary therapies: importance of dialogue to ascertain the client's goals and access to referral sources to locate knowledgeable providers
- Expanded access for new medications and PWA buyers' clubs

(Table continued on following page.)

TABLE 14.3.   Protocol for HIV-Related Care *(Continued)*

Clinical research	Patient education and empowerment
• Adolescent cohort studies: AMHARN	• Importance of peer support
• Clinical trials: ACTG, CPCRA	• Skill building and development of self-efficacy
• Behavioral research/secondary risk reduction	• Provider/patient relationship—partner in care
	• Ongoing access to information
Entitlements/case management	
• Initial and ongoing entitlements assessment	
• Ensure access to case management; periodic consult with case manager	

From Futterman D, Shalwitz J, Hunter J: Protocol for medical care of HIV+ Youth. Conference on the Primary Care Needs of Lesbian and Gay Adolescents. Washington, DC, Health Resources and Services Administration, December 5–6, 1994.

and pregnancy history; information on prior health care; history of transfusions and receipt of blood products; immunizations, medications, and allergies; family medical and psychiatric history; and diet and nutrition.

If the adolescent has been tested elsewhere and has presented as HIV-infected, the provider should retest to ensure HIV status. The provider should assess the adolescent's living situation and support system; mental status and psychiatric history, including depression, suicide, medications, and inpatient treatment; education, literacy level, and employment history; sources of financial and social support; and involvement with adolescent service systems, including juvenile justice and foster care.

The sexual and substance risk history should be more comprehensive than questions routinely asked during an initial primary care assessment (*see* Tables 14.4 and 14.5 in the previous chapter for assessment questions). By carefully clarifying an adolescent's risk behaviors, the provider may develop a more effective prevention and medical management plan. For example, adolescents with an active substance abuse problem require treatment and after-care that is geared to the needs of people with HIV/AIDS, including proactive relapse prevention and support from other recovering persons with HIV. Sexual history should include the sex and number of partners; sexual orientation; age at initiation, specific practices (oral, anal, and vaginal intercourse), and frequency; history of sexual abuse and experience with domestic violence, perpetrators and whether reported or not; and potential involvement with survival sex or prostitution. Substance use history should include type (alcohol, tobacco, marijuana, cocaine, crack, opiates); use of steroids or hormones; age at initiation; route (injection, smoking, sniffing, or pills); frequency, and amount. Family history should include level of cohesion; past and current interactions, including coping skills and response to health crises; knowledge of HIV status and sexual orientation; if lesbian or gay, reactions of others; and runaway or throwaway history. Providers should assess the level of available support. In addition to the immediate and extended family, the

TABLE 14.4.   Types of Questions for Eliciting Information During an Interview

Open-Ended Questions	Closed Questions
How often do you have anal sex?	Have you ever had anal sex?
Tell me about the times you have been told that you have had a sexually transmitted disease.	Have you ever had a sexually transmitted disease?

From Kunins H, Hein K, Futterman D, et al: Guide to adolescent HIV/AIDS program development. J Adolesc Health 14:1S, 1993, with permission.

TABLE 14.5. Affect of HIV Viral Load on AIDS Progression
(Percentage of Deaths During Each Time Period)

Average Viral Load (copies/ml)	5 Years (%)	7 Years (%)	10 Years (%)
< 5,300	0	4.4	38
5,300–12,900	2	13	56
12,900–37,000	10	63	71
> 37,000	66	69	76

From Mellors J, et al: Prognosis in HIV-1 infection predicted by the quantity of virus in plasma. Science 272:1167, 1996, with permission.

support network includes friends, partners, and adult role models (e.g., teachers, counselors). Access to AIDS-related support is particularly important; providers should assess the adolescent's awareness of community-based AIDS programs and involvement with other people with HIV.

Many providers feel uncomfortable talking about sexual behaviors with adolescents. Acknowledging this difficulty is one way to introduce the topic: "Some of the questions I need to ask are very personal, and you may not have discussed them with anyone before. You may feel uncomfortable talking about sex, but I need this information to provide care. Remember, whatever you tell me is private."

Providers also should reassure adolescents that the information that they share is confidential and will be disclosed only if they are suicidal or homicidal or are the victims of sexual or physical abuse. Using simple, nonmedical terms to explain clinical concepts ensures that adolescents understand what you are saying. The interview and risk assessment should include both closed and open-ended questions. Closed questions limit dialogue by eliciting a yes or no answer, whereas open-ended questions encourage discussion (Table 14.4). Both are useful to elicit risk behaviors and sensitive information.

REVIEW OF SYSTEMS AND PHYSICAL EXAMINATION

An HIV-specific review of systems should include assessment for fatigue, fever, weight loss, night sweats, lymph node enlargement (note number, size, location, and consistency), and skin lesions or rashes. Assess for diarrhea, abdominal pain or masses, anal, vaginal, or penile pain, itching or discharge, or persistent infections. Check for persistent cough or shortness of breath. Head, neck, ear, nose, and throat examination (HEENT) includes inspection of nasal passages and palpation for sinus tenderness (sinusitis is a frequent problem among adolescents with HIV); visual changes which may indicate cytomegalovirus (CMV); and dysphagia (thrush), tooth or gum disease, mouth sores, ulcers, or inflammation. Neuromuscular review should assess for weakness, myalgia (abnormal pain), or sensations. A careful assessment of weight is warranted. Unlike in adults, stable weight in adolescents who are undergoing significant growth is not necessarily an indicator of health. Growth failure during puberty may be an indicator of HIV progression even without declining CD4 counts.

The physical examination should include vital signs and general appearance. Nutritional status should be noted. Skin examination should include a search for seborrhea, eczema, tinea, molluscum, and bruising. Assess for visual acuity and perform a fundoscopy to screen for CMV or toxoplasma retinitis. Tanner staging should be done for breasts and genitalia. External genitalia and anus should be inspected for sores, lesions, or warts (condyloma); both males and females should be examined because they may be reluctant to admit to having anal intercourse but may have anal warts or herpes. Genital, cervical, or anal neoplasia may occur in immunocompromised persons who have been infected with certain types of human papilloma virus (HPV). Females who have had sexual intercourse, pelvic pain, or are over age 18 should have a pelvic examination every 6 months. Cardiac status should be assessed at baseline in all patients, particularly in those who have used injection drugs. Adolescents who use injection drugs are at risk for bacterial endocarditis.

A baseline mental status is helpful for assessing neurological changes associated with HIV. Assessment should include evidence of personality changes, dementia, depression, anxiety, thought disorders, and headaches. If neurologic involvement is suspected, testing may be indicated.

LABORATORY ASSESSMENT

Laboratory assessment is essential to help determine the stage of HIV infection. When available, adolescent-specific values should be used; however, the normal range for immune system markers has not been determined for this age group. The level of virus (viral load) has been shown to be the single most predictive indicator of course of disease. Tests (*see* Tables 14.6 and 14.7) are used for (1) assessing risk of HIV disease progression; (2) deciding when to initiate antiretroviral treatment; and (3) monitoring effectiveness of treatment. Testing should include total CD4 lymphocyte count, percentage of total lymphocytes, and CD4:CD8 ratios. Establishing the CD4 level helps to guide prophylaxis and antiviral treatment. Viral load and CD4 counts should be monitored every 3 months, at a minimum. HIV-positive status should be confirmed before initiating clinical care.

A tuberculin skin test (PPD) with anergy panel (Merieux multitest or candida and tetanus antigen) is important because TB infection can occur early in HIV disease. If found to be positive or anergic, a chest x-ray should be done to rule out tuberculosis. All sexually active teens should be screened with the following workups: 1) gonorrhea culture from three sites (penile urethra or cervix, anus, and pharynx); (2) chlamydia test of genital fluids (immunofluorescent slide test or culture) or urine ligase chain reaction to screen for gonorrhea and chlamydia; (3) herpes culture of suspicious lesions; (4) Gram stain of genital fluids to detect gonorrhea or inflammation (in males); (5) potassium hydroxide preparation of vaginal secretions for candida; (6) wet preparation for trichomonas or clue cells (bacterial vaginosis) in females; (7) syphilis serologic test (rapid plasma reagin with confirmatory fluorescent treponemal antibody);

TABLE 14.6. Consensus Recommendations for Initiating Treatment

Status	Recommendation
Symptomatic HIV disease	Therapy recommended for all patients.
Asymptomatic, CD4 < 500/mm³	Therapy recommended (some may defer therapy if CD4 = 350–500/mm³ and viral load < 10,000 copies/ml.
Asymptomatic, CD4 > 500/mm³	Therapy recommended for patients with viral load > 30–50,000 or rapidly declining CD4
Asymptomatic, CD4 > 500/mm³	Therapy should be considered if viral load > 5–10,000 copies/ml

From Carpenter C, Fischl M, Hammer S, et al for the International AIDS Society USA: Consensus statement: Antiretroviral therapy for HIV infection in 1996. JAMA 276:146–154, 1996, with permission.

TABLE 14.7.   Antiretroviral Medications

Medication (Generic)/*Brand Name*, FDA Approval Date	Dosage	Side Effects/Considerations
Nucleoside Analogues		
Zidovudine (AZT/ZDV)/ *Retrovir*, 1986	200 mg (2 capsules) every 8 hours	Anemia, headache, malaise
Didanosine (ddI)/ *Videx*, 1991	200 mg (2 tabs) every 12 hours	Diarrhea, rash, pancreatitis, neuropathy Take on empty stomach.
Zalcitabine (ddC)/ *Hivid*, 1992	0.75 mg (1 pill) every 8 hours	Neuropathy, mouth ulcers
Stavudine (d4T)/ *Zerit*, 1992	40 mg (1 capsule) every 12 hours	Neuropathy
Lamivudine (3TC)/ *Epivir*, 1995	150 mg (1 tablet) every 12 hours	Headache, malaise, nausea
Protease inhibitors		
Saquinavir (SAQ)/ *Invirase*, 1995	600 mg (3 capsules) every 8 hours	Nausea, diarrhea, headache Must take with food.
Indinavir (IDV)/ *Crixivan*, 1996	800 mg (2 capsules) every 8 hours	Nausea, vomiting, diarrhea, kidney stones, rash Must take on empty stomach, drink lots of water.
Ritonavir (RIT)/ *Norvir*, 1996	600 mg (6 capsules) every 12 hours	Bitter taste, nausea, vomiting, diarrhea, tingling around mouth Refrigerate, take with food.
Non-nucleoside reverse transcriptase inhibitors		
Nevirapine (NVP)/ *Viramune*, 1996	200 mg (1 tablet) every 12 hours	Rash, fever, nausea, headache

(8) hepatitis serologic test (Hep B sAg, cAb); and (9) cervical cytology (Pap smear) to assess for dysplasia every 6–12 months.

Although decreased antibody response and short-term increase in viral load are seen in some immunocompromised persons, the following immunizations are recommended by the CDC for HIV-infected children, adolescents, and adults: influenza (yearly); baseline pneumococcal, tetanus and diphtheria (Td), measles, mumps, rubella (MMR), and hepatitis B vaccine if nonimmune. Pregnancy should be ruled out before giving rubella vaccine. Pregnant adolescents also should receive counseling on antiretroviral therapy to reduce perinatal transmission. Pregnant adolescents under age 21 represent 1 of 4 participants in the AIDS Clinical Trials Group protocol 076 that studied use of ZDV to interrupt perinatal transmission of HIV. In addition, a 1994 follow-up study of women with AIDS reported to the CDC found that 90% had been pregnant at some time; of these, three quarters had their first pregnancy by age 25, and half were less than 20 years old during their first pregnancy.[2] Federal guidelines for offering and implementing ZDV therapy with pregnant women and adolescents have been developed for use in clinical and community settings;[10] new guidelines for combination antiretroviral treatments during pregnancy are currently under development.

Treatment

During 1996, major clinical advances enabled providers to assess stage of illness[17] more accurately and to intervene with powerful new drugs (protease inhibitors), which, in combination with other antiretroviral medication, can significantly improve longevity and quality of life.[1,3] These advances were based on an important long-term prospective study (and related findings) that documented measurement of viral load (amount of virus in the blood) as the most accurate predictor of course of disease.[14] According to the study, people with a high viral load are much more likely to progress to AIDS or die, regardless of their CD4 (T-cell) count (Table 14.5).[14]

Current suggestions for frequency of viral load monitoring include 2 baseline tests (to establish a reliable starting point), with repeat testing every 3 months and/or within 3–4 weeks of a change in treatment. The goal of antiretroviral treatment is to reduce viral load to undetectable levels using the most up-to-date viral load test. Table 14.6 provides the most recent consensus recommendations for initiating treatment.

COMBINATION THERAPY

Combination therapy (the use of 2 or more antiretroviral drugs) is the standard of care for treating HIV disease and the most effective way to lower viral load and help prevent drug resistance. Combinations must be adjusted for each individual, taking into account current disease status, prior antiretroviral use, other current medications/ drug interactions, side effects, and dosing schedules. Because knowledge is rapidly increasing and new medications are continually being approved by the Food and Drug Administration, providers should seek current publications and consensus panels for the latest treatment recommendations regarding combination therapies. Guidelines for initiating treatment and medications licensed as of January 1997 are summarized in Tables 14.6 and 14.7.

DETERMINING DOSAGE

Because few adolescents have been included in clinical trials, treatment guidelines for adolescents are based on experiences with adults. However, changes in body composition and metabolism that occur during puberty may affect drug distribution and dosage. As a result, dosages should be determined by Tanner stage rather than by age.[4,5] Adolescents in Tanner Stages I and II should receive pediatric dosing schedules, and teens in Tanner Stages IV and V should receive adult dosages, regardless of age. Youth in Tanner Stage III should be monitored closely for signs of efficacy and toxicity. Because clinical care guidelines change rapidly, providers should consult the most recent guidelines for treatment indications and dosing information.

TREATMENT ADHERENCE

Although all age groups show a drop in adherence with complex regimens for chronic illnesses, adolescents need additional assistance and support from providers in developing skills to manage drug therapy. Compliance may be complicated by many factors, including denial and fear of HIV infection, misinformation, distrust of the medical establishment, fear and lack of belief in the effectiveness of medications, low self-esteem and self-efficacy, unstructured and chaotic lifestyles, and lack of social support.

Adolescents often approach illness differently from adults. Concrete thought processes make it difficult to face the long-term implications of being infected with HIV. Youth need time to accept the reality of their new health status and assistance developing support systems and making plans for disclosure. As youth mature or achieve mastery in some aspect of their lives, adherence often improves.

Abstract long-term treatment goals are less likely to motivate teens than strategies that generate positive feedback and bolster self-esteem. Compliance is especially difficult for multiproblem youth, including those who are homeless or drug-addicted,

TABLE 14.8. Adherence/Compliance Goals for Treating Adolescents

Treatment regimens should combine the goals of maximizing therapeutic potency with realistic assessment and support for adherence.

KISS: Keep it simple and safe.

whose primary concern may be finding a place to sleep or ensuring day-to-day survival.

Unlike many adults with HIV disease or parents/caregivers of HIV-infected children, many adolescents do not actively seek the latest antiretroviral treatments. In fact, they often need to be convinced of the importance of taking medication. Thus, providers must play an active role in giving adolescents comprehensible information about antiretrovirals, prophylaxis for opportunistic infections, and skills training, and development of individualized strategies and plans to enhance medication adherence (Tables 14.8, 14.9 and 14.10).

Providers may promote adherence by helping to simplify the treatment regimen and by strategizing with youth about the most practical way to develop a medication schedule. The strategy may include figuring out how best to adapt medication to the adolescent's routine (for example, taking morning medications after brushing teeth), rather than basing dosage on an arbitrary treatment schedule. Use of pill timers may also be effective. Providers may need to prioritize medication for homeless youth who are likely to discontinue treatment early. Anticipating and discussing specific obstacles to compliance may help an adolescent manage difficult situations, such as friends who may ask why he or she is taking medication or not having a safe place to keep it. Encouragement and positive reinforcement help build self esteem and feelings of competence—important steps in developing self-care skills. Paying for care and drug therapy remain major barriers for many adolescents, particularly those who want to protect their confidentiality. Assisting adolescents with obtaining medication through Medicaid, the state AIDS Drug Assistance Program (ADAP), or Ryan White services can help them follow a treatment regimen.

Psychosocial Care

Adolescents with HIV have significant psychosocial needs that require ongoing attention from providers and other supportive adults. At the same time, an HIV/AIDS diagnosis directly challenges age-appropriate developmental strivings for independence and autonomy. The capacity for abstract thinking and ability to set and achieve long-term goals—essential to the development and maintenance of skills for self-care and treatment adherence during chronic illness—are still evolving in adolescents with

TABLE 14.9. Enhancing Treatment Adherence for Adolescents

Give simple instructions for taking medication.
Help develop strategies for remembering when to take medication (e.g., after brushing teeth).
For multiproblem and homeless youth, prioritize medication.
Discuss obstacles to compliance (e.g., what to say if someone asks what the pills are for).
Reward gains, no matter how small.
Identify and address financial barriers.

From Kunins H, Hein K, Futterman D, et al: Guide to adolescent HIV/AIDS program development. J Adolesc Health 14:1S, 1993, with permission.

TABLE 14.10. Considerations in Developing a Treatment Regimen for Adolescents with HIV

Medication issues
Size and number of pills, complexity of regimen, side effects, drug interactions, risks of noncompliance

Health status
Level of wellness/symptoms, strength, coordination, vision, ability to swallow

Cognitive function
Understanding the function of medication in treating disease, understanding dosing regimens, cognitive level, literacy, time and future orientation, memory

Psychological issues
Understanding health status and stage of HIV disease, belief that medications will help, trust in caregivers, social support and degree of disclosure, daily routine, resources, denial and other coping mechanisms, degree of readiness to change

HIV. Coping with a diagnosis of HIV infection or AIDS is devastating for an adult; for an adolescent with more limited access to resources and life experiences, the news can be overwhelming.

Adolescents need access to a range of psychosocial and support services. Communities with large populations of persons living with HIV generally offer a wide selection of AIDS-related services, including programs specifically geared to adolescents with HIV. In smaller or more rural communities, finding programs and providers with expertise in serving people with HIV is much more difficult, and finding programs targeted to adolescents is often impossible.

Staff at the Montefiore Adolescent AIDS Program have identified a five-stage model of coping challenges for adolescents, extending throughout the course of HIV disease (Table 14.11). Each stage introduces new tasks, which at times may conflict with normal adolescent developmental strivings. Although each adolescent responds differently psychologically and emotionally, these stages represent HIV-related milestones that require specific interventions from providers. Stages include (1) being informed of one's HIV-positive status; (2) making decisions about disclosure; (3) learning about viral load and CD4 marker changes; (4) becoming symptomatic; and (5) coping with death and dying.

Among adolescents and adults, being informed that they are HIV-positive triggers a range of emotional and psychological reactions, including fear, guilt, anger, depression, and denial. For many, learning that they are HIV-positive represents a death sentence. Although suicidal thoughts are common among newly diagnosed persons, an assessment of adolescents' responses to HIV-positive results found no increase in suicide attempts and only a minimal increase in suicidal thoughts after learning the test results[6]—responses that coincide with those of HIV-positive adults.[15] For gay adolescents, learning that they are HIV-positive often reinforces negative self-perceptions and internalized homophobia. Some may perceive HIV infection as a punishment for being gay. In addition to offering ongoing emotional support and assessing levels of psychological distress, providers should help youth identify their support system, plan their response for the next 48 hours, and make appointments for follow-up counseling and medical care.

Making decisions about disclosure is an important part of incorporating HIV status into various aspects of the adolescents' lives and ultimately normalizing that status. Although disclosure is an ongoing process, it represents the first major decision they have to make related to their new health status. Many youth fear loss of support or potential rejection by their families and friends as well as current and future sexual

TABLE 14.11. Coping with HIV Infection: Stages and Tasks for Adolescents and Providers

Stage	Task	Adolescent's Response	Intervention
Being informed of HIV-positive status	Begin to respond and identify resources	Range of emotions: denial, anxiety, fear, guilt, shame, anger, regression, depression, suicidal thoughts	Provide immediate emotional support Encourage adolescent to express feelings and identify level of psychological distress Request assistance from mental health provider, if necessary Help to identify existing coping strategies Help to identify support system and available resources, and encourage adolescent to use support system Discuss adolescent's feelings about being HIV-infected and talk about how they expect to cope during the next 48 hours Provide phone numbers for 24-hour hotlines Provide referrals and arrange appointments for emotional support and followup medical care
Making decisions about disclosure	Find appropriate support to assist in decision-making	Fear of rejection by family, friends, and present or future sexual partners Fear of disclosure of homosexuality or other risk behaviors (for heterosexual youth)	Initiate discussion about disclosure Discuss critical need to involve supportive adult (preferably a parent) in treatment and care Role play conversation with parents—explore advantages and disadvantages of telling them Help to plan for possible reactions Arrange a meeting with youth and parents to provide support during disclosure Provide followup meetings to help family discuss issues and concerns Provide referral to family therapist to work through feelings and develop coping strategies Discuss disclosure to close friends or others in the adolescent's support system
Learning about CD4 and viral load changes	Begin to understand more about complexity and course of HIV disease Attempt to increase sense of control through access to information	Fear, anxiety, difficulty understanding that viral load is an important predictor and that CD4 counts are a relative indicator of health and not a fixed determinant Loss of control, reinforcement of "patient" status	Explain role of viral load and CD4 count in making treatment decisions (e.g., prophylaxis); apply to adolescent's medical status and level of functioning Clearly state that high viral load and low CD4 counts do not mean immediate debilitation or death (e.g., many people with low CD4 counts lead active, satisfying lives) Explain the concept of a spectrum of HIV disease, which can have a different course with each person Explain CDC guidelines for the expanded AIDS definition and the rationale Discuss how often adolescent's viral load and CD4 counts will be measured and reviewed

(Table continued on following page)

TABLE 14.11. Coping with HIV Infection: Stages and Tasks
for Adolescents and Providers *(Continued)*

Stage	Task	Adolescent's Response	Intervention
Becoming symptomatic	Need to incorporate new identity (person with HIV) Need to manage stress and obtain support Need to learn self-care skills	Range of emotional responses from fear to determination to fight HIV Denial is actively challenged	Explore the adolescent's perceptions and feelings about each symptom; validate feelings; correct misconceptions and distortions Help youth put symptom(s) in perspective (all infections are not equally serious and not all are AIDS-defining conditions) Make inpatient visits, if hospitalization is required, to provide support and avoid feelings of abandonment Deal realistically and honestly with need for restricted functioning or strict medication schedule Ensure that adequate support is available; explore involvement with community AIDS programs and access to other people with HIV
Coping with death and dying	Explore spiritual needs Resolve relationships. Prepare living will	Reluctant to discuss death; may fear he or she will upset others (e.g, family and friends) May have limited understanding of death	Explore adolescent's conceptions about death (may be very infantile) Ask if he or she has thought about death and if he or she needs help with making plans Discuss options for dying: hospital or home Discuss health-care proxy Discuss developing a living will and assist with planning Discuss preferences for funeral, burial/cremation Discuss need to resolve relationships with family, close friends, others

From Kunins H, Hein K, Futterman D, et al: Guide to adolescent HIV/AIDS program development. J Adolesc Health 14:1S, 1993.

partners. Lesbian and gay youth face additional stigma on the basis of their sexual orientation. Some families tolerate an adolescent's HIV infection but are unable to deal with homosexuality. Heterosexual youth exposed through sexual activity or needle-sharing have to disclose sexual activity or drug use. Helping adolescents understand the importance of involving a supportive adult (preferably a parent) in their treatment and care is an essential task for providers. This may involve role playing a conversation between the adolescent and his or her parents, helping plan for possible responses; arranging a meeting between adolescent and parent(s) to provide support during disclosure; and providing a referral for family therapy to assist with coping.

Adolescents need additional support in learning to interpret tests that provide information about the course of HIV disease, particularly viral load and CD4 markers. A careful explanation requires use of jargon-free language that helps adolescents put their test results into perspective as an indicator, rather than a fixed determinant, of a serious infection or imminent death. Because many adolescents think concretely, providers should explain that viral load and CD4 counts may vary widely and that even when they change significantly, people can lead satisfying, productive lives.

The appearance of HIV-related symptoms introduces a major shift in how youth perceive their health status, actively challenging their denial. Some may initially become aware that they are HIV-infected after symptoms develop. Reactions range from anxiety and obsession over health status to determination to fight disease progression actively. Providers may help adolescents adjust to their changing health status by exploring and validating the adolescents' feelings about each symptom, correcting misconceptions and distortions, dealing realistically and honestly with limitations and restricted functioning, and ensuring availability of adequate support, including involvement with community AIDS programs and access to others living with HIV. Community-based AIDS organizations provide various services, including psychosocial support, recreational activities, home health aides, hospice, transportation, and home-delivered meals. Located in all states, metropolitan areas, and many smaller cities, these services reduce isolation, increase socialization, and help normalize the lives of people with HIV/AIDS. Increasingly, such services are available for adolescents with HIV (Table 14.12). (*See* Appendix B for resource information.)

Just as it is important for providers to help adolescents know that they can live for years with HIV disease with appropriate self-care and medical monitoring, they need to help adolescents think about and plan for death. Many adolescents have limited experiences with death and have naive perceptions about what to expect. As their disease progresses, adolescents may avoid the topic to protect family members, friends, or even providers, who often have difficulty dealing with the deaths of young people. Providers can assist by exploring adolescents' perceptions of dying and helping with planning, including options for dying in the hospital or at home, talking about funeral or memorial services, and discussing child custody or permanency plan-

TABLE 14.12. Components of Psychosocial Care

Based on assessment, care may include any of the following:

Alternative treatments (e.g., biofeedback, acupuncture, immune enhancements)
Care for the caregiver (supportive counseling, respite care, training, support groups)
Childcare (daycare, babysitters, child custody/permanency planning)
Community involvement (speaker's bureaus, volunteer activities, AIDS organizations, participation on advisory boards)
Educational/vocational services (school reentry, tutoring, GED, job readiness)
Financial assistance (Medicaid, food vouchers, rent, transportation)
Food/nutrition (home food delivery, dietary counseling, special diets, TPN, supplements)
Hospital alternatives (hospice, visiting nurse, infusion treatment)
Housing (shelter; transitional, independent, and group living)
Legal services (discrimination, emancipation, power of attorney, wills, living wills)
Mental health (crisis intervention, individual or group therapy, bereavement, psychotropic medication)
Outreach (information dissemination, condom and needle distribution)
Prevention/education (peer education/support groups, relapse prevention, ongoing risk reduction, partner notification)
Recreation (activities, exercise, retreats, supportive environments for lesbian/gay youth)
Spiritual needs (organized religion, spirituality, meditation)
Substance abuse treatment (detox, methadone maintenance, clean and sober clubs, NA and AA, residential programs for dually and triply diagnosed)
Support networks (HIV+ youth groups, peer support, parents, and partners)
Transportation (bus tokens, taxi vouchers, handicapped access, transportation programs)

From Shalwitz J: Psychosocial care. In Futterman D, Shalwitz J, Hunter J: Protocol for medical care of HIV+ youth. Conference on the Primary Care Needs of Lesbian and Gay Adolescents, Health Resources and Services Administration, Washington, DC, December 5–6, 1994.

ning for adolescents who are parents. Introducing the topic by talking about a living will or health-care proxy is a practical way to help youth organize their thoughts and deal with these difficult issues. A health-care proxy is a signed document, included in the medical record, that allows the adolescent to designate an adult to make treatment decisions should the youth become unable or unwilling to do so. A living will specifies the level of medical intervention that a person desires as his or her health condition deteriorates, ranging from no intervention other than nutrition and hydration to full life support.

Although the overall needs of lesbian and gay adolescents with HIV are no different from the needs of adolescents in general, the prevalence of HIV/AIDS within the gay community intensifies many of their feelings and experiences. AIDS bereavement is a routine occurrence in the lives of all lesbians and gay men; loss of peers is common in all age groups from their 20s through 50s. Lesbian and gay adolescents who have access to the broader gay community through service organizations and the media are socialized into a culture in which chronic illness and premature death have become the norm. The impact on their psyches and emerging identity is significant. Many feel that they cannot avoid infection and do not bother to protect themselves. Increasing visibility as a result of the AIDS epidemic has led to a rise in gay bashing and anti-gay sentiment, which reinforce negative self-perceptions and the need to hide. Access to sensitive providers who understand the additional stressors that increase vulnerability for lesbian and gay youth is essential to increase proactive prevention efforts to reduce risk for HIV infection.

References

1. Carpenter C, Fischl M, Hammer S, et al for the International AIDS Society USA: Consensus statement: Antiretroviral therapy for HIV Infection in 1996. JAMA 276:146–154, 1996.
2. Centers for Disease Control: Supplement to the HIV/AIDS Surveillance Project. Unpublished data, March 1994.
3. Deeks S, Smith M, Holodny M, Kahn J: HIV-1 Protease inhibitors: A review for clinicians. JAMA 277:145–153, 1997.
4. El-Sadr W, Oleske J, Agins B, et al: Evaluation and Management of Early HIV Infection. AHCPR Publication no. 94-0572. Rockville, MD, U.S. Department of Health and Human Services, January 1994.
5. Futterman D, Hein K: Medical management of adolescents. In Pizzo P, Wilfert C (eds): Pediatric AIDS: The Challenge of HIV Infection in Infants, Children and Adolescents, 2nd ed. Baltimore, Williams & Wilkins, 1994.
6. Futterman D, Hein K, Reuben N, et al: Human immunodeficiency virus-infected adolescents: The first 50 patients in a New York City program. Pediatrics 91:730, 1993.
7. Futterman D, Rogers A, Abdalian S, et al: Higher CD4 counts in HIV-infected female than male youth in care in the U.S. Presented at the Eleventh International Conference on AIDS, Vancouver, July 1996.
8. Futterman D, Shalwitz J, Hunter J: Protocol for medical care of HIV+ youth. Conference on the Primary Care Needs of Lesbian and Gay Adolescents, Washington, DC, December 5–6, 1994.
9. Grubman S: Older children and adolescents living with perinatally acquired human immunodeficiency virus infection. Pediatrics 95:657, 1995.
10. Health Resources and Services Administration: Use of Zidovudine to reduce perinatal HIV transmission in HRSA-funded programs. Rockville, MD, U.S. Department of Health and Human Services, December 1995.
11. Ho D: Time to hit HIV, early and hard. N Engl J Med 333:450, 1995.
12. Kaplan J, Masur H, Holmes K for the USPHS Prevention of Opportunistic Infections Working Group: USPHS/IDSA Guidelines for the prevention of opportunistic infections in persons infected with HIV. Clin Infect Dis 21(Suppl):S1, 1995.
13. Kunins H, Hein K, Futterman D, et al: Guide to adolescent HIV/AIDS program development. J Adolesc Health 14:1S, 1993.

14. Mellors J, Rinaldo C, Gupta P: Prognosis in HIV-1 infection predicted by the quantity of virus in plasma. Science 272:1167, 1996.
15. Perry S, Jacobsberg L, Fishman B: Suicidal ideation and HIV testing. JAMA 263:679, 1990.
16. Rodgers AS, Futterman D, Levin L, D'Angelo L: A profile of human immunodeficiency virus-infected adolescents receiving health care services at selected sites in the United States. J Adolesc Health 19:401, 1996.
17. Saag M, Holodny M, Kuritzkes D, et al: HIV viral load markers in clinical practice. Nature Med 2: 625, 1996.
18. Shalwitz J: Psychosocial care. In Futterman D, Shalwitz J, Hunter J: Protocol for medical care of HIV+ youth. Conference on the Primary Care Needs of Lesbian and Gay Adolescents, Health Resources and Services Administration, Washington, DC, December 5–6, 1994.

Conclusion

So many of the health and mental health concerns of lesbian and gay youth are associated with how they are perceived in the social environment. And stigma has a powerful impact on self-perception, behavior, and health outcomes. However, the experiences of lesbian and gay youth *can* be mediated and enhanced by sensitive, informed, and nonjudgmental providers. Moreover, appropriate care for lesbian and gay adolescents does not require special skills or extensive training. Rather, awareness that all youth are not heterosexual, sensitivity in conducting routine interviews, and understanding the stressors that affect lesbian and gay youth will enable providers to assess and address their needs. In fact, quality care for lesbian and gay youth is quality care for *all* youth. Routine screening recommended in this book, including asking adolescents about their sexual orientation, is also recommended as part of routine preventive assessment by the American Medical Association's Guidelines for Adolescent Preventive Services.

Providing comprehensive health and mental health guidelines for lesbian and gay youth is an essential step in ensuring quality care for an underserved and medically neglected population, but it is only part of an overall service delivery, research, and policy effort. Unless these guidelines get into the hands of providers who work with families and youth, and unless they are consistently applied, the kinds of inappropriate and insensitive care reported by many lesbian and gay youth and described repeatedly in studies of adolescents and adults will be perpetuated and the preventive and life-affirming interventions that could make a profound difference in the lives of these youth will continue to be denied.

Future Directions

Although researchers and scholars have traveled light years during the past two decades in exploring sexual identity, risk behavior, and the emotional and social effects of stigma, in many ways this work has just begun. Much of what we know today is based on cross-sectional studies (studies done at one point in time with different age groups), and we know little about the evolution of identity over time. Longitudinal studies (over time) are needed to answer many questions about adolescent and adult development.

The following represent key areas for further research in understanding the needs and experiences of lesbian, gay, bisexual, and transgendered youth:

- Longitudinal studies on the development and evolution of sexual identity and life course outcomes, including bisexual and transgendered identity and identity in ethnic and racial minority youth.
- Longitudinal studies to understand the impact of stigma, ethnicity, and sexual identity among ethnic and racial minority youth.
- Studies of coping behaviors and adjustment in non-heterosexual youth who "come out" at various stages of adolescence and the role of families and institutions in their identity development.
- Comparative studies of mental health and psychosocial adjustment among lesbian, gay, and heterosexual youth, including suicide risk and prevention and HIV prevention.

- Studies of the rate and impact of violence and harassment among lesbian, gay, bisexual, and transgendered youth.
- Help-seeking behaviors for health and mental health care in lesbian, gay, bisexual, and transgendered youth, and, in particular, accessing HIV-related care.

In addition to research on the needs of lesbian, gay, bisexual, and transgendered youth and the inclusion of questions on sexual orientation in mainstream studies of adolescents and adults, government, schools, public agencies, and youth-serving organizations must acknowledge the presence of these youth in their client populations. What is still urgently needed is training for practitioners, teachers, and staff to dispel myths and misconceptions and sensitize them to the level of harassment and abuse routinely experienced by non-heterosexual youth, together with policies to protect youth from harassment and abuse and to facilitate access to care.

Much is made on the eve of a new century of the challenges of change and diversity facing our society. Although lesbians and gay men have increasingly gained in visibility and public acceptance during the latter part of the twentieth century, the next frontier entails shattering myths about sexuality, including the capacity of adolescents to form a non-heterosexual identity. During the past century, the concept of sexual identity has evolved and with it a diverse and vibrant community that enriches the broader society in new and creative ways. For the most part, however, that community has existed as a parallel world--separate and apart from mainstream culture. Until now.

As Gil Herdt and Andy Boxer and the lesbian and gay youth of Horizons so clearly demonstrated in a pioneering study conducted in 1987,[1] lesbian and gay youth are evolving a new concept of identity while leading a new way out of the closet. When they are free to come out and integrate their lives, they leave behind the costs of compartmentalized and hidden lives experienced by earlier generations of lesbians and gay men. There is no doubt that lesbian and gay youth are coming out at younger ages and are in need of appropriate care and support. What remains to be seen is if they will receive it.

In leading a new way out of the closet, lesbian and gay youth are also the community of tomorrow. It seems appropriate to close as we began with the voices of youth, hopeful and proud:

> We are the community of tomorrow. How we are treated now, our experiences now, who we are able to become will affect the world of tomorrow. Even though we're young and gay, we're people just like you.
>
> Chris, age 17

Reference

1. Herdt G, Boxer A. Children of Horizons, 2nd ed. Boston, Beacon Press, 1996.

Appendix A

Steering Committee
HRSA Conference on the Primary Care Needs
of Lesbian and Gay Adolescents
December 5–6, 1994

Conference Co-Chairs

Donna Futterman, MD
Director
Adolescent AIDS Program
Montefiore Medical Center
Bronx, NY

Joan Holloway
Director
Division of Programs for Special Populations
Bureau of Primary Care, HRSA
Bethesda, MD

Co-Chairs, Primary Care Task Group

Neal Hoffman, MD
Medical Director
Adolescent AIDS Program
Montefiore Medical Center
Bronx, NY

David Ocepek, MD
Medical Director
Mariposa Community Health Center
Nogales, AZ

Co-Chairs, Mental Health & Substance Abuse Task Group

Andrew M. Boxer, PhD
Director, Evelyn Hooker Center for
Gay and Lesbian Mental Health
University of Chicago, Department
of Psychiatry
Chicago, IL

Joan Haas, LCSW
Director of Social Work
Chicago Lakeshore Hospital
Chicago, IL

Co-Chairs, HIV/AIDS Task Group

Joyce Hunter, DSW
Director, Community Liaison
Program
HIV Center for Clinical/Behavioral
Studies
New York State Psychiatric Institute
New York, NY

Donna Futterman, MD
Director
Adolescent AIDS Program
Montefiore Medical Center
Bronx, NY

Janet Shalwitz, MD
Medical Director
Maternal, Child & Adolescent
Health
SF Department of Public Health
San Francisco, CA

Co-Chairs, Linkages Task Group

Frances Kunreuther
Executive Director
Hetrick-Martin Institute
New York, NY

Darrel LeMar
Family Support Specialist
Massachusetts Department of Social Services
Boston, MA

Steering Committee Member

Gary Remafedi, MD, MPH
Director
Youth and AIDS Project
Minneapolis, MN

HRSA Liaison

Maria Lago, MSW
Division of Special Populations
Bureau of Primary Health Care, HRSA

Conference Coordinators

Caitlin C. Ryan, MSW, ACSW
Washington, DC

Katherine Perkins, MPA
Kennebunk, ME

Appendix B

Resources for Primary Care Needs of Lesbian and Gay Adolescents

Youth-serving agencies for lesbian and gay adolescents are available throughout the United States. Fc referral information, call agencies listed below or contact The National Youth Advocacy Coalition, Bridge Project, at 202-319-7596 for access to a comprehensive national data base of youth services and infor mation. The following agencies provide a range of services for lesbian and gay adolescents.

Service and Resource Agencies

Adolescent AIDS Program
Montefiore Medical Center
111 E. 210th Street
Bronx, NY 10467
Contacts: Donna Futterman, MD
Neal Hoffman, MD
Telephone: 718-882-0023; Fax: 718-882-0432

Sidney Borum, Jr. Health Center
130 Boylston Street
Boston, MA 02116
Telephone: 617-457-8140; Fax: 617-457-8141

Health Initiatives for Youth, Inc.
1242 Market Street
San Francisco, CA 94102
Telephone: 415-487-5777; Fax: 415-487-5771

Hetrick-Martin Institute
2 Astor Place
New York, NY 10003
Telephone: 212-674-2400; TTY 212-674-8695
E-mail: hmi@hmi.org

HIV Center for Clinical & Behavioral Studies
New York State Psychiatric Institute
722 West 168th Street, Unit 29
New York, NY 10032
Contact: Joyce Hunter, PhD
Telephone: 212-740-7291; Fax: 212-795-4222

Horizons Community Services
Youth Services & Anti-Violence Program
961 West Montana Street
Chicago, IL 60614-2408
Telephone: 773-472-6469; TDD: 773-472-1277
Anti-Violence 24-Hour Crisis Line: 773-871-2273

Youth and AIDS Project
University of Minnesota
Adolescent Health Project
428 Oak Grove Street
Minneapolis, MN 55403
Contact: Gary Remafedi, MD, MPH
Telephone: 612-627-6820; Fax: 612-627-6819
E-mail: yap@tc.umn.edu

Family Information/Support

Parents, Families and Friends of Lesbians and
Gays (PFLAG)
1726 M Street, NW, Suite 400
Washington, DC 20036
Telephone: 202-638-4200; Fax: 202-467-8194
E-mail: info@pflag.org
(Contact National Office for information on state
and local chapters)
http://www.pflag.org

Advocacy

AIDS Alliance for Children, Youth and Families
1600 K Street, NW
Washington, DC 20006
Contact: David Harvey, MSW
Telephone: 202-785-3564; Fax: 202-785-3579
E-mail: info@aids-alliance.org

Lambda Legal Defense and Education Fund
120 Wall Street, Suite 1500
New York, NY 10005-3904
Contact: David Buckel
Telephone: 212-809-8585; Fax 212-809-0055
E-mail: lambda@lambdalegal.org

National Youth Advocacy Coalition
1638 R Street, NW, Suite 300
Washington, DC 20009
Telephone: 202-319-7596; Fax: 202-319-7365
E-mail: nyac@nyac.org
http://www.nyacyouth.org

Youth Project
National Center for Lesbian Rights
870 Market Street, Suite 570
San Francisco, CA 94102
Contact: Shannon Minter
Telephone: 415-392-6257; Fax:415-392-8442
E-mail: info@nclrights.org

Resources for Information on HIV/AIDS

National Pediatric & Family HIV Resource Center
University of Medicine & Dentistry of New Jersey
30 Bergen Street—ADMC #4
Newark, NJ 07107
Telephone: 1-800-362-0071
http://www.pedhivaids.org

Professional Associations:

American Academy of Pediatrics
Adolescent Section
141 Northwest Point Boulevard
P.O. Box 927
Elk Grove Village, IL 60009
Telephone: 1-800-433-9016

American Counseling Association
Association for Gay, Lesbian, and Bisexual Issues
  in Counseling)
5999 Stevenson Avenue
Alexandria, VA 22304
Contact: Carol Neiman
Telephone: 1-800-347-6657, ext. 288

American Psychological Association
750 First Street, NE
Washington, DC 20002-4242
Contact: Clinton Anderson
Telephone: 202-336-6037

American Psychiatric Association
Committee on Lesbian, Gay and Bisexual
  Concerns
1400 K Street, NW
Washington, DC 20005
Contact: Janice Taylor
Telephone: 202-682-6097

American Medical Association
Section on Adolescent Health
515 North State Street
Chicago, IL 60610
Telephone: 312-464-5530

Gay and Lesbian Medical Association
459 Fulton Street, Suite 107
San Francisco, CA 94102
Contact: Maureen O'Leary
Telephone: 415-255-4547; Fax: 415-255-4784
E-mail: Gaylesmed@aol.com
http: www.glma.org

Training Resources

Gay and Lesbian Adolescent Health Resource
  Center
Telephone: 718-882-0322
http://www.adolaids.org

Online Youth Resources

Advocates for Youth—GLBT Youth Resource
  Web site
http://www.youthresource.com/
Telephone: 202-347-5700
Information on health and mental health concerns,
  access to support and information

Youth Guardian Services
http://www.youth-guard.org
Telephone: 703-734-7498
Access to supervised electronic lists for youth,
  ages 13–17, 17–21, and 21–25, for information
  and support

Gay, Lesbian and Straight Education Network
  (GLSEN)
122 West 26th Street, Suite 1100
New York, NY 10001
Contact: Kevin Jennings
Telephone: 212-727-0135; Fax: 212-727-0254
E-mail: glsen@glsen.org
http://www.glstn.org/respect

National Association of Lesbian and Gay
  Addiction Professionals
c/o NAADAC
1911 Fort Meyer Drive, Suite 900
Arlington, VA 22209
Telephone: 703-741-7686; Fax: 703-741-7698

National Association of Social Workers
National Committee on Lesbian, Gay and Bisexual
  Issues
750 First Street, NE, Suite 700
Washington, DC 20002-4241
Contact: Luisa Lopez
Telephone: 202-408-8600, ext. 287

National Education Association
1201 16th Street, NW
Washington, DC 20036
Contact: Ron Houston
Telephone: 202-822-7710

Society for Adolescent Medicine
Gay and Lesbian Special Interest Group
1916 N.W. Copper Oaks Circle
Blue Springs, MO 64015
Telephone: 816-224-8010

Appendix C

Resources for Parents and Youth

National Youth Advocacy Coalition
1638 R Street, NW, Suite 300
Washington, DC, 20009
Telephone: 202-319-7596
Fax: 202-319-7365
E-mail: nyac@nyacyouth.org
http://www.nyacyouth.org
(Referral information for youth-serving agencies, services and support groups)

Parents, Families and Friends of Lesbians and Gays (PFLAG)
1726 M Street, NW, Suite 400
Washington, DC 20036
Telephone: 202-638-4200
Fax: 202-467-8194
E-mail: info@pflag.org
(Contact National Office for information on state and local chapters)
http://www.pflag.org

Bibliography

Bernstein RA:. Straight Parents, Gay Children: Keeping Families Together. New York, Thunder Mouth Press, 1995.
Borhek MV: Coming Out to Parents: A Two-Way Survival Guide for Lesbians and Gay Men and Their Parents. Cleveland, OH, Pilgrim Press, 1993.
Bridges of Respect: Creating Support for Lesbian and Gay Youth. A Resource Guide from the American Friends Service Committee. Philadelphia, PA, American Friends Service Committee, 1989.
Brimmer LD: Being Different: Lambda Youth Speak Out. New York, NY, Franklin Watts/Grolier Publishing, 1995.
Cantwell A: Homosexuality: The Secret a Child Dare Not Tell. Rafael Press, 1996.
Dew RF: The Family Heart: A Memoir of When Our Son Came Out. Reading, MA, Addison-Wesley, 1994.
Due LA: Joining the Tribe: Growing Up Gay and Lesbian in the '90s. New York, NY, Anchor Books, 1995.
Fairchild B, Hayward N: Now That You Know: What Every Parent Should Know about Homosexuality. New York, NY, Harcourt Brace Jovanovich, 1989.
Fricke A: Reflections of a Rock Lobster: A Story of Growing Up Gay. Boston, MA, Aly Cat Books, 1981.
Griffin CW, Wirth MJ, Wirth AG: Beyond Acceptance: Parents of Lesbians and Gays Talk About Their Experiences. Englewood Cliffs, NJ, Prentice-Hall, 1986.
Griffin M, Aarons L: Prayers for Bobby: A Mother Comes to Terms with the Suicide of Her Gay Son. San Francisco, CA, Harper, 1995.
Griffin P: Homophobia in sport: Addressing the needs of lesbian and gay high school athletes. The High School Journal Oct./Nov. 1993–Dec./Jan. 1994:81–87.
Herdt G, Koff B: Something to Tell You: The Road Families Travel When a Child Is Gay. New York, Columbia University Press, 2000.
Heron A (ed): One Teenager in 10: Writings by Gay and Lesbian Youth. Boston, MA, Alyson, 1983.
Heron A (ed): Two Teenagers in 10: Writings by Gay and Lesbian Youth. Boston, MA, Alyson, 1994.
Jennings K (ed): Becoming Visible: A Reader in Gay and Lesbian History for High School and College Students. Boston, MA, Alyson, 1994.
Lambda Legal Defense and Education Fund: Stopping Anti-Gay Abuse of Students in Public Schools: A Legal Perspective. New York, Lambda Legal Defense and Education Fund, 1996.
Muller A: Parents Matter. New York, NY, Naiad Press, 1987.
Rafkin L (ed): Different Daughters: A Book by Mothers of Lesbians. San Francisco, CA, Cleis Press, 1987.
Remafedi G: Death by Denial: Studies of Suicide in Gay and Lesbian Teenagers. Boston, MA, Alyson, 1994.
Rench J: Understanding Sexual Identity: A Book for Gay and Lesbian Teens. Minneapolis, MN, Lerner Publications, 1990.
Singer B (ed): Growing Up Gay: A Literary Anthology. New York, Free Press, 1993.

Appendix D

Recommended Reading for Providers
Primary Care Needs of Lesbian and Gay Adolescents

Primary Care

Abdalian SE, Remafedi G: Sexually transmitted diseases in young homosexual men. Semin Pediatr Infect Dis 4:122–130, 1993.

American Academy of Pediatrics, Committee on Adolescence: Homosexuality and adolescence. Pediatrics 92:631–634, 1993.

Bidwell RJ: Sexual orientation and gender identity. In Friedman SB, Fisher M, Schonberg SK (eds): Comprehensive Adolescent Health Care. St. Louis, MO, Quality Medical Publishing, 1992, pp 715–724.

Cabaj RP: AIDS and chemical dependency: Special issues and treatment barriers for gay and bisexual men. J Psychoact Drugs 21(4):387–393, 1989.

Cates W Jr: Teenagers and sexual risk taking: The best of times and the worst of times. J Adolesc Health 12:84–94, 1991.

Centers for Disease Control: STD Treatment Guidelines. Washington, DC. U.S. Department of Health and Human Services, 1993.

Cheng TL, Savageau JA, Sattler AL, DeWitt TG: Confidentiality in health care: A survey of knowledge, perceptions, and attitudes among high school students. JAMA 269:1404–1407, 1993.

Council on Scientific Affairs, American Medical Association: Confidential health services for adolescents. JAMA 269:1420–1424, 1993.

Coupey SM, Klerman LV (eds): AMA Guidelines for Adolescent Preventive Services (GAPS): Recommendations and Rationale. Baltimore, MD, Williams & Wilkins, 1994.

English A: Treating adolescents: Legal and ethical considerations. Med Clin North Am 74(5):1097–1112, 1990.

Friedman SB, Fisher M, Schonberg SK (eds): Comprehensive Adolescent Health Care. St. Louis, MO, Quality Medical Publishing, 1992.

Futterman D, Casper V: Homosexuality: Challenges of treating lesbian and gay adolescents. In Hoekelman (ed): Primary Pediatric Care, 2nd ed. St. Louis, MO, Mosby, 1992, pp 777–780.

Hoffman ND, Hein K: Sexually transmitted diseases. In Tonkin R (ed): Current Issues of the Adolescent Patient, vol. 2. London, Bailliere Tindall, 1994, pp 302–330.

Ingra V, Millstein SG: Current status and approaches to improving preventive services for adolescents. JAMA 269:1408–1412, 1993.

Klein JD, Slap GB, Elster AB, Schonberg SK: Access to health care for adolescents: A position paper of the Society for Adolescent Medicine. J Adolesc Health 13:162–170, 1992.

MacKenzie RG, Kipke MD: Substance use and abuse. In Friedman SB, Fisher M, Schonberg SK (eds): Comprehensive Adolescent Health Care. St. Louis, MO, Quality Medical Publishing, 1992, pp 765–786.

McAnarney ER, Kreipe RE, Orr DP, Comerci GD (eds): Textbook of Adolescent Medicine. Philadelphia, PA, W.B. Saunders, 1992.

Paroski PA: Health care delivery and the concerns of gay and lesbian adolescents. J Adolesc Health Care 8:188–192, 1987.

Remafedi G: Fundamental issues in the care of homosexual youth. Med Clin North Am 74:1169–1179, 1990.

Remafedi G, Resnick M, Blum R, Harris L: Demography of sexual orientation in adolescents. Pediatrics 89:714–721, 1992.

Strasburger VC, Greydanus DE: The at-risk adolescent. Adolesc Med State Art Rev 1:1, 1990.

Sturdevant MD, Remafedi G: Special health needs of homosexual youth. Adolesc Med State Art Rev 3: 359–371, 1992.

Thurman PJ, Swaim R, Plested B: Intervention and treatment of ethnic minority substance abusers. In Aponte JF, Rivers YR, Wohl J (eds): Psychological Interventions and Cultural Diversity. Needham Heights, MA, Allyn and Bacon, 1995, pp 215–233.

White J, Levinson W: Primary care of lesbian patients. J Gen Intern Med 8:41–47, 1993.

150 Appendix D

HIV/AIDS

Chabon B, Futterman D: HIV infection in adolescents: prevention and treatment. Int Pediatr 10(4):311-320, 1995.

Cohen P, Sande M, Volberding P (eds): The AIDS Knowledge Base, 2nd ed. Boston, MA, Little, Brown, 1994.

El-Sadr W, Oleske J: Evaluation and management of early HIV infection. Clinical Practice Guideline No 7. Rockville MD, Agency for Health Care Policy and Research, U.S. Department of Health and Health Services, 1994.

English A: Expanding access to HIV Services for adolescents: Legal and ethical issues. In Clemente R. (ed): Adolescents and AIDS: A Generation in Jeopardy. Newbury Park, CA, Sage, 1992, pp 531-560.

Futterman D, Hein K: Medical care of HIV infected adolescents. AIDS Clin Care 4:95-98, 1992.

Futterman D, Hein K: Medical management of adolescents. In Pizzo P, Wilfert C (eds): Pediatric AIDS The Challenge of HIV Infection in Infants, Children and Adolescents, 2nd ed. Baltimore, MD, Williams & Wilkins, 1994, pp 757-772.

Hoffman ND, Futterman D: Human immunodeficiency virus infection in adolescents. Semin Pediatr Infect Dis 4(2):113-121, 1993.

Hunter J, Schaecher R: AIDS prevention for lesbian, gay and bisexual adolescents. Fam Soc J Contemp Human Serv 75:345-354, 1994.

Kelly P, Holman S, Rothenberg R, Holzemer S: Primary Care of Women and Children with HIV Infection. Boston, MA, Jones and Bartlett, 1995.

Kunins H, Hein K, Futterman D, et al: A Guide to Adolescent HIV/AIDS Program Development. J Adolesc Health July (Suppl):1-168, 1993.

Libman H, Witzburg R (eds): HIV Infection: A Clinical Manual, 2nd ed. Boston, MA, Little, Brown, 1993.

Mann J, Tarantola D, Netter T (eds): A Global Report: AIDS in the World. Cambridge, MA, Harvard University Press, 1992.

Merle S, Volberding P (eds): The Medical Management of AIDS, 3rd ed. Philadelphia, PA, W.B. Saunders, 1992.

Pizzo P, Wilfert C (eds): Pediatric AIDS: The Challenge of HIV Infection in Infants, Children and Adolescents, 2nd ed. Baltimore, MD, Williams & Wilkins, 1994.

Rotheram-Borus MJ, Hunter J, Rosario M: Coming out as lesbian or gay in the era of AIDS. In Herek G, Greene B (eds): AIDS, Identity and Community: The HIV Epidemic and Gay Men. Thousand Oaks, CA, Sage, 1995, pp 150-168.

Savin-Williams R, Lenhart R: AIDS prevention among gay and lesbian youth: Psychosocial stress and health care intervention guidelines. In Ostrow D (ed): Behavioral Aspects of AIDS. New York, Plenum, 1990, pp 77-99.

Mental Health

Boxer AM, Cohler B, Herdt G, Irvin F: Gay and lesbian youth. In Cohler B, Tolan P (eds): Handbook of the Clinical Psychology of Adolescence. New York, John Wiley & Sons, 1991.

Boxer AM, Cook J, Herdt G: Double jeopardy: Identity transitions and parent-child relations among gay and lesbian youth. In Pillemar K, McCartney K (eds): Parent-child Relations Throughout Life. Hillsdale, NJ, Lawrence Erlbaum, 1991, pp 59-92.

Cabaj RP, Stein TS (eds): Textbook of Homosexuality and Mental Health. Washington, DC, American Psychiatric Press, 1996.

Chan CS: Issues of identity development among Asian-American lesbians and gay men. J Counsel Dev 68:16-20, 1989.

Coleman E: Integrated Identity for Gays and Lesbians: Psychotherapeutic Approaches for Emotional Well-being. New York, Harrington Park Press, 1988.

D'Augelli A, Patterson C (eds): Lesbian, Gay and Bisexual Identities over the Lifespan. New York, Oxford University Press, 1994.

Espin OM: Issues of identity in the psychology of latina lesbians. In Boston Lesbian Psychology Collective (eds): Lesbian Psychologies: Explorations and Challenges. Urbana, IL, University of Illinois Press, 1987.

Garnets L, Herek GM, Levy B: Violence and victimization of lesbians and gay men: Mental health consequences. In Herek G, Berrill K (eds): Hate Crimes: Confronting Violence against Lesbians and Gay Men. Newbury Park, CA, Sage, 1992, pp 227-240.

Gonsiorek JC: Mental health issues of gay and lesbian adolescents. J Adolesc Health Care 9:114-122, 1988.

Greene B: Ethnic minority lesbians and gay men: Mental health treatment issues. J Consult Clin Psychol 62(2):243-251, 1994.

Greene B (ed): Ethnic and Cultural Diversity Among Lesbians and Gay Men. Thousand Oaks, CA, Sage, 1997.

Herdt G, Boxer AM: Children of Horizons: How Gay and Lesbian Youth Are Leading a New Way out of the Closet. Boston, MA, Beacon Press, 1993.

Hershberger SL, D'augelli AR: The impact of victimization on the mental health and suicidality of lesbian, gay and bisexual youths. Dev Psychol 31:64–74, 1995.

Hetrick E, Martin AD: Developmental issues and their resolution for gay and lesbian adolescents. J Homosex 13(4):25–43, 1987.

Hunter J: Violence against lesbian and gay male youth. J Interpers Violence 5(3):295–300, 1990.

Lambda Legal Defense and Education Fund: Stopping Anti-Gay Abuse of Students in Public Schools: A Legal Perspective. New York, Lambda Legal Defense and Education Fund, 1996.

Mallon GP: Gay and no place to go: Assessing the needs of gay and lesbian adolescents in out-of-home care settings. Child Welfare 71:547–556, 1992.

Martin AD, Hetrick ES: The stigmatization of gay and lesbian adolescents. J Homosex 15(1–20):170–175, 1988.

Morales ES: Ethnic minority families and minority gays and lesbians. In Bozett FW, Sussman MB (eds): Homosexuality and Family Relations. Binghamton, NY, Harrington Park Press, 1990, pp 217–239.

Remafedi G: Adolescent homosexuality: Psychosocial implications. Pediatrics 79:326–330, 1987.

Remafedi G, Farro J, Deisher R: Risk factors for attempted suicides in gay and bisexual youth. Pediatrics 87:869–876, 1991.

Savin-Williams RC: Gay and Lesbian Youth: Expressions of Identity. New York, Hemisphere Publishing, 1990.

Savin-Williams RC: Lesbian and gay adolescence. In D'Augelli A, Patterson C (eds): Lesbian, Gay and Bisexual Identities over the Lifespan. New York, Oxford University Press, 1994.

Sears J: Growing Up Gay in the South: Race, Gender, and the Journey of the Spirit. New York, Haworth Press, 1990.

Schneider M: Often Invisible: Counseling Gay and Lesbian Youth. Toronto, Toronto Central Youth Services, 1988.

Silverstein C: Gays, Lesbians, and their Therapists. New York, NY, W.W. Norton, 1991.

Stein TS, Cohen CJ: Contemporary Perspectives on Psychotherapy with Lesbians and Gay Men. New York, NY, Plenum Press, 1986.

Tremble B, Schneider M, Appathurai C: Growing up gay or lesbian in a multicultural context. J Homosex 17(1/2):253–267, 1989.

Wertheimer D: Treatment and service interventions for lesbian and gay male crime victims. In Herek G, Berrill K (eds): Hate Crimes: Confronting Violence Against Lesbians and Gay Men. Newbury Park, CA, Sage, 1992.

Appendix E

Adolescent HIV Counseling and Testing Protocol*

PRE-TEST COUNSELING

I. Introduction
   A. Review previous test history, if any.
   B. Clearly inform youth they will continue to receive ongoing care, whether or not they choose to be tested.
   C. Help youth to identify a supportive adult to be involved in the testing process and to provide ongoing assistance and support.

II. HIV/AIDS Knowledge
   A. Routes of transmission
   B. Affect of HIV on the immune system

III. Risk Assessment
   A. Sexual risk assessment
   B. Drug use assessment
   C. Blood products
   D. Maternal transmission

IV. Risk Reduction Education
   A. Decision making and readiness for sexual experience
   B. Safer sex
      1. Condom demonstration
      2 Dental dam
      3. Female condom
   C. Safer needle use
   D. Sex and drugs

V. Testing Issues
   A. Types of testing
      1. Anonymous
      2. Confidential
   B. Meaning of HIV test results
      1. Positive
      2. Negative
      3. Indeterminate
   C. Pros and cons of HIV testing
   D. Obtaining consent

VI. Issues for Followup and Referral
   A. Managing results
      1. Coping strategies
      2. Partner notification
   B. Medical
   C. Psychosocial
   D. School-related
   E. Other

* Adapted from Brenda Chabon, PhD, Donna Futterman, MD, Colleen Jones, FNP: Adolescent HIV Counseling and Testing Protocol, Adolescent AIDS Program, Montefiore Medical Center, 1995.

This protocol is intended for use by providers in primary care settings who have ongoing relationships with adolescents and their families. Some of the assessment information requested here may already have been obtained during routine provision of care. If a provider has already conducted a thorough risk assessment for HIV with an adolescent, the protocol should be adapted accordingly.

Pre-Test Counseling Session

I. Introduction

1. Begin session and review reasons for testing.

Allow the adolescent to verbalize his or her understanding of HIV and why he or she seeks testing, or explain why you have recommended testing. Encourage the youth to express feelings about being tested. Assure the youth that care will not be adversely affected should he or she decide not to be tested. Testing should not be coercive. When medical indications call for immediate testing, the provider should explain the need for testing, help the adolescent to deal with potential resistance, and follow the protocol for counseling and obtaining informed consent.

Help to identify a supportive adult (parent, counselor) who can be involved in the testing process.

2. Do you know anyone who is HIV+ or has AIDS? (ask youth to identify all that apply)
   a. ____ Parent
   b. ____ Friend
   c. ____ Sexual partner
   d. ____ Relative
   e. ____ Drug using partner
   f. ____ Other _____

3. Review testing history: Have you ever been tested for HIV before?

This is particularly relevant for new clients; however, some adolescents may have been tested before without telling anyone. Asking about previous HIV-testing experiences helps to assess counseling and support needs.

4. Why?_____

5. How many times?___ ___

6. Where?_____

7. When? ___ ___/___ ___   ___ ___/___ ___   ___ ___/___ ___

8. Did you go back for the results?
   ____ Yes
   ____ No (Why not?)

9. If yes, what were the results?
   a. Positive
   b. Negative
   c. Don't Know

II. HIV Knowledge

A. Routes of transmission

Ask the adolescent to identify routes of transmission for HIV. Fill in knowledge gaps, clarify misconceptions, and add risk behaviors not mentioned.

10. Can you tell me how people get infected with HIV?

Ask questions to evaluate adolescent's level of understanding for each mode of transmission:

   a. ____ Sexual transmission
   b. ──── Needle sharing/body piercing
   c. ____ Blood product transfusion before 1985
   d. ____ Maternal/child transmission
   e. ____ Tattooing
   f. ____ Not spread through casual contact

• HIV is present in blood, semen, "pre-cum" (pre-ejaculatory fluid), vaginal fluids, and breast milk.
• HIV is minimally present in saliva but is very dilute, with no known cases of transmission from kissing.
• HIV is not spread through casual contact (e.g., public toilets, touching, sharing cigarettes).
• Medical and mental health care can help to prevent life-threatening infections and help people to cope with having HIV.

B. How HIV Acts on the Immune System

11. What do you know about HIV and AIDS?

Ask the adolescent to describe what happens when someone gets infected with HIV, how the immune system responds, and how HIV affects the immune system. Ask him or her to explain the difference between HIV and AIDS and what he or she knows about the course of disease.

Include the following concepts:

• HIV does not equal AIDS, and not all persons with HIV infection have AIDS.
• Average latency period (HIV progression to symptoms of AIDS) is 10 years.
• HIV suppresses the immune system, leaving the body unable to fight certain diseases.
• Teens with HIV infection can be very healthy for a long time—attend school, get a job, have productive, active lives. Care and medication help teens with HIV live healthier lives.
• Antibodies take a while to develop, generally 3–6 months before the HIV test is able to detect them ("window period"). That is why some people who were recently exposed to HIV may have to be retested.

III. Risk Assessment

A. Sexual Risk Assessment

"I'm going to ask you some personal information to help you to understand how you may be putting yourself at risk for HIV. Some of this may make you feel uncomfortable, but it is important to talk about so that you can learn how to protect yourself."

Providers should be nonjudgmental and open to any information that the adolescent may share, and should not make assumptions about an adolescent's sexual orientation/identity or sexual behaviors.

12. Have you ever been sexually active or had any sexual experiences?
    ___ No
    ___ Yes

13. If yes, how old were you when you first had sex?
    Age: ___

14. Have you ever had?   At what age?
    a. ___ Oral sex   ___
    b. ___ Vaginal sex   ___
    c. ___ Anal sex   ___

15. How old was your first sexual partner?
    Age: ___

16. How many female sexual partners have you ever had?   ___

17. How many female sexual partners have you had in the last 3 months?   ___

18. How many male sexual partners have you ever had?   ___

19. How many male sexual partners have you had in the last 3 months?   ___

20. Do you consider yourself _____?

Providers should be aware of the distinction between "sexual identity" and "sexual behavior." Not all youth who engage in same-sex behavior self-identify as lesbian or gay. Male adolescents may have had anal intercourse but may not perceive themselves as being gay; similarly, lesbian adolescents may have sex with males, including anal intercourse.

    a. ___ Straight
    b. ___ Gay or lesbian
    c. ___ Bisexual
    d. ___ Not sure

21. Have you ever _____?

    a. ___ Traded sex for money, drugs, food, or a place to live
    b. ___ Had sex with someone who you knew was HIV+
    c. ___ Had sex with someone who has injected drugs
    d. ___ Had sex with someone who was the sexual partner of an HIV+ person
    e. ___ Had sex with someone who was the sexual partner of an IDU
    f. ___ Had sex with someone who was gay or bisexual

22. Have you ever been forced to do something sexually that you did not want to do?

Providers should be aware that many teens at risk for HIV were or currently are being sexually abused. Be alert for nonverbal cues because this type of disclosure is difficult to make. If an adolescent is being sexually abused, it must be reported, and the youth should be referred for a mental health assessment.

____ No
____ Yes (age) _____   Describe:_____

23. How often would you say that you are high on drugs or alcohol when you have sex?
   a. ____ Never
   b. ____ Sometimes
   c. ____ Always

24. If yes, which drugs? _____

25. Have you ever been told by a doctor that you had _____?
   a. ____ Syphilis   e. ____ Pelvic inflammatory disease
   b. ____ Gonorrhea   f. ____ Genital or anal warts
   c. ____ Herpes   g. ____ Other STD_____
   d. ____ Chlamydia   h. ____ Not sure

26. Do you do anything to protect yourself against HIV and other sexually transmitted diseases?
   If yes, what

27. How do you avoid pregnancy?

If no birth control is used, ask if there are religious or other reasons. Determine if the adolescent is having difficulty getting her partner to agree to birth control measures. This will be helpful for risk reduction intervention.

   a. ____ Birth control pills   e. ____ Rhythm
   b. ____ Condoms   f. ____ Depo
   c. ____ Diaphragm   g. ____ Other _____
   d. ____ Withdrawal

28. How often do you use condoms when you have sex?

Evaluate if use is consistent or inconsistent and identify obstacles.

   a. ____ Never   c. ____ Usually
   b. ____ Sometimes   d. ____ Always

29. If you do not use a condom each time, why not?
   a. ____ Does not like them
   b. ____ Does not know how
   c. ____ Partner does not like them or refuses
   d. ____ Cannot discuss it with partner
   e. ____ Opposed to birth control
   f. ____ I know my partners, and they do not have any infections
   g. ____ Other_____

B. Drug Use Assessment

Assess level of drug and alcohol use and context in which use occurs. Emphasize the risk of impaired judgement leading to unsafe sex. Review needle hygiene. Assess potential for addiction and treatment needs.

30. What drugs have you used?
   a. ____ Tobacco   f. ____ Heroin
   b. ____ Alcohol   g. ____ LSD/Ecstasy/mescaline
   c. ____ Marijuana   h. ____ Pills_____
   d. ____ Crack   I. ____ Never used drugs
   e. ____ Cocaine

31. Which of the following drugs have you used in the last 3 months?
   a. ____ Tobacco   f. ____ Heroin
   b. ____ Alcohol   g. ____ LSD/Ecstasy/mescaline
   c. ____ Marijuana   h. ____ Pills_____
   d. ____ Crack   I. ____ Never used drugs
   e. ____ Cocaine

156 Appendix E

32. Who do you usually get high with?_____

33. Have you ever used a needle for:
    a. ___ Heroin
    b. ___ Cocaine
    c. ___ Speed
    d. ___ Hormones
    e. ___ Anabolic steroids
    f. ___ Tattoos/body piercing
    g. ___ Other_____

C. Blood Products

34. Have you ever had a blood transfusion?

Explain that the blood supply has been safe since 1985. (If the adolescent has received blood or blood products prior to 1985, testing may be indicated.)

    a. No
    b. Yes (when?) _____

D. Maternal Transmission

Emphasize the following: Approximately 25% of infants born to mothers with HIV will be infected if the mother does not take medication; HIV also can be transmitted through breast milk. Children infected at birth may not be diagnosed until adolescence (several 14- and 15-year-olds have acquired HIV congenitally). Knowledge of parental risk for HIV will help one to assess the adolescent's risk for perinatal transmission.

For pregnant adolescents, review the benefits of HIV testing: (1) opportunity to make decisions about the pregnancy; (2) potential for taking antiretroviral drugs to reduce transmission of HIV to their infants (describe results of ACTG 076, which showed a two-thirds reduction in maternal-infant transmission of HIV); and (3) opportunity to provide appropriate medical care for the newborn.*

IV. Risk Reduction Education

A. Decision Making and Readiness for Sexual Experience

Discuss postponing sex for youth who are not sexually active. Assess motivation for sexual behavior (e.g., experimentation, peer pressure); some youth may need support (and assistance in building communication skills) not to be sexually active. Discuss ways to feel close or have sexual, intimate pleasure without risking exposure to HIV, i.e., "outercourse" (e.g., intimate touching, including petting, and mutual masturbation do not involve the exchange of body fluids).

B. Safer Sex

Providers should explain that sexuality is a normal and positive part of life. Review the continuum of sexual behaviors from safe to unsafe. Explain that risk for HIV is increased when other STDs cause sores or lesions. Discuss techniques for negotiating safer sex with partners; use role play to model potential responses and increase confidence. Determine specific obstacles to sexual risk reduction. Discuss the following barrier methods:

1) Condom Demonstration

- *Condoms must be 100% latex or polyurethane. Do not store them next to your body (e.g., in a wallet). Check expiration date on package before buying them.*
- *Use a water-based spermicide containing nonoxynol-9, both on the inside tip of the condom and on the outside, during anal or vaginal intercourse (use non-lubricated condoms for oral sex).*
- *Do not use oil-based lubricants such as Crisco or Vaseline, which may cause holes in condoms, allowing transmission of HIV.*
- *Penis must be erect; leave room at tip of the condom when rolling it on; hold on to base of condom while withdrawing, using extra care if penis becomes soft.*

2) Dental Dam Usage

- *Used for mouth-to-vagina or mouth-to-anus sexual contact. Can substitute nonmicrowavable saran wrap.*
- *Use only with water-based lubricants such as K-Y Jelly; never use Vaseline.*
- *Place dental dam completely over mouth or anus.*
- *Use a different dental dam with each new partner and/or sexual activity.*
- *Do not use a dental dam more than once.*
- *Do not use it for vaginal or anal intercourse.*
- *Do not puncture it.*

---

* Guidelines for offering the ZDV perinatal regimen to pregnant women are available from HRSA. (Health Resources and Services Administration: Use of Zidovudine to Reduce Perinatal HIV Transmission in HRSA-Funded Programs. Rockville, MD, Department of Health and Human Services, 1995.)

3) Female Condom

- *Female condoms enable women to make the decision to use protection; male partners do not have to be erect or maintain erection to have intercourse. Product name is "Reality."*
- *Condom is inserted in the vagina (or anus); during intercourse, the penis must enter the condom.*
- *A new condom is needed for every sexual encounter. Condoms are not reusable.*

4) Partner Negotiation

Role play scenarios and appropriate responses to help adolescents to learn ways to talk with their partner about practicing safer sex.

C. Safer Needle Use

- *Consider demonstrating how to clean injection equipment. Explain that this is an important skill to reduce their risk for infection.*
- *Discuss availability of needle exchange programs.*
- *Tell youth not to share tattoo or ear-piercing equipment.*
- *Encourage drug treatment and assist in making needed referrals.*

D. Sex and Drugs

Discuss increased risk due to impaired judgement. Help adolescent develop strategies to minimize or eliminate use of alcohol and drugs before and during sex.

V. Testing Issues

A. Types of Testing

1) Anonymous Testing

Explain that anonymous test sites do not use any names or other identifying information; test recipients receive a code number that identifies the blood sample sent to the lab. Information is given only to the person who gives the code number when he or she returns for results. Describe the pros and cons: although this method guarantees anonymity, it also makes it much more difficult to ensure that medical and support services are provided, especially for adolescents who have greater difficulty accessing care. Clearly explain that adolescents who test positive need to receive follow-up care, which will be provided confidentially, not anonymously. (Some adolescents may ask for anonymous testing because they falsely assume that being "anonymous" will prevent others from learning their HIV status.)

2) Confidential Testing

Confidential testing can be offered in the provider's office (or in a counseling and testing site where the sample is identified by name). In most cases, the results are available only to health providers and the person tested. Providers should be familiar with state laws related to HIV counseling and testing and provide accurate information about required or potential disclosure of results to others (e.g., parents or other agencies). Although this option may not ensure anonymity, it does enable adolescents to receive appropriate referrals for care, advocacy, and support services.

B. Meaning of HIV Test Results

1) Positive Test

A positive result means that you are infected with HIV and can infect others; it does not necessarily mean that you have AIDS. Other tests are needed to show how HIV has affected your immune system and whether or not you have AIDS.

2) Negative Test

A negative result means that you are probably not infected, but you can become infected later if you do not protect yourself. Remind adolescent of the "window period" and potential and need for retesting.

3) Indeterminate

Very rarely, test results are indeterminate, which means we are not sure if results are negative or positive. If this happens, the test must be repeated.

C. Pros and Cons of HIV Testing

35. What do you think are some of the benefits of knowing you are HIV positive?

Providers should be sure that the adolescent understands the benefits of early medical intervention, avoidance of reexposure and/or reinfection with HIV, and ability to protect others, including infants from becoming infected. Finding out early allows the adolescent to get used to the idea of having HIV before the disease progresses and to learn skills for taking care of himself or herself.

36. What do you think some of the drawbacks are to finding out that you are HIV+?

Providers should point out that this news is devastating and hard to handle. Assess potential for self-harm and/or harming others. Family may be rejecting; people with HIV are stigmatized and discriminated against.

37. If you are HIV+, what would you do?

Assess for potential suicide risk. Has the youth ever attempted suicide? Does he or she have a plan? A brief role play may be helpful to anticipate reactions to test results and to identify positive coping strategies. This may elicit strong emotional reactions from some youth.

38. Whom would you inform about the positive test result? Who knows that you are being tested? On whom do you rely for support when you have problems?

If providers have not already done so, they should help to identify and to involve a supportive adult in the youth's testing decision.

D. Obtaining Consent

39. Do you feel ready to be tested today?

Determine if the youth is ready to be tested; take into account responses during the counseling session, support systems, current emotional stability, and potential for suicide.

   a. ____ Yes
   b. ____ No   Why?_____
   c. ____ Unsure Why?_____

Use following checklist:

   a. Does the adolescent understand that he or she has a choice about being tested, and that care will not be jeopardized if he or she decides not to be tested?
   b. Does he or she indicate an understanding of the purpose and significance of the test?
   c. Does he or she show an ability to anticipate a possible positive outcome?
   d. Has a supportive person been identified?
   e. Do they seem suicidal or homicidal?

40. Obtain written consent.

If the youth is not ready to be tested, schedule another appointment for further counseling. Be sure that he or she reviews and signs a consent form prior to drawing blood.

E. After Testing

Ask the adolescent if he or she has any questions, and assess need for interim counseling.

VI. Issues for Follow-Up and Referral

1) Strategies for Coping

Discuss how the youth anticipates coping during the waiting period. Explore ways to relieve stress and anxiety in productive ways. Give the youth a phone number to call if he or she becomes anxious or has any questions while waiting for results.

2) Partner Notification

Discuss the implications of indiscriminately telling others about having been tested (e.g., risk of discrimination). Suggest that the youth tell sexual or injection drug-using partners, and encourage partners or friends who are at risk to be tested.

3) Make Appointment for Results

Make an appointment to return for test results. (This usually takes approximately 2 weeks.) Explain that you will give results in person.

4) Follow-up and Referral

Review needs for referral and followup identified during the session and initiate as many as possible.

   a. Medical
   b. Psychosocial
   c. School-related
   d. Other

POST-TEST COUNSELING

Negative

   I. Introduction

  II. HIV Test Results
     A. Meaning of negative HIV test result
     B. Window period/retesting

 III. Risk Reduction Review and Treatment Plan

 IV. Skills Building
     A. Condom demonstration and condom use
     B. Substance abuse
     C. Negotiating with partner

  V. Discrimination and Disclosure

 VI. Referral and Follow-up

Post-Test Counseling—Negative

I. Introduction

Post-test counseling may take one or more sessions. The goal is to help the youth to understand the meaning of his or her results and to reinforce healthy behavioral changes and awareness of risk behaviors. Discuss the objectives of the session, assess affect, and determine if the youth is intoxicated. If so, do not proceed with counseling until the youth is sober; this may require waiting for a period of time or rescheduling the appointment and asking him or her not to use substances before the session.

II. HIV Test Results

"I am going to give you your results, and we will discuss what they mean. Your HIV test came back negative, which means you do not have antibodies to HIV right now. But we need to make sure you stay negative."

Allow time for the youth to respond; show the lab slip to reinforce understanding of results. Ask if the youth is surprised, and what his or her expectation was. Explore reactions (e.g., "survival guilt"—some may feel guilty or disbelieving, particularly if a partner is infected).

A. Meaning of negative result
Discuss and clarify meaning of negative HIV test result. Explain that the test results do not mean that he or she is immune to HIV.

B. Window period/retesting
Explain the window period and need for retesting within 6 months if the youth has engaged in risky behavior during the past 6 months.

III. Risk Reduction Treatment Plan

"You have had a negative result. We need to make sure it stays that way. Let's develop a simple plan to help to keep you from getting infected."

Review and reinforce the adolescent's knowledge of risk reduction behaviors. Assess commitment to practicing them. Develop an individualized risk-reduction treatment plan on the basis of changes (or lack of changes) adopted since the pre-test. Remain open and nonjudgmental to create a safe environment for discussion.

Goal	Strategy	Obstacles	Success

IV. Skills Building

A. Condom demonstration and condom use
Review condom demonstration, supply condoms, initiate role play to help youth to introduce them during sexual encounters. Help to identify ways to eroticize condom use.

B. Substance Abuse

Review risks created by substance use before and during intercourse. Although sharing needles represents the most direct route for HIV infection, other substances (e.g., alcohol, marijuana, intranasal heroin, and cocaine) impair judgment and increase potential for risky behaviors.

C. Negotiating with Partner

Encourage the adolescent to discuss HIV with his/her sexual and/or drug-injecting partner. Use a role play to discuss bringing the partner in for counseling, risk-reduction education, and testing.

V. Disclosure and Discrimination

Caution the youth about indiscriminately telling others that he or she has been tested, because people can be discriminated against just for being at risk for HIV. Provide information about what to do if he or she experiences discrimination, including advocacy referral resources.

VI. Referral and Follow-up

Ask the youth if there are any questions. Make appropriate referrals for follow-up care, mental health services, or social services while the youth is still in your office. Ask how the youth would like to be contacted (e.g., in some cases, the adolescent may not want parents to know that he or she is seeking certain kinds of services).

Provide health education literature. Schedule another post-test counseling session, if indicated; schedule follow-up testing in six months, if required.

POST-TEST COUNSELING

Positive

   I. Introduction

   II. HIV Test Results

   III. Implications of Positive HIV Test Result

   IV. Risk Reduction Review

   V. Skills Building
      A. Condom demonstration and condom use
      B. Substance abuse
      C. Negotiating with partner

   VI. Discrimination and Disclosure

   VII. Referral and Follow-Up

Post Test Counseling—Positive

I. Introduction

Assess the adolescent's affect and determine if he or she is intoxicated. (If so, do not proceed with counseling until the youth is sober; this may require waiting for a period of time or rescheduling the appointment.) Explain the goals of the counseling session (to help the youth to understand the meaning of his or her results and to reinforce healthy behavioral changes and awareness of risk behaviors).

"I am going to give you your results, and we will discuss what they mean."

II. HIV Test Results

Give the test results and show the laboratory slip. Allow time for the youth to respond; ask if the youth is surprised, and what his or her expectation was. Provide emotional support. Allow him or her time to react and to express feelings. Assess level of shock and denial. Do not push the youth to proceed until he or she clearly is ready to. Assess potential for traumatic emotional reaction and suicide throughout the session.

"Your test results show that you have antibodies for HIV; this means that you have been infected with HIV."

III. Implications of a Positive Result

Discuss the difference between being HIV-infected and having AIDS. Offer hope/optimism for continued health and quality of life. Explain that AIDS is a chronic illness, not a death sentence, and that regular medical care will help to maintain health and help to identify health problems before they become serious.

"A positive result means that you have antibodies to HIV in your blood. This means that you are infected with HIV. Another way to say this is that you are HIV-positive or seropositive. It is important to get regular medical care so that you can find out what stage of HIV infection you are in and receive appropriate treatment. When you are infected with HIV, the virus slowly weakens your body's ability to fight other infections. New medical treatments can help your body to fight HIV by slowing the growth of the virus and delaying or preventing certain life-threatening conditions. If you get prompt and regular medical care, you can delay getting AIDS and prevent serious infections. It is important to remember that HIV infection is a chronic illness, not a death sentence. People can live healthy and productive lives, even though they are infected with HIV."

A. Antiretroviral perinatal risk reduction (pregnant adolescents)

If the adolescent is pregnant, discuss the option of taking antiretroviral drugs to reduce the risk of perinatal transmission. Provide patient education materials; review benefits and potential risks; answer questions; and provide an opportunity for followup and family counseling to support decision-making.

IV. Risk Reduction Review

The emphasis of an initial post-test visit for HIV-positive adolescents is coping with their new health status and linking with services and care. Risk reduction skills can be mentioned but are not the focus of the visit. Review of dos and don'ts includes the following:

Do not donate blood, semen, tissue, or body organs.
Do not share razors or toothbrushes.
Do not breast feed.

Do not share needles
Do practice safer sex
Assess risk behaviors and commitment to risk reduction strategies.

V. Skills Building

Emphasize the importance of engaging in safer sex, even if youth is not ready to notify his or her partner.

A. Condom demonstration and condom use

Review condom demonstration, supply condoms, initiate role play to help youth to introduce them during sexual encounters. Help to identify ways to eroticize condom use.

B. Substance abuse

Make sure the adolescent understands that sharing needles (IV drug use) represents the most direct risk for HIV infection, but use of alcohol and other drugs (e.g., marijuana, intranasal heroin, and cocaine) impairs judgment and increases the potential for risky behaviors.

C. Partner negotiation/notification

Encourage the adolescent to discuss HIV with his/her sexual and/or drug-injecting partner. Use a role play to discuss bringing the partner in for counseling, risk reduction education and testing.

VI. Disclosure and Discrimination

Discuss the need for disclosure to the adolescent's past partners, family, and dentist. Offer to provide assistance and support in notifying others, if needed. Caution the youth about disclosing his or her HIV status more extensively because discrimination against people with HIV is widespread. Provide information about what to do if discrimination occurs.

VII. Referral and Follow-up

Discuss referral and follow-up needs identified during the session (e.g. general medical care, rape crisis, battered women's services, drug treatment); schedule a follow-up appointment; and initiate referrals while the youth is still in your office. Discuss appropriate entitlement programs, e.g. ADAP (AIDS Drug Assistance Program). Be clear about how the youth would like to be contacted by other agencies.

Review the adolescent's support system and develop a plan for getting appropriate support during the next week. If a supportive adult has not accompanied the youth for test results, ask: "What are you going to do when you leave this office? Are you going to call _____ (identified support person)?" Provide emergency contact numbers (e.g., 24-hour crisis hotline, emergency mental health services) and information on how to contact you, if necessary.

Ensure that the adolescent is emotionally stable before terminating the session. At a later date discuss legal, housing, school, and employment rights.

Appendix F

Clinical Care Protocols
HRSA Conference on the Primary Care Needs
of Lesbian and Gay Adolescents

Mental Health Care for Lesbian, Gay, and Bisexual Adolescents
Andrew Boxer, PhD, and Joanne Haas, LCSW

Mental Status

(May include the following)

Current stressful life events
Physical appearance
Sleep and appetite
Manner of relating and relationships
Orientation to time, place, person
Current medical problems; medications

Emotional states/affects
    General
    Anxiety
    Depression
    Anger
    Other

Speech and language
Reading/writing
Quality of thinking and perception
Intelligence
Memory
Fantasies and conflict(s)
Impulsivity and risk-taking
Coping resources/defenses
Judgment and insight
Adaptive capacities
Positive attributes/resilience

Mental Health Assessment

Background/Family History

1. Family
    a. Relationships
2. Living situation
3. Work
4. School
    a. Academic
    b. Activities and interests
5. Social relationships
    a. Adults and peers
    b. Social networks
6. Disclosure
7. Self-concept/self-image
8. Conscience/values

Background/Family History *(cont.)*

    a. Capacity for judgment and decision-making
    b. Personal values: what is important/
        worthwhile?
9. Emotional states
    a. General feelings
        What makes you happy/sad?
    b. Anxiety (duration, severity, frequency)
    c. Depression (duration, severity, frequency)
    d. Anger
    e. Other
10. Reality testing
    a. Judgment and insight
    b. Impulsivity
11. Fantasy—imagination
12. Future time orientation/expectations
    a. Goals

Past Psychiatric/Mental Health History

Mental health treatment/counseling history
    a. Inpatient
    b. Outpatient
    c. Medications
    d. Experience with mental health
        professionals/counselors
Family History
    a. History of severe and persistent mental ill-
        ness
    b. Family use of mental health services
        – Inpatient, outpatient
    c. Youth's perception of these experiences

Substance Use

Drug
    a. Cigarettes
    b. Alcohol
    c. Marijuana
    d. Cocaine
    e. Amphetamines
    f. Nonprescribed narcotics
    g. Inhalants
    h. Tranquilizers
    i. Hallucinogens

Substance Use *(cont.)*

Mode of administration
a. Oral
b. Nasal
c. Intravenous/intramuscular
Age at initiation
Duration/frequency of use

Sexuality

Sexual orientation/sexual identity
a. Sexual desires/attractions
b. Sexual behavior and experience
   — Sexual readiness
   — Types and number of partners
   — Frequency and range of sexual behavior
   — Knowledge and use of safer sex practices
c. Sexual fantasies
d. Sexual identity/labeling (heterosexual, gay/lesbian, bisexual, homosexual, "queer")
e. Psychological conflicts

Sexual Development

a. Awareness of desires—age, context
b. First sexual experience(s)—gender, age, age of partner
c. Sexual abuse
d. Disclosure of sexual identity (consequences + response)
   — Parents/family/guardians
   — Peers
   — School environment
   — Workplace
   — Adults
e. Decision-making about disclosure
   — Is it safe?
   — Consequences
   — Who to tell and when

Gender Identity

Core gender identity
a. Sense of masculinity and femininity
Cross gender behavior
a. History and personal significance
Gender Dysphoria
a. History
b. Current status

Emotional Response/Psychological Responses to Sexuality Issues

a. Changes in sociability
   — Social engagement or withdrawal
   — Changes in peer group (loss of close friends?)

Sexual Development *(cont.)*

b. Emotional responses
   — Emotional changes (temporary or long-lasting?)
   — Knowledge of help-seeking + response
   — Substance use related to sexual experience
   — Nature of responses
   — Temporary or significant duration?

Evaluation of Suicide Risk

Current/past suicidal actions/feelings/fantasies
a. Methods
Concepts/intentions of outcome
Life circumstances/situation at time of attempt
Past experience/history of suicidality
Motivations for suicidal behavior
Experiences/concepts of death
Depression and other predominant emotional states/affects
Family and environmental circumstances
Assessment of impulsivity
Assessment of suicide within the peer network

Victimization/Abuse/Exposure to Violence

Victimization and harassment related to sexual orientation
a. Verbal (insults, harassment)
b. Physical (assault)
c. Sexual (sexual abuse/rape)
d. Nonverbal/nonphysical experiences with stigma

Victimization based on ethnicity, gender, or other characteristics
a. Verbal
b. Physical
c. Sexual abuse

Childhood abuse history
a. Corporal punishment
b. Sexual abuse
   — Family members
   — Others
c. Emotional/verbal abuse

Exposure to crime/violence
a. Relationship to violence
   — Family
   — Intimate relationship(s)
   — Peers—in school/out of school/community
   — Gang participation

Traumatic events
a. Accidents
b. Major illnesses
c. Family dissolution
d. Other

Primary Care for Lesbian and Gay Adolescents
Neal Hoffman, MD, and David Ocepek, MD

Physical Examination

1. Height and weight with percentiles
2. Blood pressure and pulse
3. Eyes, ears, nose, mouth, teeth, and gums
4. Thyroid
5. Lymph nodes
6. Breasts
7. Heart, lungs, and abdomen
8. Back/spine
9. Tanner staging of pubertal development
   Breasts and pubic hair pattern
     for females
   Testicular volume and pubic hair pattern
     for males
10. Ano genital exam/inspection (in all)
    – Testicular exam
    – *Anal exam, if indicated*
    – Pelvic exam, if symptomatic, sexually
    experiences or > 18 years old
      a. Speculum and bimanual
11. Skin
12. Neurologic and mental status examination

Patient Education

1. Breast or testicular self-examination
2. Genital examination (internal and
   external)
3. Menstrual history
4. Guidance (parenting, injury prevention, diet
   and fitness, adolescent development, and
   healthy lifestyles)

Laboratory Screening

1. Hemoglobin or hematocrit (sickle cell screen,
   if indicated) (Consider CBC for youth
   with chronic illness, such as HIV.)
2. Urine analysis
3. Liver function tests (SGOT, SGPT) for
   substance-using adolescents
4. Cholesterol screening, if indicated by obesity,
   other history
5. Pregnancy-related tests
   – Serum hCG, if history or clinical examination
   indicative
   – Rubella serology, before pregnancy

Immunizations

1. dT
2. MMR
3. Hepatitis A, Hepatitis B
   (Prescreen sexually active gay male,
   homeless and HIV+ youth for exposure to
   hepatitis B with HepB sAg, cAb, sAb)

Immunizations *(cont.)*

4. Influenza, yearly, for adolescents with chronic
   illness (including HIV) and homeless youth
5. Varicella, if nonimmune

Tuberculosis Evaluation (use CDC guidelines)

1. Skin testing
2. Baseline chest x-ray if PPD+
3. Facilitating completion of evaluation

Vision Testing and Audiometry

Referral for Dental Care

Other Referrals

Sexual History and Screening

Sexual Identity

1. Behavior
   – Same sex and opposite sex partners
   – Age of coitarche and age of partners
   – Consensual and non-consensual sex
   – Types of sexual experience
     Outercourse
       a. Kissing
       b. Massage and petting
       c. Masturbation
     Intercourse
       a. Vaginal-penile
       b. Oral-genital, oral-anal
       c. Anal-genital
   – Condom use (settings and partner type)
   – Concurrent substance use
   – Survival sex
2. Disclosure of sexual orientation
   – Family
   – Friends/partner(s)/roommates
   – Classmates/co-workers
   – Teachers/supervisors/counselors
   – Role of health care provider

Sexually Transmitted Diseases

1. Screening
   – Gonorrhea (triple site—genital, oral, anal)
   – Chlamydia
     a. Cervical
     b. Urine sediment versus urethral swab
   – Vaginal wet mount (candida, vaginosis,
   trichomoniasis), if indicated by history or
   examination

Sexually Transmitted Diseases *(cont.)*

  - Hepatitis B (HBV) prevaccination screen
    HepB sAg, cAb, sAb (Consider hepatitis C
    serology if HBV+ or partner has HCV)
  - HIV antibody (consent and confidentiality)
  - Human papillomavirus (HPV)/dysplasia
  a. Cervical Papanicolaou (Pap) smear
  b. *Consider anal Pap and anoscopy if perianal
     warts present*
  - Syphilis
  - *Intestinal parasites, if clinically indicated, but
    not routine*
2. Treatment issues

Sexually Transmitted Diseases *(cont.)*

  - Adherence
  - Test of cure
  - Partner issues
3. Prevention
  - Readiness for sexual experience
  - Risk reduction

Reproductive Health

1. Contraception
2. Pregnancy decision-making
3. Parenting skills

Medical and Psychosocial Care of HIV+ Adolescents
Donna Futterman, MD, Janet Shalwitz, MD, and Joyce Hunter, DSW

Protocol for HIV-Related Care

Overview

1. Medical and psychosocial history
2. Review of systems
3. Physical examination
4. Laboratory assessment
5. Immunizations
6. Medications/treatment
7. Access to clinical research
8. Entitlements/case management
9. Patient education and empowerment
10. Referral to support services

Medical History

- Allergies (particularly medication related)
- Childhood and family illnesses
- Hospitalization and medication history
- Sexual history: sexuality, sexually transmitted/ gynecologic diseases, sexual abuse, pregnancy/parenting history
- Tuberculosis/pneumonia and other infections
- Substance use

Psychosocial History

- HIV risk behaviors (sex and substance use)
- Psychosocial status and needs (comprehensive history)
- Coping behaviors and skills
- Access to counseling and support
- Disclosure: family, partners, friends
- Living will
- Child custody/permanency planning

Review of Systems

- Sense of well-being/illness
- Symptoms of seroconversion illness
- Appetite, weight loss or gain, nausea, vomiting, diarrhea
- Lymphadenopathy: presence or regression, tenderness
- Oral health: dentition, gum disease, thrush, herpes, lesions
- Sino-pulmonary: cough, shortness of breath, wheezing, sinusitis
- Ano-genital complaints
- Skin or hair changes
- Mental status or neurologic changes
- Visual changes
- Unusual bleeding

Physical Exam

- General: appearance, weight, fever
- Skin: HIV-related lesions appear throughout course of HIV, dermatologic problems common among adolescents
- HEENT: visual fields and thorough retinal exam (consider referral for ophthalmologic examination when CD4 < 100/mm³), oral examination: dentition, gums, thrush, herpes
- Lymph nodes: note presence and regression
- Breast: masses, discharge, enlargement 2' hormones
- Lungs and cardiac function
- Abdominal: hepatosplenomegaly
- Gynecologic: speculum and bimanual examination incorporated into full examination, not referred out
- Genital: inspection for lesions
- Anal: inspection for all youth (including lesbians and males denying male-male sex)
- Neurologic/mental status: may be difficult to sort out HIV issues from substance use in active users; assess developmental/cognitive level

Laboratory Assessment *(at entry and suggested minimal interval; as clinically indicated and needed to monitor medication)*

- Repeat HIV Ab for confirmation
- CD4 and viral load count every 3 months and with medication changes
- Complete blood count every 3–12 months
- Chemistry and enzyme panel every 12 months
- Urinalysis every 12 months
- Toxoplasmosis titer every 2–3 years in unexposed patients when CD4 < 200/mm³
- Tuberculosis: PPD with anergy every 12 months unless anergic for 2 years (chest x-ray if anergic)
- Syphilis serology every 6–12 months
- Gonorrhea (genital, oral, anal) every 6–12 months
- Chlamydia (genital) every 6–12 months
- Cervical cytology (Pap) every 6–12 months (colposcopy when indicated)
- Vaginal wet preparation every 6–12 months

Treatment

- In partnership with youth, develop most effective regimen youth will reliably take
- Concrete problem solving to enhance adherence

Appendix G

American Academy of Pediatrics Statement on Homosexuality and Adolescence

Committee on Adolescence

The American Academy of Pediatrics issued its first statement on homosexuality and adolescence in 1983. The past decade has witnessed increased awareness of homosexuality, changing attitudes toward this sexual orientation, and the growing impact of the human immunodeficiency virus (HIV). Therefore, an updated statement on homosexuality and adolescence is timely.

Homosexuality is the persistent sexual and emotional attraction to members of one's own gender and is part of the continuum of sexual expression. Many gay and lesbian youths first become aware of and experience their sexuality during adolescence. Therefore, pediatricians who care for teenagers need to understand the unique medical and psychosocial issues facing homosexually oriented youths (see Table 1 for definition of terms).

Etiology and Prevalence

Homosexuality has existed in most societies for as long as recorded descriptions of sexual beliefs and practices have been available. Societal attitudes toward homosexuality have had a decisive impact on the extent to which individuals have hidden or made known their sexual orientation.

In 1973, the American Psychiatric Association reclassified homosexuality as a sexual orientation/expression rather than as a mental disorder.[1] The etiology of homosexuality remains unclear, but the current literature and the vast majority of scholars in this field state that one's sexual orientation is not a choice; that is, individuals no more choose to be homosexual than heterosexual.[2,3] However, the expression of sexual behaviors and lifestyle is a choice for all teenagers regardless of sexual orientation.

During the adolescent years, many youths engage in sexual experimentation. Sexual behavior during this period does not predict future sexual orientation. Gay, lesbian, and heterosexual youths may engage in sexual activities with members of the

same or opposite sex. Kinsey et al.,[4,5] from their studies in the 1930s and 1940s, reported that 37% of men had at least one homosexual experience resulting in orgasm. From the same cohort, Kinsey reported that 4% of women and 10% of men were exclusively homosexual for at least 3 years of their lives. Sorenson[6] surveyed a group of 16- to 19-year-olds and reported that 6% of females and 17% of males had at least one homosexual experience. While the Kinsey data suggest that 4% of adult men and 2% of adult women are exclusively homosexual in their behavior and fantasies, the current prevalence of homosexual behavior and identity among adolescents remains to be defined.

Special Concerns

Gay and lesbian adolescents share many of the developmental tasks of their heterosexual peers. These include establishing a sexual identity and deciding on sexual behaviors, whether choosing to engage in sexual intercourse or to abstain. Due to the seriousness of sexually transmitted diseases (STDs), abstinence should be promoted as the safest choice for all adolescents. However, not all youths will choose abstinence. The current reality is that a large number of adolescents are sexually active. Therefore, all adolescents should receive sexuality education and have access to health care resources. It is important to provide appropriate anticipatory guidance to all youths regardless of their sexual orientation. Physicians must also be aware of the important medical and psychosocial needs of gay and lesbian youths.[7]

HIV

The epidemic of the HIV infection highlights the urgency of making preventive services and medical care available to all adolescents regardless of sexual orientation or activity. Heterosexual and homosexual transmission of HIV infection is well established. The role of injectable drugs of abuse in HIV transmission is also well known.[3,8] Sex between males accounts for about half of the non-transfusion-associated cases of acquired immunodeficiency syndrome (AIDS) among males between the ages of 13 and 19 years.[8] While not all gay adolescents engage in high-risk sex (or even have sex), their vulnerability to HIV infection is well recognized. The pediatrician should encourage adolescents to practice abstinence. However,

This statement has been approved by the Council on Child and Adolescent Health.

The recommendations in this policy statement do not indicate an exclusive course of treatment or serve as a standard of medical care. Variations, taking into account individual circumstances, may be appropriate.

TABLE 1. Definitions of Terms

Coming out	The acknowledgment of one's homosexuality and the process of sharing that information with others.
Gender identity	The personal sense of one's integral maleness or femaleness; typically occurs by 3 years of age.
Gender role	The public expression of gender identity; the choices and actions that signal to others a person's maleness or femaleness; one's sex role.
Heterosexist bias	The conceptualization of human experience in strictly heterosexual terms and consequently ignoring, invalidating, or derogating homosexual behaviors and sexual orientation.[19]
Homophobia	The irrational fear or hatred of homosexuality, which may be expressed in stereotyping, stigmatization, or social prejudice[18]; it may also be internalized in the form of self-hatred.
In the closet	Nondisclosure or hiding one's sexual orientation from others.
Sexual orientation	The persistent pattern of physical and/or emotional attraction to members of the same or opposite sex. Included in this are homosexuality (same gender attractions); bisexuality (attractions to members of both genders); and heterosexuality (opposite-gender attractions). The terms preferred by most homosexuals today are lesbian women or gay men.
Transsexual	An individual who believes himself or herself to be of a gender different from his or her assigned biologic gender (gender identity does not match anatomic gender).
Transvestite	An individual who dresses in the clothing of the opposite gender and derives pleasure from this action. This is not indicative of one's sexual orientation.

many will not heed this important message. Thus, practical, specific advice about condom use and other forms of safer sex should be included in all sexuality education and prevention discussions.

Issue of Trust

Quality care can be facilitated if the pediatrician recognizes the specific challenges and rewards of providing services for gay and lesbian adolescents. This care begins with the establishment of trust, respect, and confidentiality between the pediatrician and the adolescent. Many gay and lesbian youths avoid health care or discussion of their sexual orientation out of fear that their sexual orientation will be disclosed to others. The goal of the provider is not to identify all gay and lesbian youths, but to create comfortable environments in which they may seek help and support for appropriate medical care while reserving the right to disclose their sexual identity when ready. Pediatricians who are not comfortable in this regard should be responsible for seeing that such help is made available to the adolescent from another source.

Special Aspects of Care

History

A sexual history that does not presume exclusive heterosexuality should be obtained from all adolescents.[3,9] Confidentiality must be emphasized except in cases in which sexual abuse has occurred. It is vital to identify high-risk behavior (anal or vaginal coitus, oral sex, casual and/or multiple sex partners, substance abuse, and others).

Physical Examination

A thorough and sensitive history provides the groundwork for an accurate physical examination for youths who are sexually experienced.[10] Depending on the patient's sexual practices, a careful examination includes assessment of pubertal staging, skin lesions (including cutaneous manifestations of STDs, bruising, and other signs of trauma), lymphadenopathy (including inguinal), and anal pathology (including

discharge, venereal warts, herpetic lesions, fissures, and others). Males need evaluation of the penis (ulcers, discharge, skin lesions), scrotum, and prostate (size, tenderness). Females need assessment of their breasts, external genitalia, vagina, cervix, uterus, and adnexa.

Laboratory Studies

All males engaging in sexual intercourse with other males should be routinely screened for STDs, including gonorrhea, syphilis, chlamydia, and enteric pathogens. The oropharynx, rectum, and urethra should be examined and appropriate cultures obtained when indicated.[3,9]

Immunity to hepatitis B virus should be assessed. Immunization is recommended for all sexually active adolescents and should be provided for all males who are having or anticipate having sex with other males.[11] HIV testing with appropriate consent should be offered; this includes counseling before and after voluntary testing.

Women who have sex exclusively with other women have a low incidence of STDs, but can transmit STDs and potentially HIV if one partner is infected. Since lesbian women who engage in unprotected sex with men face risks of both sexually acquired infections and pregnancy, the pediatrician should offer them realistic birth control information and counseling on STD prevention.

Psychosocial Issues

The psychosocial problems of gay and lesbian adolescents are primarily the result of societal stigma, hostility, hatred, and isolation.[12] The gravity of these stresses is underscored by current data that document that gay youths account for up to 30% of all completed adolescent suicides.[13] Approximately 30% of a surveyed group of gay and bisexual males have attempted suicide at least once.[14] Adolescents struggling with issues of sexual preference should be reassured that they will gradually form their own identity[15] and that there is no need for premature labeling of one's

TABLE 2. Stages of Homosexual Identity Formation

Sensitization	The feeling of differentness as a prepubertal child or adolescent. The first recognition of attraction to members of the same gender before or during puberty.
Sexual identity confusion	Confusion and turmoil stemming from self-awareness of same-gender attractions. Often this first occurs during adolescence. This confusion usually is not so much due to a questioning of one's feelings as it is to the attempt to reconcile the feelings with negative societal stereotypes. The lack of accurate knowledge about homosexuality, the scarcity of positive gay and lesbian role models, and the absence of an opportunity for open discussion and socialization as a gay or lesbian person contribute to this confusion. During this stage the adolescent develops a coping strategy to deal with social stigma.
Sexual identity assumption	The process of acknowledgment and social and sexual exploration of one's own gay or lesbian identity and consideration of homosexuality as a lifestyle option. This stage typically persists for several years during and after late adolescence.
Integration and commitment	The stage at which a gay or lesbian person incorporates his/her homosexual identity into a positive self-acceptance. This gay or lesbian identity is then increasingly and confidently shared with selected others. Many gays and lesbians may never reach this stage; those who do are typically in adulthood when this acceptance occurs.

* From Troiden RR: Homosexual identity development. J Adolesc Health Care 9:105–113, 1988.

sexual orientation.[16] A theoretical model of stages for homosexual identity development composed by Troiden[17] is summarized in Table G.2. The health care professional should explore each adolescent's perception of homosexuality, and any youth struggling with sexual orientation issues should be offered appropriate referrals to providers and programs that can affirm the adolescent's intrinsic worth regardless of sexual identity. Providers who are unable to be objective because of religious or other personal convictions should refer patients to those who can.

Gay or lesbian youths often encounter considerable difficulties with their families, schools, and communities.[16,18,19] These youths are severely hindered by societal stigmatization and prejudice; limited knowledge of human sexuality, a need for secrecy, a lack of opportunities for open socialization, and limited communication with healthy role models. Subjected to overt rejection and harassment at the hands of family members, peers, school officials, and others in the community, they may seek, but not find, understanding and acceptance by parents and others. Parents may react with anger, shock, and/or guilt when learning that their child is gay or lesbian.

Peers may engage in cruel name-calling, ostracize, or even physically abuse the identified individual. School and other community figures may resort to ridicule or open taunting, or they may fail to provide support. Such rejection may lead to isolation, runaway behavior, homelessness, domestic violence, depression, suicide, substance abuse, and school or job failure. Heterosexual and/or homosexual promiscuity may occur, including involvement in prostitution (often in runaway youths) as a means to survive. Pediatricians should be aware of these risks and provide or refer such youths for appropriate counseling.

Disclosure

The gay or lesbian adolescent should be allowed to decide when and to whom to disclose his/her sexual identity. In particular, the issue of informing parents should be carefully explored so that the adolescent is not exposed to violence, harassment, or abandonment. Parents and other family members may derive considerable benefit and gain understanding from organizations such as Parents and Friends of Lesbians and Gays (PFLAG).[3,18]

Concept of Therapy

Confusion about sexual orientation is not unusual during adolescence. Counseling may be helpful for young people who are uncertain about their sexual orientation or for those who are uncertain about how to express their sexuality and might profit from an attempt at clarification through a counseling or psychotherapeutic initiative. Therapy directed specifically at changing sexual orientation is contraindicated, since it can provoke guilt and anxiety while having little or no potential for achieving changes in orientation. While there is no current literature clarifying whether sexual abuse can induce confusion in one's sexual orientation, those with a history of sexual abuse should always receive counseling with appropriate mental health specialists. Therapy may also be helpful in addressing personal, family, and environmental difficulties that are often concomitants of the emerging expression of homosexuality. Family therapy may also be useful and should always be made available to the entire family when major family difficulties are identified by the pediatrician as parents and siblings cope with the potential added strain of disclosure.

Summary of Physician Guidelines

Pediatricians should be aware that some of the youths in their care may be homosexual or have concerns about sexual orientation. Caregivers should provide factual, current, nonjudgmental information in a confidential manner. These youths may present to physicians seeking information about homosexuality, STDs, substance abuse, or various psychosocial difficulties. The pediatrician should ensure that each youth receives a thorough medical history and physical examination (including appropriate laboratory tests), as well as STD (including HIV) counseling and, if necessary, appropriate treatment. The health care professional should also be attentive to various potential psychosocial difficulties and offer counseling or refer for counseling when necessary.

The American Academy of Pediatrics reaffirms the physician's responsibility to provide comprehensive health care and guidance for all adolescents, including gay and lesbian adolescents and those young people struggling with issues of sexual orientation. The deadly consequences of AIDS and adolescent suicide underscore the critical need to address and seek to prevent the major physical and mental health problems that confront gay and lesbian youths in their transition to a healthy adulthood.

Committee on Adolescence, 1992 to 1993
Roberta K. Beach, MD, Chair
Suzanne Boulter, MD
Marianne E. Felice, MD
Edward M. Gotlieb, MD
Donald E Greydanus, MD
James C. Hoyle, Jr., MD
I. Ronald Shenker, MD

Liaison Representatives
Richard E. Smith, MD, American
    College of Obstetricians and
    Gynecologists
Michael Maloney, MD, American
    Academy of Child and Adolescent
    Psychiatry
Diane Sacks, MD, Canadian Paediatric
    Society

Section Liaison
Samuel Leavitt, MD, Section on
    School Health

Consultants
Donna Futterman, MD, Albert Einstein
    College of Medicine
John D. Rowlett, MD, Children's
    Hospital of Savannah, GA
S. Kenneth Schonberg, MD, Albert
    Einstein College of Medicine

References

1. American Psychiatric Association: Diagnostic and Statistical Manual of Mental Disorders, 3d ed, revised. Washington, DC: American Psychiatric Association, 1987.
2. Savin-Williams, RC: Theoretical perspectives accounting for adolescent homosexuality. J Adolesc Health Care 9:2, 1988.
3. Rowlett J, Patel DR, Greydanus, DE: Homosexuality. In Greydanus DE, Wolraich M, eds: Behavioral Pediatrics. New York, NY: Springer-Verlag, 1992, pp 37–54.
4. Kinsey AC, Pomeroy WB, Martin CE: Sexual Behavior in the Human Male. Philadelphia, PA, W.B. Saunders, 1948.
5. Kinsey AC, Pomeroy WB, Martin CE: Sexual Behavior in the Human Female. Philadelphia, PA, W.B. Saunders, 1953.
6. Sorenson RC: Adolescent Sexuality in Contemporary America. New York, NY, World Publishing, 1973.
7. Remafedi GJ: Adolescent homosexuality: Psychosocial and medical implications. Pediatrics 79:331–337, 1987.
8. Centers for Disease Control: AIDS Surveillance Update. Atlanta, GA, March 1991.
9. Remafedi GJ. Sexually transmitted diseases in homosexual youth. Adolesc Med State Art Rev 1:565–581, 1990.
10. Brookman RR: Reproductive health assessment of the adolescent. In Hofmann AD, Greydanus DE, eds: Adolescent Medicine, 2nd ed. Norwalk, CT, Appleton-Lange, 1989, pp 347–351.
11. Centers for Disease Control: Hepatitis B virus: A comprehensive strategy for eliminating transmission in the United States through universal childhood vaccination: Recommendations of the Immunization Practices Advisory Committee. MMWR 40(No. RR-13):13–16, 1991.
12. Martin AD: Learning to hide: The socialization of the gay adolescent. In Feinstein SC, Looney JG, Schwarzenberg AZ, Sorosky AD, eds: Adolescent Psychiatry. Chicago, IL, University of Chicago Press, 1982, pp 52–65.
13. US Department of Health and Human Services: Report of the Secretary's Task Force on Youth Suicide. Washington, DC: US Department of Health and Human Services, 1989.
14. Remafedi GJ, Farrow JA, Deisher RW: Risk factors for attempted suicide in gay and bisexual youth. Pediatrics 87:869–875, 1991.
15. Remafedi GJ, Resnick M, Blum R, et al: Demography of sexual orientation in adolescents. Pediatrics 89:714–721, 1992.
16. Greydanus DE, Dewdney D: Homosexuality in adolescence. Semin Adolesc Med 1:117–129, 1985.
17. Troiden RR: Homosexual identity development. J Adolesc Health Care 9:105–113, 1988.
18. Peterson PK, ed: Special symposium: Gay and lesbian youth. In American Academy of Pediatrics, Adolescent Health Section Newsletter 12(1):3–41, 1991.
19. Herek GM, Kimmel DC, Amaro H, et al: Avoiding heterosexist bias in psychological research. Am Psychol 46:957–963, 1991.

Index

Entries in **boldface** type indicate complete chapters.

parental notification about, 33–34
screening for, 80–84, 163–164
substance abuse and, 44
Sexual orientation, 7–10
attempts to reverse. *See* Conversion (reparative)
therapy
disclosure of. *See* Disclosure, of sexual orientation
Sexual readiness, assessment of, 84
Sexual risk history, of HIV-infected youth, 115
Smoking, 3, 43, 44, 80, 86
Social isolation. *See* Isolation
Socialization, 45, 74, 107
Somatic disorders, 55, 57
Stereotypes, of gays and lesbians, 4, 11, 22, 69, 70, 72–73
effect on career development/job choice, 74–75
effect on identity consolidation, 20–23, 72–73
Steroid use, 105–106, 130
as HIV transmission route, 105–106
Stigma, of gay and lesbian youth, 9, 11, 20–24, 27, 28, 55, 138
of ethnic and racial minority youth, 9, 14, 15, 20–21
HIV seropositivity-related, 115, 118
of the mentally ill, 53
parents' reactions to, 68
psychological reactions to, 29
as substance abuse risk factor, 28, 95
visible and invisible, 20–21
as vulnerability risk factor, 59, 94, 142
Stress, 73–74
assessment of, 81, 92, 142
chronic, 58–59
coming out-related, 29, 58–59, 107
HIV seropositivity-related, 118
homophobia-related, 58–59
stigma-related, 28
as suicide risk factor, 61
Substance abuse, 3–4, 13, 21, 27–28, 43–45, 58, 85–88, 90, 132
anticipatory guidance about, 73
assessment of, 85–87, 92, 161–162
consent to treatment for, 33
as HIV risk factor, 28, 159, 160
by homeless and runaway youth, 26, 85
by incarcerated youth, 4
referrals for, 87–88, 89
risk factors for, 85, 86
screening for, 85–87
services for HIV-infected youth, 130
stages of, 86–87
as suicide risk factor, 56, 62
treatment of, 87–88, 90
twelve-step programs, 88
Suicidal ideation and attempts, 29, 60–63, 73–74, 86, 93, 136
referrals for, 94

Suicide, 29, 56–57, 60–62
alcohol abuse-related, 43
closeted status-related, 17
by homeless and runaway youth, 52, 85
by incarcerated youth, 208
Massachusetts Youth Risk Behavior Survey, 60
Paul Gibson's report on, 61
prevention of, 55
rates of, 4, 29, 56–57, 60–62
risk assessment of, 81, 93–94, 162
risk factors for, 29, 56–57, 60, 61, 94
substance abuse-related, 29, 86
twin studies, 61–62
Support systems and groups, 4, 12, 22, 74, 95
for ethnic and racial minority youth, 9, 13–15
for HIV-infected youth, 122, 127, 129, 130, 136, 139
lack of, 4–5, 13, 20
for parents, 70–71, 74
peers as, 74
referrals to, 73, 74
Survival sex, 44, 105, 130
Syphilis, 39, 41, 83, 132, 164

Throw-away youth, 25, 51–52, 130
Transgendered youth, xiii, **48–50**, 59, 63, 94, 105–106, 142, 143
cross-gendered, 61
Transsexuals, 48, 49
Transvestites, 48, 49
Trauma, 42–43, 85
assessment of, 94–95, 162
sexual assault-related, 42–43
Trichomonas, 39, 83, 132
Truancy, 24
Tuberculosis, 80, 132, 163, 165

Urethritis, 40–41

Vaginosis, 39, 132
Verbal abuse, 23–24, 42
Victimization, 22–27, 43, 48, 51, 52, 53, 54, 57, 85, 92
buffers to, 94
effects of, 24–25, 28
sexual assault, 42–43
Violence, anti-gay. *See* Anti-gay violence
Vulnerability, 29
to HIV infection, 107, 140
of incarcerated youth, 3–4
to sexually transmitted diseases, 39
social stigma-related, 58, 94–95
to stress, 58–59
to substance abuse, 45, 85
to suicide, 61

Youth Risk Behavior Survey, 60